Leadership and Transformative Ambition in International Relations

NEW HORIZONS IN LEADERSHIP STUDIES

Series Editor: Joanne B. Ciulla, *Professor and Coston Family Chair in Leadership and Ethics, Jepson School of Leadership Studies, University of Richmond, USA*

This important series is designed to make a significant contribution to the development of leadership studies. This field has expanded dramatically in recent years and the series provides an invaluable forum for the publication of high quality works of scholarship and shows the diversity of leadership issues and practices around the world.

The main emphasis of the series is on the development and application of new and original ideas in leadership studies. It pays particular attention to leadership in business, economics and public policy and incorporates the wide range of disciplines which are now part of the field. Global in its approach, it includes some of the best theoretical and empirical work with contributions to fundamental principles, rigorous evaluations of existing concepts and competing theories, historical surveys and future visions.

Titles in the series include:

The Quest for a General Theory of Leadership
Edited by George R. Goethals and Georgia L.J. Sorenson

Inventing Leadership
The Challenge of Democracy
J. Thomas Wren

Dissent and the Failure of Leadership
Edited by Stephen P. Banks

Corporate Governance and Ethics
An Aristotelian Perspective
Alejo José G. Sison

Rethinking Leadership
A New Look at Old Leadership Questions
Donna Ladkin

Leadership Studies
The Dialogue of Disciplines
Edited by Michael Harvey and Ronald E. Riggio

Poor Leadership and Bad Governance
Reassessing Presidents and Prime Ministers in North America, Europe and Japan
Edited by Ludger Helms

Leadership by Resentment
From *Ressentiment* to Redemption
Ruth Capriles

Critical Perspectives on Leadership
Emotion, Toxicity, and Dysfunction
Edited by Jeanette Lemmergaard and Sara Louise Muhr

Authentic Leadership
Clashes, Convergences and Coalescences
Edited by Donna Ladkin and Chellie Spiller

Leadership and Transformative Ambition in International Relations
Mark A. Menaldo

Leadership and Transformative Ambition in International Relations

Mark A. Menaldo

Assistant Professor of Political Science, Texas A&M International University, USA

NEW HORIZONS IN LEADERSHIP STUDIES

Edward Elgar
Cheltenham, UK • Northampton, MA, USA

Published by
Edward Elgar Publishing Limited
The Lypiatts
15 Lansdown Road
Cheltenham
Glos GL50 2JA
UK

Edward Elgar Publishing, Inc.
William Pratt House
9 Dewey Court
Northampton
Massachusetts 01060
USA

A catalogue record for this book
is available from the British Library

Library of Congress Control Number: 2013938067

This book is available electronically in the ElgarOnline.com Social and Political Science Subject Collection, E-ISBN 978 1 78100 947 5

ISBN 978 1 78100 946 8

Printed and bound in Great Britain by T.J. International Ltd, Padstow

Contents

Acknowledgments   vi

Introduction   1

1   Realism and ambition: Otto von Bismarck reconsidered   11
2   The strategic perspective of leadership: ambition as political
    survival   35
3   Personality and political ambition   54
4   Transformational leadership: a theoretical critique   81
5   Aristotle's idea of magnanimity and transformative
    ambition   100
6   Pericles' transformative ambition (1): regime politics and
    character   127
7   Pericles' transformative ambition (2): democracy, empire,
    and the Peloponnesian War   146

Conclusion   172

References   177
Index   186

Acknowledgments

I must give thanks to the friends, colleagues, and teachers that have contributed to my formation as a student and scholar. From Colorado College, I thank Jeff Livesay and Jonathan Lee for their friendship and tutelage. As an undergraduate, they encouraged me to be creative and think beyond the bounds of any specific discipline. I have applied this philosophy throughout my graduate study, academic, and teaching career. This book is an example of such liberal learning. At Michigan State University, I had very fine teachers including Mohamed Ayoob and Michael Colaresi who taught me about international relations, and Steven Kautz, Arthur Melzer, and Jerry Weinberger, who molded my thought, introduced me to the beauty of close reading, and, through example, taught me how to teach.

Special thanks go to Michael Colaresi, Arthur Melzer, and Richard Zinman who each read and commented on earlier versions of individual chapters. I am indebted to Steven Kautz who read earlier versions of most of the chapters and provided helpful criticism. I would like to thank Mark Garner and Lorena Zapata for their invaluable assistance as graduate assistants in the preparation of the manuscript. Many thanks goes to my colleagues, especially Frances Bernat, Thomas Mitchell, and Stephen Duffy at Texas A&M International University who have provided great support and advice through all the phases of writing the manuscript.

Many thanks go to the faculty at the Jepson School of Leadership, including Gary L. McDowell, Sandra J. Peart, Terry L. Price, Thad Williamson, and J. Thomas Wren, for recognizing the value of my ideas for the study of leadership. I am especially grateful to Joanne Ciulla who encouraged me to write this book and included it in her series. Alan Sturmer, Jennifer Wilcox, and Bob Pickens and the rest of the topnotch team at Edward Elgar were the book's shepherds and made the experience an easy and pleasant one for its writer.

I must thank my wife Kary who shared her perceptive criticism and helped me clarify and improve the whole manuscript. Without her love, support, and patience I could not have completed this project. Lastly, I owe gratitude to my parents Victor and Frances for if it wasn't for them I wouldn't be the man I am today. I dedicate this book to them.

Parts of Chapters of 6 and 7 appear in an article that was previously published in *Leadership, Accountability, and Ethics* by the North American Business Press. I thank the Press for permission to incorporate that article into two more extensive chapters.

Mark A. Menaldo

Introduction

We princes … are set upon stages, in the sight and view of the world.
Queen Elizabeth II

It is almost impossible to think about international affairs without invoking the major figures involved and their distinguishing character traits. How else can the Sicilian Expedition (AD 415–413) be understood, its audacious planning and catastrophic failure, if not seen as the product of Alcibiades' daring and Nicias' paralyzing caution? Can we make sense of the onset of World War II without considering Hitler's imperial ambition? Or understand its final resolution without summing his strategic blunders, or Churchill's steadfast resolve and prudence? Are both Gulf Wars fathomable without Saddam Hussein's lust for regional dominance and overestimations of his strength? Could a 'Bush Doctrine' have emerged in the aftermath of a Gore administration's 9/11?

In this book I explore what has become a neglected topic in the contemporary study of international politics: the role of statesmanship. Prevailing realist, rational choice, and personality theories of international relations conceive of leadership too narrowly. The realist perspective subjects all political leaders to the same functional necessity, state survival in the international system, thus limiting their scope of autonomous action. Rational choice theories attribute leaders' preferences to the domestic political system, the constituencies they are beholden to, and assume that their foreign policies are universally motivated by their desire to gain and remain in power. These abstract models of action, particularly foreign policy action, based on the assumption of self-interest and the calculation of cost and benefits, provide overly simplistic explanations of leader behavior. Moreover, this theoretical gap is poorly addressed by existing theories that tend to emphasize the idiosyncratic role of personalities.

I argue that each approach neglects the crucial role of leaders' political ambition. I develop a theory of transformative ambition to describe leaders who, motivated by a particular political and moral understanding, seek to change and redefine their domestic polity and use foreign policy as a means to achieve domestic ends. Drawing on Aristotle's idea of magnanimity and Niccolò Machiavelli's lessons to princes through his examples of great founders, I examine the character traits that surround and amplify transformative ambition. I argue that these leaders are guided by their desires and beliefs about what can be accomplished through international politics. They are not blind to constraints, but use their state capabilities and the art of statesmanship to shape their societies and the world. Through the force of their initiative, personalities, and the practice of statesmanship, leaders with transformative ambition try to accomplish great goals despite international and domestic constraints. When successful they manage to change the conventions and rules of domestic and international politics and (re)set the relations between states.

THE PROBLEM OF AMBITION

I begin with the crucial but undeveloped idea in foreign policy theories that a leader's political ambition matters. Political ambition in international politics can manifest in war, diplomacy, empire, and the normative and legal shaping of the international order: Hitler's will to dominate Europe and promote his radical ideology through aggressive expansion; Churchill's great desire to practice statesmanship in order to save Britain and the rest the world from the dangers of Nazism and tyranny; Woodrow Wilson's grand moral hope to practice international leadership by transforming the anarchic order into a moral and legalistic one; Mikhail Gorbachev's stunning reversal of the Soviet Union's traditional Cold War foreign relations through his policy of 'New Thinking,' an attempt at reform via conciliatory policies with the West and loosening the Soviet Union's grip on Eastern Europe. Pericles channeled his enormous aims into a vision of Athens as an imperial ruler and civilizing force in the Greek world. Alcibiades' ambition, on the other hand, knew no bounds; filled with a desire to achieve greatness through unlimited imperial expansion, he lacked Pericles' patriotism, not to mention his prudence.

Ambition is not just a drive but a complex phenomenon because it is highly individualistic but, to some degree, is also nurtured by the leader's domestic regime. Constitutions, social mores, and the passions and habits of the polity favor particular qualities in their leaders and so have a hand in shaping and constraining political ambition. At the same time, it is on account of what I call transformative political ambition that leaders seek to transcend the constraints of domestic politics by bringing in new modes and orders, transforming and redefining existing constitutions, or shaping the polity's moral and political understanding. These kinds of leaders turn to international affairs to accomplish their ambitions and find it quite necessary to rise above the limits of the international environment as well. Domestically, transformative ambition surpasses the desire for political survival, and such leaders seek to change the concrete political and material elements of a regime.

So what is the nature of ambition, where does it come from, and what effect does it have on leaders' political behavior? From the perspective of individual psychology, ambition is a product of unconscious motives and personal experiences. Seen in this way, it is the displacement of unconscious emotional needs upon public objects. As such, its origin is very idiosyncratic. Yet, ambition in political life, unlike other forms, is both personal and public. Once in power, the less ambitious remain satisfied with their posts, while others may set their sights beyond political power. This book pays particular attention to the idea that transformative ambition not only differs in degree but also in kind. This categorical difference is clearly and forcefully articulated by Abraham Lincoln (1953 [1992]) in his Lyceum Address, which he gave at the age of 28:

> Many great and good men sufficiently qualified for any task they should undertake, may ever be found, whose ambition would inspire to nothing beyond a seat in Congress, a gubernatorial or a presidential chair; but such belong not to the family of the lion, or the tribe of the eagle. What! Think you these places would satisfy an Alexander, a Caesar, or a Napoleon? Never! Towering genius disdains a beaten path. It seeks regions hitherto unexplored. It sees no distinction in adding story to story, upon the monuments of fame, erected to the memory of others. It denies that it is glory enough to serve under any chief. It scorns to tread in the footsteps of any predecessor, however illustrious. It thirsts and burns for distinction; and, if possible, it will have it, whether at the expense of emancipating slaves, or enslaving freemen.

Lincoln draws our attention to those individuals with boundless ambition and the spiritedness to go with it; only bold and path-breaking political actions that increase their power and glory can satisfy them. Lincoln understood such transcendent desire for eternal renown that is achieved through worldly accomplishments. Figures such as Alcibiades and Napoleon displayed the restive and grand ambition of the family of the lion and tribe of the eagle. Each leader possessed great ambition and set his sights beyond the bounds of his context but lacked magnanimity, a rare virtue that may be coupled with grand ambition. It is this combination of grand ambition and virtue that is the cornerstone of transformative ambition.

TRANSFORMATIVE POLITICAL AMBITION

The political leaders that I examine here are cut from the same fabric as Lincoln's 'tribe of the eagle' because they try to make bold and sweeping changes to domestic and international politics in order to accomplish a principled aim for their countries. Their ambition and concomitant behavior cannot be explained by current political-science theories that posit political necessity as the source of behavior. Since such acts of transformation are rarely necessary, I take an alternative approach and make the case that some of history's leaders have purposely tried to change the course of politics. On account of their ambition and statesmanship, they gained a mastery over politics and transformed their political environments.

Leaders with transformative ambition are moved by principles, such as the establishment of a new political regime, the defense of free politics, and desire to raise the rank of one's nation, which drive them to boldly reshape fundamental features of domestic society. In order to accomplish such tasks, they may seek to reorder domestic institutions, to propose new policies and establish new doctrines, and to rethink the ideals that animate their countries. A leader with transformative ambition feels elevated by a grand goal or project and therefore tries to infuse ordinary politics with nobler purposes by pushing the regime's political and moral elements further, challenging, and elevating them toward that which has not yet been realized.

One way that this is achieved is by the proper articulation of a leader's goals. The leaders with transformative ambition that I concentrate on accomplished their goals by making appropriate use of oratory, whose purpose is 'to describe the people as they are in such a way as to inspire them to be what they should be' (Newell, 2009, p. 51). Leaders such as Pericles of Athens and Charles de Gaulle aimed for a redefinition of the national character that not only influenced citizens' beliefs but also shaped their habits and practices. However, empirically, I am interested in a more specific political transformation, the kind that ties the success of domestic goals to foreign policy. Thus, transformative ambition manifests itself on two levels: the leader's ability to foster domestic and international institutions while they also prepare the polity for a psychological and moral acceptance of the new domestic and international orders they seek.

Although I argue that leaders' ambition is a unique quality that catalyzes historical change, I closely examine how leaders develop their unique attributes and art of leadership within the context of their regimes. I focus mainly on leaders who have risen to the pantheon of great statesmen and pay careful attention to how they engaged in the rough and tumble politics of their days. Even when scrutinized in relation to their regimes, my analysis shows that leaders with transformative ambition still managed to introduce new political ideas and novel practices that changed the established principles and customs that had governed their nations' domestic politics as well as the structure of global affairs.

Transformative ambition needs content and direction, which flows from a leader's personal ambitions, his moral opinions, and political deliberation about the challenges and opportunities presented to him. In this book, I do not make the simple distinction between self-interested leaders and public-spirited ones. Leaders with transformative ambition often combine a desire for personal achievements with service to the common good, as they understand it. From time immemorial, leaders with grand ambition have sought stages on which their virtues may shine. The leaders with transformative ambition examined here tend to manifest this dualism: they are genuinely moved by public service and the common weal, but they also seek their self-satisfaction. As Waller Newell has deftly observed, in politics outstanding personalities confront the greatest issues and crises of their eras while also pursuing great honors through preeminent public service (2009, pp. 26–8).

Through Aristotle's idea of magnanimity, I provide a model of leadership that demonstrates how self-regarding leaders reconcile their great personal ambition with the demands of public-minded statesmanship. Magnanimous leaders aspire to great honors and wish to act on a grand scale, but they often have a sober view of power; they limit their honor seeking to the kind that can also be dedicated to justice. Although their ambition is dedicated to the grandeur of their nations, their strength of character and prudence of judgment provides them with the capacity to think and act at a distance from ordinary citizens. The ability to remove themselves from quotidian matters and base self-interest enables them to translate their ambition into a productive vision that can transform the existing elements and principles of a regime toward greater and nobler purposes.

To illustrate the Aristotelian dimension of transformative ambition, I discuss the example of Charles de Gaulle. De Gaulle channeled his ambition toward public service; he sought to transform the state through the promotion of a distinct French unity, achieved by pursuing national greatness. He turned deliberately toward foreign policy to increase the nation's glory, its prestige, and a shared sense of national purpose. He believed that the success of domestic transformation, de Gaulle's idea of French unity, resided in elaborating a grand foreign policy. In the Cold War era that was divided into two blocs, de Gaulle sought to recapture French grandeur for the sake of unity. He did this by increasing France's international role by transforming the global order at the margins: he attacked the Cold War status quo, made inroads into the Third World, and sought to maximize France's influence and freedom of maneuver despite the fact that its relative power did not warrant such a forceful foreign policy.

My key examples of transformative ambition, Charles de Gaulle and Pericles, show how leaders can be the driving force for political change in their regimes and they often deliberately turn to foreign policy to achieve their ambitions. I argue that these leaders are not blind to the conditions that international relations impose on states and that they use artful diplomacy and harness their states' capabilities to pursue innovative and beneficial transformation of their nations. Through their actions, moreover, the world of states is partly of their own making, reflecting their ideas about what the world is like and how it should be.

AMBITION IN INTERNATIONAL RELATIONS, LEADERSHIP STUDIES AND POLITICAL PHILOSOPHY: CARVING A MIDDLE GROUND

In Chapters 1, 2, and 3, I examine neorealism, institutional theories that assume leaders are motivated foremost by a concern for political survival, and personality theories that assume that the motivations influencing foreign policy are the product of psychological idiosyncrasies. In Chapters 4 and 5, I place my idea of transformative political ambition within theories of moral and political leadership as discussed by leadership scholars and political philosophers. Lastly, in Chapters 6 and 7, I apply my theory of transformative political ambition to a sustained case study of Pericles.

For realists, states have to protect themselves from other states because no other state or governing body will do so. In this sense, all states perform the same functions for their citizens, and leaders represent the authoritative voice of the state in foreign policy. As a result, realists argue that a unitary state should be assumed in matters pertaining to international politics. In a realist world, the state's motivation for survival is a leader's too. Political ambition is coupled with the leader's obligation to respond to the demands imposed on the state by anarchy. Realist leaders select foreign policies while working in the realm of 'high politics,' which means that they worry about the international environment, and state security is the overriding preoccupation of their statecraft.

In Chapter 1, I argue that realists' portrayal of Bismarck as a quintessential realist fails to do justice to his statesmanship and ambition, which had a profound effect on the state, geopolitics, and the rules and practices of statecraft. Bismarck's political skill and genius was unmatched. He accomplished extraordinary changes not only by outmaneuvering domestic and foreign rivals, but also by taking it upon himself to apply a novel scientific outlook to international politics. Bismarck held to the notion that in the service of the state an amoral concept of power was required in the practice of domestic and international politics. He introduced Realpolitik, which prioritized power and opportunity over ideology. By abandoning established rules and beliefs, he led Germany toward unification. In the process, Bismarck radically reshaped the geopolitical landscape in Europe, revolutionized diplomacy, and overturned the established rules that had held the international order together. Although he transformed Germany and Europe, I do not classify him as a leader with transformative ambition because his statecraft was not animated by any moral principle. However, Bismarck had a complicated view of politics and I examine it closely in order to discern the content of his ambition.

Rational choice theorists that focus on the effect of domestic institutions are skeptical of realism's depiction of 'high politics' and argue that political leaders are not only beholden to the state, but to themselves and their desire to remain in power. No matter which political regime is under observation, these theorists assume that leaders are always intent on maintaining power. As a result, their policy preferences are not independent of the citizens who are in command of the institutions that select them into power.

Chapter 2 critically examines the theory of strategic political survival, which assumes that the ambition of democratic and autocratic leaders is strategic because they practice statecraft with a view to satisfy the preferences of citizens who control their political fates. The incentives of political actors at the level of 'low politics' are the most influential factors in political decisions. I critique this view by turning to Niccolò Machiavelli's *Prince*, which speaks directly to leaders who found new regimes or refound existing ones. I reexamine cases of political leaders, particularly in Latin America, that either subvert existing political institutions or create them from the ground up.

Finally, personality scholars think that political ambition reflects behavior that is based on psychological needs, the most pervasive of which is the need for power although the need for approval and affiliation are also prevalent. For these theorists, ambition precedes political life because it is a function of psychological needs and drives that are well developed long before leaders enter politics. Strong internal motives combine with personality traits and produce individual orientations that determine leaders' behavior in international politics. For personality scholars, foreign policy behavior is largely idiosyncratic: personal characteristics affect their foreign policy behavior. In Chapter 3, I examine the personality approach's study of leadership by turning to its classic application of Woodrow Wilson's personality and foreign policy, specifically his role in the failed ratification of the League of Nations Treaty in the United States Senate. I am critical of the view that Wilson's political personality was one that was defined by compensating for low self-esteem, which led to the failed ratification of the League of Nations. Rather, I argue that personality scholars fail to understand that Wilson's intractability with the Senate was not a function of a flawed personality as much as his desire to do immortal work, and he used prerogative and his belief in presidential rhetoric to try and achieve this goal.

The nature of political ambition and the problems it poses in politics and to societies are major subjects in political thought and are broached by classical and modern thinkers. In Chapter 4, I show how the idea of transformative political ambition is distinct from theories of transformational leadership. I specifically critique James Macgregor Burns' (1978) theory of transformational leadership, which is widely considered to be the foundational work for modern leadership studies. The critique contains three parts: the problem with the idea that leaders elevate values and aim to achieve self-actualization; Burns' insufficient treatment of political ambition and how it is shaped and expressed in regimes, and his neglect of how leaders act differently in both domestic and international contexts.

For Burns, there is a difference between individuals who hold positions of power and leaders. He views leaders as visionary moral guides who are capable of transforming the lives of followers. In this sense, Burns and I share a common ground. Leaders are not merely reactive; rather they are purposeful and may try to accomplish the highest political goals despite their constraints. Yet, I understand purposeful leadership through the perspective of political theory. I argue that political ambition, a leader's moral compass, and intention for transformation are tied in complicated ways to the particular regime.

The regime determines the goals of a society; it both influences and is affected by leadership. The relationship between political ambition and the study of regimes raises normative questions about justice and the proper role of leadership within a government. Thus, while Burns seeks a general theory of leadership, I argue that leadership aimed at moral and institutional change must be examined in the fine grain of regime politics, especially when the change is political. Leaders that possess transformative ambition in politics are spurred by a combination of personal and public concerns. Leaders want political power and need it to get things done. However, scholars tend to simplify ambition as an impulsive desire for power or as a calculated interest in political power that is held by rational and self-interested individuals. I do not argue against the plausibility of these claims.

However, I propose that individual ambition can have a public scope beyond private aggrandizement. Leaders can seek honor that is gained from the esteem of respectable citizens. When leaders seek some public recognition, it can lead them to refuse power for its own sake. Moreover, such aspirations can result in leaders bearing themselves with responsibility toward office. Responsibility does not amount to a denial of ambition, but it does enable some leaders to distinguish between their sense of worthiness and the limits that political power presents to fulfilling their ambition. As I discuss in Chapter 5, Aristotle's idea of magnanimity helps us to understand how leaders with transformative ambition hold high notions of their merit and a desire for greatness while also permitting them to consider moral goals, such as duty and justice, in their self-assessments. Aristotle's magnanimous man represents a leader of great ambition who acts for great political purposes and simultaneously restrains himself from overstepping his regime's laws.

In Chapters 6 and 7, I illustrate Pericles of Athens as a representative case study of a leader with transformative ambition who restrained the power-seeking motive and showed both great ambition and magnanimity, which I contrast with Donald Kagan's (2009) biography of Pericles. In Chapter 6, through the example of Pericles, I demonstrate how the interaction of personal characteristics and regime politics indelibly shapes some leader attributes. Ancient Athens fostered an environment where the better qualities of individuals could flourish, which enabled some of its leaders to stand above the morass of politics. Athens produced leaders who were very competitive, cunning, and bold. They were molded by the empire's ascendance, and they behaved in ways that added to its glory and strength.

Pericles possessed superior leadership qualities, virtues, and the inner sense of greatness and his worth. With his sights set on political goals that did justice to his pride and notions of dignity, he found that the opportunity to fulfill his ambitions arose through energetic service to the city. Pericles was superior to his contemporaries in many ways. He was a natural imperialist like other leaders, but he acted as an independent force in policy and was able to shape and curb his followers' political aims. Thus, he could define the Athenian imperial project in a way he believed was both sustainable and did justice to the Athenian character. Pericles was acutely aware that the democratic regime he helped bring into being had a distinct daring character, which was both the source of Athens' imperial success and a potential security risk.

Chapter 7 examines Pericles international leadership, specifically how his vision of Athenian democracy gave shape to Athens's imperial project. Pericles had the difficult task of managing an expanding empire's power. He did his best to turn the desire for expansion and wealth toward Athens' more noble activities, such as political participation, public works, and philosophical and aesthetic achievement. Moreover, his diplomatic decisions were instrumental in precipitating the war against Sparta and his military strategy revolutionized the conduct of ancient Greek warfare. Pericles met an untimely end, however, and much of his project was undermined by lesser leaders, who could not lead the democracy after his death. In this last chapter, I raise issue with the longevity and unintended effects of the projects inaugurated by leaders with transformative ambition.

1. Realism and ambition: Otto von Bismarck reconsidered

> Politics is not a science, as the professors are apt to suppose. It is an art.
>
> **Otto von Bismarck**

Otto von Bismarck is trotted out by realists as the quintessential realist statesman and as an artful practitioner of *realpolitik*, "the notion that relations among states are determined by raw power and the mighty will prevail" (Kissinger, 1994, p. 104). Realists concentrate on his diplomatic and wartime accomplishments. He opposed the Vienna settlement because in designating Austria as the central state in the newly formed German Confederation, it "locked Prussia into being Austria's junior partner" (1994, p. 104). Bismarck lived unhappily with this arrangement and strove to advance Prussian interests. In doing so, he bypassed domestic political forces that sought to unify Germany through parliamentary institutions and forged unification on the basis of the preeminence of Prussian power.

His actions shifted the power dynamics in the region; after his deliberately orchestrated war between Austria and Prussia, Austria was forced to withdraw from Germany. In the aftermath, Bismarck deposed the rulers of states that had sided with Austria, challenging Klemens von Metternich's principle that in the interest of stability, the legitimate rulers in Europe had to be preserved. The North German States became subject to Prussian leadership "in everything from trade legislation to foreign policy" (1994, p. 117).

Why did Bismarck pursue these policies? For realists, his ambitions were calibrated precisely to Prussia's national interest. The scholars attribute Bismarck's policies to his well-timed reaction to the international environment; that is, he responded correctly to the competitive nature of the system that Germany inhabited.[1] An offensive realist explanation suggests that Bismarck sought to expand Prussia's borders in order to make it more secure and was determined to create a unified

German state.[2] With Germany's borders enlarged enough to guarantee its security, Bismarck appropriately changed gears from war to diplomacy; he made use of both open and secret alliances that prevented any hostile alliance from forming against Germany, bringing peace and stability to the nation for the next two decades.

The argument I present here is critical of the neorealist view that international order is properly characterized as an unchanging systemic structure and that leaders like Otto von Bismarck are constrained by that structure. Whether the world is populated by tribes, empires, small city-states, or modern nation-states, neorealists argue that the behavior of political actors only leads to changes in the distribution of power. Despite such changes, this kind of behavior only serves to confirm that anarchy, which is the basic ordering principle of international relations, is a continuous feature of the international system. Neorealism denies the possibility of system transformation, or treats such transformation as an unpredictable accident. It is highly skeptical of the idea that individuals can act as creative forces that redefine the parameters under which states operate. Among realists, only Henry Kissinger understands the complexity of Bismarck's statesmanship, yet he extols his statecraft because it worked strictly within the bounds of power politics.

In contrast, I emphasize how Bismarck introduced change into the nature of international politics as he grappled with politics and foreign affairs while applying the creative and practically oriented view that interests and facts trump precedent and principle. Bismarck's ambition disdained opposition to his goals; he had supreme confidence in his intellect and an intuitive grasp of political reality. In short, Bismarck played politics as a high stakes game and sought to constitute the new rules of statecraft: to anticipate developments before they happen and try to steer circumstances in a favorable direction.

During the periods of war and consolidation, Bismarck broke with traditional alliances, orchestrated a war against Austria, revolutionized diplomacy, and upset the international status quo. His path-breaking application of the tools of statecraft made him a historical force of significance. This chapter questions the received wisdom of neorealist (Kenneth Waltz and John Mearshiemer) and classical realist (Henry Kissinger) theory by examining closely Otto von Bismarck's political thought and ambition. Through the example of Bismarck, I show how statesman with transformative ambition stretch or override the constraints of the international system.[3]

When transformative ambition is observed in leaders who make foreign policy decisions it can have a profound effect on the state, geopolitics, and the rules and practices of statecraft. Bismarck's transformative ambition is distinct from the one examined later on, such as the cases of Pericles, Woodrow Wilson, and Charles de Gaulle. In contrast to these statesmen, Bismarck's ambition was unmoored from the sense of public duty and principle. While he completely altered the map of Europe and was the main driver of German unification, he did not do so for the sake of moral ideals or for the greater good of his polity. Bismarck wanted his politics to triumph and to achieve this required freedom of maneuver: he made alliances, foreign and national, for the sake of convenience, yet just as quickly turned on individuals who could no longer render him any service. In his lifetime, Bismarck's political skill and genius was unmatched. Without occupying a post that wielded power, and without qualifications or experience, Bismarck accomplished extraordinary changes not only by outmaneuvering domestic and foreign rivals, but also by taking it upon himself to apply a novel outlook to international politics. Bismarck's political outlook was shaped by his widely ranging understanding of history, artful politics, and radical skepticism toward principled politics.[4]

Bismarck held to the notion that an amoral concept of power was required in the practice of domestic and international politics. He developed and implemented the rules and ideas of *realpolitik* over the course of his political career.[5] This was a novel application of the ideas that power and opportunity trumped tradition and principle. By abandoning established rules and beliefs, he led Germany toward unification. In the process, Bismarck radically reshaped the geopolitical landscape in Europe, revolutionized diplomacy, and overturned the established rules that had held the international order together.

Bismarck's success was not limited to his perspicuity about the international environment. His gift for international politics was evenly matched by his ability to lead internal elements within the German state, as he consistently restrained the more ambitious and aggressive goals of the military leadership. Throughout his life and political career he thrived by never being in one single camp and, while he sowed conflict against liberalism, he surprised everyone in his career by uniting what were believed to be irreconcilable domestic elements: nationalism and conservatism. Through his policies, Bismarck completely reordered Central Europe and united Germany through wise diplomacy.

Bismarck was the lone figure who defined Prussia's interests on the basis of utility, while Liberals and Conservatives rested on Metternich's conservative principle of legitimacy. This meant that lawful monarchs had to be restored to power, which in practice led to the suppression of revolts across Europe and democratic sentiments. For a man of Bismarck's ambition and political skill, the existing domestic institutions and international structure proved inadequate for his goals and type of statecraft. His transformative ambition and skillful leadership helped dismantle the status quo. In practice, this meant that Bismarck would oppose Prussia's partnership with Austria and the Holy Alliance. Moreover, he advocated that Prussia become an ally of its natural enemy, France. Bismarck overturned its public policies through foreign policy and by 1871 had concluded German unification through war and a diplomatic compact among sovereigns. Ultimately, Germany did not become unified by the slow march of parliamentary consensus that the Liberals had expected.

LEADERS IN A REALIST WORLD

For decades, international relations theory was dominated by system theories, especially neorealism. Neorealism is considered an advance over Hans Morgenthau's classical realism because rather than rely on assumptions about human nature, it examines how the anarchic international system constrains state behavior and how the interactions between states produce predictable patterns. According to neorealism, under anarchy, states cannot trust each other so they must vie for security and self-sufficiency. Under these conditions, states unwittingly produce a balance of power.

A balance of power exists when one state does not dominate the international system and is marked by stability, while deviations from a balance of power create international instability that put some states at strategic disadvantages. These shifts can lead to destructive wars. From a structural perspective, the prelude to World War I was marked by Germany and Russia's ascendancy and the decline of the Austrian–Hungarian Empire. The power of the Triple Alliance (Germany, Austria–Hungary, and Italy) and the Triple Entente (Britain, France, and Russia) was roughly equal; thus, any change to the balance of power either through an ally's defeat or defection could lead to major conflict. As a result, each state had to adjust its strategy and capabilities to the aims and fears of its partners; state behavior was strictly determined by the fear that the balance of power could be undermined by the defeat or defection of a major ally (Waltz, 1988, p. 621).

Leaders' miscalculations may also create instability in the balance of power.[6] For example, under Hitler's leadership, Germany began to rearm. Hitler then went further, remilitarizing the Rhineland in 1936 and marching into Austria in 1938 without resistance. Finally, when he invaded Poland in 1938, England and France declared war on Germany. Although his aggressive actions incited a war, he had borne the costs and by 1940 had defeated and occupied the major powers of continental Europe. However, with an insatiable appetite for conquest, and an overoptimistic view of his military forces combined with an underestimation of the Soviet Union's, Hitler launched Operation Barbarossa, a massive invasion of the USSR that aimed to defeat the great power in a single, quick campaign. Hitler relied on his knowledge of the German Army, *blitzkrieg* warfare, and his estimates of the Red Army. He miscalculated the strength of the Soviet Army, especially its ability to replenish its defeated forces, the capacity of the centralized government to conduct the war, and the fierce resistance of the Russians toward the German invaders. Eventually, the Soviet Army took back the conquered territory and brought the fight to Germany proper.

If deviations in the balance of power dispose states to conflict, then we may ask: is the lesson for leaders that they should become balancers of power? Neorealists would say no, it is not the responsibility of other leaders to right the ship when a Hitler comes onto the scene; rather, the balance of power is produced by the uncoordinated actions of states, much as economists think that market price is determined by unfettered competition between suppliers and consumers.

Neorealists do not support the idea that a statesman can consciously guide the balance of power. They argue, for example, that Winston Churchill mistakenly believed that Britain's international role was as a "holder of the balance" (Sheehan, 1989). Nor is a disruption in the balance of power by influential nations and ambitious leaders who are tempted to overreach proof that leaders can willingly change the international structure, since eventually other states will engage in balancing. For realists, state decision-makers are prone to mistakes when they seek to reestablish the balance of power (unless it is clearly in their favor), but those errors are eventually corrected by other actors in the system, as Wilhelm II and Hitler learned when coalitions formed to check their expansion. According to realists, the anarchic international structure causes state behavior and also provides a self-corrective to any instability, which results in a reproduction of the existing structure. There is no role for enlightened leadership to either keep international politics as it is or try to change it.

Classical realists like Morgenthau and Kissinger still believe that it is within the statesman's purview to skillfully apply the lessons of *realpolitik* to statecraft. Kenneth Waltz's neorealism completely expunges the necessity for leaders to be conscious and self-disciplined practitioners of *realpolitik*. Instead, he argues that we can expect state leaders to behave like realists because of the demands imposed on a state under anarchy. State survival is the primary goal of international politics, so all foreign policy decisions should take into consideration the relative power of the state and other states. For Waltz, it is not a question as to whether leaders should act like realists. They simply do.

Neorealism is pessimistic about the idea that individuals can transcend the necessities of power politics and create an alternative international structure. It regards the balance of power as the most influential factor in state behavior. State leaders really only have two paths they can choose. They either defend the balance of power when change favors another state or undermine it when the direction of change is in their favor (Mearsheimer, 2001, p. 3).

While Waltz's theory of international politics does not explain foreign policy, his understanding of international relations bears on the foreign policies of nations. As Waltz (1988) writes, it can: "explain only certain aspects of them. It can tell us what international conditions national policies have to cope with" (p. 619). What is not accounted for by neorealism must be understood through theories of foreign policy, which do not try to explain state interactions and patterns of behavior but, rather, the individual behavior of states and decision-makers. This is why among neoclassical realists, who blend the lessons of classical and neorealist thought, the idea that leaders are vital in shaping foreign policy has resurged because "systemic imperatives can only influence a state's behavior in the international arena through calculations and perceptions of the 'flesh and blood' officials who act on the state's behalf" (Taliaferro, 2004, p. 228).

The neoclassical realists agree with neorealists that basic systemic forces such as a state's relative power and its position in the international system determine foreign policy. However, neoclassical realists contend that a theory of international politics, such as the balance-of-power theory, cannot explain why states and leaders pursue particular foreign policies and grand strategies. For neoclassical realists, systemic forces are constant, but the combination of international opportunities and existing threats are "translated through unit-level intervening variables such as decision-makers' perceptions and the domestic state structure" (Rose, 1998, p. 152).[7]

I also examine how leaders work within domestic politics to respond to their international environment. But I disagree with neoclassical realists that leaders' foreign policy responses that are not appropriately realist are clear evidence of poor judgment, irrationality, or folly. In other words, I do not contend that anarchy in the system, the relative distribution of power, and pervasive uncertainty are simply filtered by intervening variables such as domestic politics and leaders' perceptions. Leaders redefine interests and state identities because their perceptions and beliefs are also constitutive.[8]

In the next section I discuss the relationship between neorealist theory and leadership in greater detail. I first argue that, contrary to what neorealists claim, their assumption about the state is contingent on leaders who act on behalf of the state. I then outline the main neorealist theories, Waltz's structural or defensive realism and John Mearsheimer's offensive realism, which propose radically opposite views of ambition. Waltz predicts that a minimum of security guarantees state survival so leaders are cautious and not ambitious (unless they are irrational), while Mearsheimer thinks that leaders' ambition is incessant and cannot be satisfied.

DEFENSIVE AND OFFENSIVE REALISM: RESTRAINED VERSUS UNLIMITED AMBITION

In international relations studies, Waltz's structural realism and Mearsheimer's offensive realism both share the systemic approach. These scholars draw on the assumption that the international system's structure and its defining feature, anarchy, compel states to pursue strategies that enhance security (Waltz) or to behave aggressively and maximize power over rivals (Mearsheimer). States are compelled to act in these ways because while anarchy persists, no international body can effectively adjudicate disputes, enforce agreements, and prevent conflict.

While Waltz stresses that states seek security and are cautious not to upset the balance, Mearsheimer argues that they can never be certain that their current power will make them safe in the future, so powerful states have an incentive to seek hegemony. These theories lead to divergent views about what leaders should desire for their states under anarchy. In Waltz's world conflict is rare and can be avoided, but a few ambitious leaders spoil it for everyone else. Individual ambition is atypical because it is irrational; leaders' ambition is bound by the necessities of the international structure, which calls upon leaders to seek only as much power as necessary to make the state secure.

For Waltz, leaders are defensive realists when they rely on an offense–defense strategy, which can be understood as the ease or difficulty of conquest. When defensive military capabilities hold an advantage over offensive ones, major wars can be avoided.[9] With uncertain intentions worldwide, leaders should prefer defense to offense.

Balanced power is a statesman's preferred outcome, as he is motivated to acquire only enough to ensure survival and will hesitate if other states begin to collaborate to arrest the increase in his state's power. Security, being a statesman's highest aim, will lend itself to a world of satisfied states, or at least the satisfaction of the status quo powers. In short, power is a means to security and not an end in itself. Rational leadership avoids the self-defeating "excessive accumulation of power"; if a statesman proves too ambitious, other states should react by balancing against the "unreasonable" leader (Waltz, 1988).

Defensive realism enjoins leaders to follow a moderate foreign policy on account of the sobering effects of the international struggle for power. Moderation is not an independent characteristic of individual leaders. Rather, in their pursuit of security, states are mindful of not pushing the limits that could spark a war since war is expensive (unless the state is willing to bear the cost). However, miscalculation or rogue and expansionist states unsettle this balance, which leads to the outbreak of conflict. For Waltz, the presence of ambition that exceeds what other states' leaders are willing to permit is unreasonable ambition because all other states should always unite against the ambitious leader.

For example, expansionist states, such as France under Louis XIV and Napoleon, and Germany under Wilhelm II and Hitler, accumulated excessive power. They perhaps were misguided or irrationally hoped that an opposition would not form. However, in each case, alarmed leaders created coalitions to push these states back. Waltz (1998, p. 627) has an explanation for this kind of behavior:

The lessons of history would seem to be clear: In international politics, success leads to failure. The excessive accumulation of power by one state or coalition of states elicits the opposition of others. The leaders of expansionist states have nevertheless been able to persuade themselves that skillful diplomacy and clever strategy would enable them to transcend the normal processes of balance-of-power politics.

For Waltz, a leader should prefer to balance power by making alliances or strengthening internally. States may increase their power, but they must show restraint and acquire as much power as appropriate to enhance security and not exacerbate the security dilemma: "where one state's measures to increase security diminish that of another state and when the latter state responds in kind, this reaction serves to confirm the former's suspicion that there was a reason to worry" (1998, p. 619). Although peace is fragile in Waltz's world and conflict is frequent, he believes states are risk averse.

For Waltz, miscalculation and irrational ambition lead to conflict, while Mearsheimer contends that lulls in aggressive behavior are evidence of missed opportunities or that leaders are just biding their time. Since Mearsheimer's theory examines states that have offensive capabilities, he attends primarily to great powers. Ironically, the most powerful states are also the most disgruntled about the relative distribution of power, and their leaders must actively seek opportunities to increase their state's power.

The substantive difference between offensive and defensive realists is reminiscent of that among human beings in Machiavelli's *Prince* (1998). While Machiavelli thinks that all people share the desire to acquire, only some actively seek more (offensive realists), while the majority simply wants to keep what they have (defensive realists). Offensive realism presumes a persistent and unrestrained ambition among the leaders of great powers. A satisfied leader quickly learns to adjust to the offensive nature of the world since all leaders are ready to take advantage of rivals as they seek to become hegemons in their regions and in the international system.

Mearsheimer describes his theory as genuinely tragic because under uncertainty states have to pursue power and dominate others. No amount of power can guarantee security, so states should actively seek new opportunities to expand their power. At all times, leaders should craft ambitious foreign policies that maximize power. Mearsheimer's world is populated by revisionist states, and even if a state already has an advantage in its region, it will behave aggressively "because it has the capability as well as the incentive to do so" (2001, p. 34). Among great powers, such behavior is more prevalent because leaders are rationally bedeviled by the fear of what other states might do to them. They must operate on worst-case assumptions, and "states are disposed to think offensively toward other states even though their ultimate motive is simply to survive" (2001, p. 34). Yet, survival requires ambitious foreign policies and the readiness to seize opportunities, best rivals, and try to dominate the region. Even if their states become regional hegemons, leaders cannot rest satisfied because they must be vigilant and actively prevent the rise of ambitious rivals.

When leaders act as defensive realists, they aim to limit state ambition, keep what they have acquired, and maintain their position in the international system. A skillful defensive realist can still gain advantages for his state, but he must do so "without antagonizing other states and frightening them into united action" (Waltz, 1988, p. 622).

How does an offensive realist behave differently? First, security is much more tenuous if increases in power are not being consistently attained. Leaders will assess threats by calculating the difference in power between states. They also assume that others are primed to use their power offensively. Leaders should want to maximize state power because its accumulation creates an incentive for more power rather than the restraint that Waltz proposes. When leaders have gained more power, they should use it.

Offensive realists pursue policies of conquest through territorial expansion. Although conquest is necessary given the incentives in the international environment, offensive realists usually carry it out in the name of national glory, personal ambition, and economic gain. For example, Bismarck, Wilhelm II, and Hitler all acted as offensive realists should, and Germany made it a priority to increase its power through expansion from 1862 to 1870, then again in 1903, and, subsequently, under Hitler until 1945. Its aggressive *Weltpolitik* was a function of strategic security calculations. Yet, from 1871 to 1890, Germany remained pacific, and it seems that it was satisfied with the balance of power in the way Waltz would argue.

According to Mearsheimer, however, Germany unhappily accepted the status quo during this period simply because it could not risk a major war with either France or Russia. The practice of offensive realism was in a period of dormancy, but the desire to act like an offensive realist was held constant. German leaders were biding their time as they increased the country's relative capabilities.

Mearsheimer is explicit about the prescriptive implications of offensive realism: "states should behave according to the dictates of offensive realism, because it outlines the best way to survive in a dangerous world," and failure to act in this way is tantamount to foolishness (2001, pp. 10–11). Neorealism takes leaders' political ambition for granted: ambition is tightly coupled to the international structure, and it is muted and unreasonable in Waltz's theory. In addition, Waltz thinks that too much ambition defies the precepts of defensive realism. In Mearsheimer's world, all leaders are ambitious. Those who show what I call transformative ambition are not unique because this kind of ambition will be matched and checked by another leader. Much like a game of chess, to win one must play aggressively, and when one player embarks on such a strategy, the other player must respond in kind. Even though Mearsheimer brings ambition back into realism, it is ultimately reined in by structure because all leaders are behaving in the same way.

Neorealists take leader ambition for granted and by doing so fail to acknowledge that varying kinds and degrees of ambition shape the paths to the balance of power. I propose that leader ambition is independent of the incentives and constraints of the international structure. I am not arguing that leaders are blind to the international reality, but that, for some, ambition transcends the tight coupling of the state's motivations under anarchy. For Waltz, the idea of transformative ambition is tantamount to folly, so we should scarcely witness it. Yet, for Mearsheimer, all leaders of great powers should have a healthy dose of transformative ambition because they are actively seeking to change the balance of power to their advantage.

Neorealist theorists need to acknowledge that ambition matters in a way that cannot just be explained away as a series of mistakes, irrational behavior, or lulls in the active pursuit of power. Political ambition is a phenomenon that requires an independent explanation from the international structure. The theories of Waltz and Mearsheimer cannot help us with the independent nature of political ambition since a realist leader's ambition is derived from the international structure. Realist leaders are constants as they act on considerations of state survival. However, realists leave much unexamined in the realm of foreign policy. Once we relax the assumption that leadership is completely determined by structure, we can separate the motivations of the state under anarchy from the political ambition of state leaders.

Realist assumptions about leaders' ambition are a convenient conceptual device, but they do not do justice to the way political ambition, and especially transformative ambition, can overcome structural constraints. Realists never would admit that structural constraints are surpassed. When scholars reconsider whether structure determines political ambition, they conceive of various other goals that leaders entertain when conducting foreign policy. For example, decision-makers who value political power should rank their personal political welfare over any other goal. A more individualistic view of political ambition emerges when we understand leaders in this way. They are held accountable not by the international system, but by the people who grant them political power. The way in which they maximize their welfare, however, requires a more precise examination of domestic institutions and their influence on leaders' behavior.

BISMARCK'S REALIST AMBITION REVISITED

Here, I return to the example of Bismarck in order to prove how both defensive and offensive theses of Bismarck's ambition are inadequate. I concentrate on the events and decisions in his early career that culminated in the war of Prussia against Austria, which led to German unification. Bismarck's actions on the domestic and international levels forever changed Europe and cemented his reputation as a genius statesman, and the realists appropriate all his successes as a verification of their theories because they were applications of *realpolitik*.

From 1862 to 1871, Bismarck embarked on the grandest diplomatic and political achievements of any leader in Europe in the last two centuries, and he did this without possessing any of three major tools at a statesman's disposal: holding a position of authority, the backing of any major political party, and command of an army. Bismarck sidestepped parliament and reorganized the army; exploited political conditions so as to declare war against Austria; dissolved the German Diet; subdued the minor states and in doing so created German unity under Prussian leadership.

However, were Bismarck's realist policies a product of structure or did they flow from his independent ambition? Here I make a case for the latter and argue that to understand Bismarck's ambition we must understand the statesman as he understood himself. Yet, Bismarck did not pursue his interest at the expense of all else; he tied his statecraft to the state's permanent interest, which for Henry Kissinger is the incontrovertible proof of Bismarck's application of the laws of realist politics.

According to Henry Kissinger, Bismarck's understanding of *realpolitik* provided him the clear-sightedness that led him to subordinate his personal ambition to the practice of dutiful statesmanship. With his ambition fixed on statesmanship, Bismarck reordered Central Europe and dominated European affairs. Kissinger (1994, p. 127) describes Bismarck's worldview and understanding of restrained ambition:

> In the world of realpolitik, it was the statesman's duty to evaluate ideas as forces in relation to all other forces relevant to making a decision; and the various elements needed to be judged by how well they could serve the national interest, not by preconceived ideologies.

Kissinger makes two disputable assumptions however: (1) assuming that the world of *realpolitik* conditioned Bismarck's foreign policy and (2) that the statesman is obliged to the state's interest. I argue that it was Bismarck's comprehension of *realpolitik* as a vehicle for his ambition, which was to practice politics on a grand scale: power and opportunity trumped ideology, flexibility in diplomacy stood over any convention, and proportionality dictated the limits of state ambition. As a result, Bismarck practiced *realpolitik* but he was unmoored; the benefits to the state were epiphenomenal.

I argue here that he deliberately chose realist goals and power for his state, because it provided the greatest platform of maneuver for him to operate. He was genuinely indifferent to the internal makeup of the state and for this reason did not possess the deliberate and public-spirited, transformative ambition of statesman like Pericles and Charles de Gaulle, despite the fact that his statecraft transformed Europe and the rules of international politics. He was a conservative absolutist when it suited him, since the foundation of his achievements was based on the approval of the King. However, the arrival of constitutional government offered him the flexibility to engineer policies that constrained the King, which is why "Bismarck sprang the idea of universal suffrage on a startled German public in 1863 in order to prevent King William from going to a congress of princes called by the Emperor of Austria" (Steinberg, 2011, p. 8). In the process of playing internal and external elements against each other, Bismarck unified Germany and transformed the geopolitical landscape by changing the character of European diplomacy.

How did the nature of Bismarck's ambition contribute to this radical change? His ambition lacked an honorable devotion to moral ideals yet realists believe that he was bound by notions of dutiful statesmanship.

How is it possible that a man without any moral compass still entertained the notion of duty to Prussia? Bismarck's statesmanship was marked by what only seems like the self-denial of personal ambition; as a result, Kissinger argues that the exercise of *realpolitik* proves that Bismarck was duty bound. I argue that his ambition was directed toward the project of imposing his rules and practices on Prussian politics and European diplomacy.

Bismarck's ambition was guided by an unashamed sense of self-interest and lack of restraint. Though highly aware of his social standing in Prussian society, Bismarck did not seek material or political gain for its own sake. He wanted to rule and dominate the political scene and best foes and friends alike. Unlike Otto Pflanze (1972), whose Freudian interpretation of Bismarck grew the more he learned about Bismarck's foibles, resentment, paranoia, and hypochondria, I do not argue that his principal ambition was driven by mere drives of his personality to dominate and rule over others.

BISMARCK'S POLITICAL THOUGHT

Despite his clashing and problematic personality, Bismarck had the rare combination of colossal ambition and political genius. He was easily bored with the humdrum of day-to-day politics and bureaucracy. Only high stakes politics proved a worthy challenge for him. To achieve his ambition he maintained a sober outlook and relativity of all belief and understood politics as the continuous flux of forces that were animated by the interests of actors, and both human beings and states were alike in this way. "In politics," he argued, "no one does anything for another, unless he also finds it in his own interest to do so" (Pflanze, 1958, p. 495).

As such, Bismarck's motives were partly based on a desire to dominate, but, primarily, he consciously wanted to take part in a highly calculating and rational game, in which he saw circumstances as opportunities and thought of political actors of all different stripes (foreign and domestic) as players on a chess board. Nothing else suited him. Bismarck observed later in life:

> My entire life was spent gambling for high stakes with other people's money. I could never foresee exactly whether my plan would succeed ... Politics is a thankless job because everything depends on chance and conjecture. One

has to reckon with a series of probabilities and improbabilities and base one's plans upon this reckoning. (Steinberg, 2011, p. 130)

Kissinger (1968) has described Bismarck as a "White Revolutionary," a rare statesman who profoundly altered the history of his society. Bismarck's innovation was unconventional; he did not seek revolutionary change and furthered his goals from a position of inferior strength. Kissinger argues that Bismarck's substantial political change was a triumph of the will as he subjected contemporary institutions to "strains for which they were not designed" (1968, p. 869). Kissinger calls Bismarck's revolution "strange" because it appeared in the guise of conservatism; "the scale of its conception proved incompatible with the prevailing international order, it triumphed domestically through the vastness of its successes abroad" (1968, p. 889). For Kissinger, it is clear that German unity was accomplished by Bismarck's force and practice of *realpolitik*.

However, Bismarck did not first discover realist principles and then apply them to policy. Rather, he was responsible for bringing realist principles into practice against conservative and liberal critics. The foundations of his statecraft were philosophical and practical; he understood history as a universal movement and the myriad of political circumstances as a game of chance. Bismarck's practical application of what he calls probabilities and improbabilities should not be mistaken for an early application of game theory to politics.[10] He developed his view of politics and history, which includes the role of states and people, through a combination of political thought and experience. Moreover, as a political practitioner Bismarck understood politics as an art, while criticizing academic and theoretical approaches to politics. Conversely, since its foundation, realists have sought to establish realism as an "objective science" of politics.[11]

At some level, this giant of European diplomacy believed that the individual mattered little. The force of circumstance, not a single person's action and moral predilections, dictates history. As such, Bismarck saw politics as the art of the possible and not a stage for gaining high honors or personal glory. His policies did not just respond to actual events but were also designed to meet all unforeseen contingencies. Although he did not think an individual could make history, he believed that a statesman could learn from history and lead the state to some greater purpose.

Bismarck's realism was lodged between his view of a destined but undisclosed history and his understanding of human freedom. While history follows a definite and rational trend, the content of history is not disclosed fully to statesmen. This limit of human understanding also constrains leaders' freedom since a political actor can never be sure if he is acting for or against his state's historical destiny. Nevertheless, Bismarck did believe he possessed a historical sense; he could discern the relations among forces and events but it was impossible to master them. Bismarck's skepticism shaped his political ambition differently from the transformative ambitions of statesmen who desire to do immortal work and build lasting monuments through institutional and moral change. The latter consciously wish to leave a mark on the world, which they try to do by bringing a novel and coherent political order into being.

NEITHER CONSERVATIVE OR LIBERAL

In 1861 Prussia was undergoing liberal political reform: it had a constitution and a bevy of electoral activity had doubled the German Progressive Party's representation. The party's cornerstone policy was centered on the Landtag's (German parliament) right to control the army's budget (Steinberg, 2011, p. 172). In his first speech as Minister-President in 1862, at a time when rumors were swirling that the King would abdicate his throne because of the growing power of the parliamentary majority, Bismarck astonished parliament in the most famous speech he ever made:

> Prussia must build up and preserve her strength for the advantageous moment, which has already come and gone many times. Her borders under the treaties of Vienna are not favourable for the healthy existence of the state. The great questions of the day will not be settled by speeches and majority decisions – that was the great mistake of 1848 and 1849 – but by blood and iron. (Steinberg, 2011, p. 181)

Although Bismarck appears retrograde, his political and moral compass is difficult to pin down because he did not rigidly adhere to any policy, political order, or moral code. Throughout his career he seemed to prefer a conservative order. However, as events unfolded in Europe, many of his own making, he breached Prussia's traditional alliances with conservative Austria. Bismarck ended the slow march for German unity through the process of consent; rather, he unified by conquest. As long as Bismarck had a strong grasp over foreign affairs, relations of power would dictate Germany's politics and shape the continent. As a result, Bismarck turned Prussia into a large and successful military monarchy.

While liberal politics declined, Germany's state power grew at a tremendous pace as the forces of the economy and industry were unleashed. Between 1862 and 1871, Prussia became the dominant continental power after winning wars against Denmark, Austria, and France. His international statecraft did not follow historical precedent; he forced Prussia to abandon its traditional alliance with Austria and her native hostility to France. Otto Pflanze explains why Bismarck chose such a course: "[a]mid conflicting forces Bismarck usually sought to occupy the middle ground: that is, the pivot position from which alternative alliances with either of two hostile interests was possible or the fulcrum position from which they could be brought into equilibrium" (1958, p. 503).

Bismarck had no passion for ideology; he was a pragmatist who pursued the Prussian state's interest at every turn. He chose German unity not because of nationalist sentiments, but because of its advantages to Prussia, despite the fact that Prussian identity was sacrificed for the sake of unity. As such, he strongly rejected the conservative unity that linked states on the basis of legitimate crowned heads. Specifically, Bismarck opposed his conservative associate Leopold von Gerlach's – to which he owed his political position – principal political strategy that politics had to rest on principle. Jonathan Steinberg (2011) perfectly sums up Gerlach's counter-argument to Bismarck's view that opportunity should dictate alliances: "because only principle provided the steady foundation of alliances and initiatives" (p. 132).

Against Gerlach and the rest of the conservative establishment, Bismarck did not tie political decisions to preconceived ideas and traditional moral categories. Moreover, neither conservative principles nor dutiful service to the Prussian monarchy, as Kissinger (1994) argues, guided his political choices. Under Bismarck's *realpolitik*, foreign policy became a contest of strength. He forged alliances in all directions, "so that Prussia would always be closer to each of the contending parties than they were to one another" (Kissinger, 1994, p. 122). At the same time, he altered Germany's liberal, progressive path toward unification: "he rested Prussia's claim to leadership in Germany on its strength rather than on universal values" (1994, p. 128).

Kissinger's emphasis on Bismarck's service to the state, above all else, is belied by the statesman's lack of interest in creating firm domestic institutions for Prussia's future. At the beginning of his career,

Bismarck reversed liberal progress by leading a conservative transformation of Prussia's politics. He resisted the identification of Prussian nationalism with liberalism and opposed a democratic constitution. Bismarck's ambition only seemed conservative because he sought to rescue what he thought was Prussia's traditional political order over and against liberalism. Yet, as mentioned earlier, the King's complete control over the armed forces was necessary for Bismarck's plans. Only a powerful monarchy could grease Bismarck's wheels.

For example, in 1862 Bismarck reacted intransigently when it seemed that William I might have to compromise with parliament over the reorganization of the armed services. Bismarck had pushed for a three-year, from a two-year, service obligation. When the Landtag voted against the measure by 150 to 17, Bismarck, as Minister-President, went on the offensive in an attempt to crush a liberal constituency: "he withdrew all compromise proposals ... and began an attack of the civil service" (Steinberg, 2011, p. 186). Bismarck's aggressive style was not due to personality foibles; it flowed from the fact that he did not have a fixed principle on which he based his conservatism.

The year following his contentious fight with Liberals, he looked for a new avenue to pursue his policies: universal suffrage. The flux of forces had shifted, which now favored his use of liberal policy. In an attempt to delegitimize the German princes, Bismarck used the "people" as leverage against them, since he predicted, correctly, that the majority of German-speaking people would choose unity over the irrevocable sovereignty of many princes. Bismarck's end was to strengthen Prussia's position in Germany, and the King against "the posturing of the liberal classes or the presumption of smaller princes" (Steinberg, 2011, p. 191). By the end of 1880s, Bismarck planned to roll back universal suffrage because it strengthened the hand of non-conservative elements in the state: Catholics and Social Democrats (2011, p. 247).

GERMAN UNIFICATION

Over the course of the 1850s, the Prussian parliament believed that the slow march of progress and consensus politics would eventually produce German unification. The pillars of Prussian foreign policy rested on the belief that relations among states should be based on common interests and shared principles. Bismarck was adamantly opposed to the liberal view: Prussia needed to be a strong and internationally ambitious power. In order to influence public policy, Bismarck urged a new direction in foreign policy that would guide Prussia based on an assessment of the state's relative strength. As a consequence, Prussia would enter and break alliances when it proved useful. But such a policy required it to abandon the self-restraint that had been in force since 1815. For Bismarck, a change in policy was necessary to see Prussia become a great power, and only this goal served as a justification for German unity. However, as I discussed previously, the Metternich system previously informed Prussian and European policy. Bismarck would need to overturn it.

Bismarck could only fulfill his ambition if Prussia rose to become the dominant German state. He bested the liberal proposal by finding a pretext to declare war with Austria while undermining the crown princes. In 1866, when that war finally came and Prussia was victorious, Bismarck had thoroughly discredited the liberal opposition. Simultaneously, against the desire of many conservatives for a punitive peace against Austria, Bismarck made peace without annexation or a victory parade in Vienna (Steinberg, 2011, p. 254).

As a result of the war, Austria had to withdraw from the association of German states and Prussia assumed the leadership of the formation of a Federation of North German States. Even though Bismarck's policies enhanced the state by amassing power, he did not pursue power like a zealot. On the one hand, he subjected the European balance of power to a relativistic analysis that discovered ways to exploit opportunities for Prussian gain. On the other hand, the forces massed against the state restrained Bismarck's pursuit of power. But his politics was not a conservative, liberal, or nationalist: "Bismarck changed colour like certain deep pools of water refract the light in various hues" (Steinberg, 2011, p. 261).

In 1866, with a new structure to command, Bismarck made peace with the Liberals in order to secure a budget that would help him construct a new Germany. His foreign policy success had led to great publicity and reverence in political circles, the popular press, and among German people. He became a media personality and a national symbol (Steinberg, 2011, pp. 263–4). To control domestic politics Bismarck had to find a way to control both the Prussian state ministry and the new Federal Government of the North German Federation. In order not to cede any power to the new Federation, Bismarck drafted a new constitution, mostly by himself, designed to keep the political balance of power in the hands of the individuals and structures on which his power rested (Steinberg, 2011, p. 267). Rather than build institutions that would withstand turbulence and change, Bismarck put together a fragile structure that suited him. The new Federation pivoted on sovereignty of the King of Prussia, the Minister-President, and the new head of the German Federation: the Federal Chancellor, a position that he occupied from 1867 to 1871 when he became Chancellor of the German empire.

To complete the unification of Germany, Bismarck sought to provoke a war with France that would bring about the end of the Napoleonic Empire. In 1868 he found that opportunity by engineering a crisis over the candidacy of Leopold, Prince of Hohenzollern, for the throne of Spain. After forcing King William I to retract his support of Leopold, Napoleon III made a diplomatic blunder by ordering his ambassador to get a public promise from the King that Prussia would not renew the Prince of Hoehnzollern's candidacy in the future. Offended, the King rebuffed the French ambassador and at Bismarck's urging, the new demand and the King's refusal were communicated to embassies abroad and to the press. Bismarck ensured that the language of the publicized statement would provoke war with France. On 19 July 1870, France declared war.

With superior numbers and organization, Prussia won a series of battles over France and on 2 September 1870, the French army was defeated at Sedan and Napoleon III was taken prisoner. France did not capitulate until January 1871, because French citizens proclaimed the French Third Republic and waged a guerilla war for months after Napoleon III's defeat. When the French Republic finally capitulated, Bismarck sought to conduct peace terms between France and Germany on his own. Germany extracted 5 billion francs in war reparations. In addition, the newly established German Empire annexed Alsace-Lorraine, which gave Germany a new strategic frontier over the French. Bismarck was opposed to the move, since it limited his diplomatic flexibility. France would never ally with Germany as long as these lands were not in its possession. With the unification of Germany under the German Empire and the victory over France, Bismarck reached the apex of his career. From 1871 to 1914, the German Empire became a superpower: it had the greatest coal, steel, and iron production on the continent, the largest, and most educated population, and by 1914 the largest army and second most powerful navy (2011, p. 313).

Bismarck spent the remainder of his career trying to hold his vast project intact, which required moderation in foreign policy and a firm hand domestically. Domestically, he was more ruthless and prone to conflict than in the past. For example, from 1873 to 1875, he spent considerable time and energy trying to crush Catholics because, as a growing demographic, they represented a powerful counterweight to Bismarck in parliament. Bismarck helped craft and pass legislation, known as the May Laws of 1873, which governed the legal status of Catholic religious orders and controlled future clergymen's nationalities, the disciplinary power of the church, and ecclesiastical appointments. Another instance that demonstrated the Chancellor's grip on domestic affairs occurred in 1876, when Bismarck, who had supported Liberals' insistence on free trade, engineered a great shift to conservatism by abandoning free trade, adopting tariffs, and ending the relationship between the Crown and the liberal parties (Steinberg, 2011, p. 349).

On the international level, he did not desire unlimited expansion, "Bismarck said that from the mistakes of Napoleon I he learned to exercise 'wise moderation after the greatest successes'" (Pflanze, 1958, p. 500). From 1871 to 1879, Bismarck focused on managing a complex set of alliances while trying to isolate France diplomatically. As such, he forged a formal alliance with Austria and then helped cement the Three Emperors League between Prussia, Austria, and Russia despite Austria and Russia's rivalry over the Balkans. In 1877, Bismarck published the Kissigen Dictation, in which he succinctly outlined the complex diplomacy of the Bismarckian system:

1. Gravitating of Russian and Austrian interests and mutual rivalry toward the East;
2. An occasion for Russia to need the alliance with us in order to achieve a strong defensive position in the Orient and on its coasts;
3. For England and Russia a satisfactory status quo, which would give both the same interest in maintaining the existing situation that we have;
4. Separation of England because of Egypt and the Mediterranean from France, which remains hostile to us;
5. Relations between Russia and Austria, which make it hard for both to create anti-German coalitions, which centralizing or clerical forces at the Austrian court are somewhat inclined to pursue (Steinberg, 2011, p. 355).

From 1881 to 1890, Bismarck worked arduously to bring Italy, Spain, and England into a dominant coalition to further isolate France (McDonald and Rosencrance, 1985, p. 58). His predecessors lacked his sense of measure in foreign affairs. He was sensitive to both the failure to take advantage of opportunity and the need to stave off coalition-building against Germany; the concern for countries uniting to balance against a powerful Germany was absent in his more aggressive fore-bears. Such aggressive impulses, and their consequences, were on display twice in the first half of the twentieth century as coalitions formed to fight and defeat Germany. In 1890, the German leadership changed. Kaiser Wilhelm II came to power, dismissed Bismarck, and abandoned the Chancellor's moderate foreign policy program. Wilhelm II undid Bismarck's alliances and his foreign policy of restraint. Under Bismarck, Germany was in a defensive alliance with Russia, which Wilhelm II ended, increasing the likelihood that conflict with France would foster a dangerous Franco-Russian alliance. Wilhelm II also introduced a policy of expansion and a naval program to match Britain's, leading to Germany's isolation as it drove Britain, France, and Russia into the Triple Entente to combat German expansionism.

CONCLUSION

While the neorealist view of ambition and statecraft presumes a structurally constrained leadership, Bismarck's statecraft was balanced between a response to the international environment and his desire to fulfill what he believed was Prussia's natural role in Europe, a position his contemporaries did not share. It was Bismarck's insatiable ambition to be an actor in high stakes politics that led Prussia to achieve supremacy over Austria and in Europe. It was his ambition coupled with genius that set his international statecraft in motion.

For realists like Kissinger, Bismarck's foreign policy not only affirms the central precepts of realist theory, but it also proves that leaders who master the art of *realpolitik* do best. Thus, a realist can conclude that Bismarck was prudent and skilled because he was an astute practioner of *realpolitik*. Thus, realist scholars tend to elevate Bismarck's leadership because he perfectly exploited opportunities but could also show restraint. In other words, he did not let his personal ambition or foibles get in the way of calibrating Germany's security needs to accurate assessments of state power. In addition, realists applaud his shrewd ability to enter into active alliances in all directions; and his genius for the art of *realpolitik* simply proves he was capable of discerning and applying realist principles. What they fail to realize is that Bismarck's superior realism can be explained by the fact that he created a world governed by *realpolitik*. Realism flowed from Bismarck's deliberation and constitutive perceptions about world.

Bismarck's rejection of traditional politics and acceptance of amoral superior force as the final arbiter gave him a steely view of international politics. This unromantic political disposition and his practice of *realpolitik* are why realists have placed him in the pantheon of realist statesmen. Yet, his realism, which transformed the international system, undermines some key realist premises. Germany's sole political aim became power: Germany for the sake of German power. Yet among German leaders, only Bismarck, whose political relativism gave him a sense of measure, reined in this force that became unhinged from any moral or political purpose. Bismarck was a political and moral relativist. His successors however did not accept a relativistic analysis of German power. They inherited what they believed was limitless might. Pride trumped sobriety. This pride gave way to the belief that power was the just desert of German supremacy, which, to the disastrous consequences witnessed in the twentieth century, was the dangerous ideology that replaced the Bismarckian order.

Realist theorists need to acknowledge that ambition matters in a way that cannot just be explained away as a series of mistakes, irrational behavior, or lulls in the active pursuit of power. Political ambition is a phenomenon that requires an independent explanation from the international structure. Waltz and Mearsheimer's theories cannot help us with the independent nature of political ambition since a realist leader's ambition is derived from the international structure. Realist leaders are constants as they act on considerations of state ambitions. However, realists leave much unexamined in the realm of foreign policy. For example, since realist leaders respond only to external constraints and opportunities, they do not calculate the impact of foreign policy on their political fates (Mesquita and Lalman, 1992, p. 12).

Realist assumptions about leaders' ambition are a convenient conceptual device, but they do not do justice to the way political ambition, and especially transformative ambition, can overcome structural constraints. Realists never would admit that structural constraints are surpassed. When scholars reconsider whether structure determines political ambition, they conceive of various other goals that leaders entertain when conducting foreign policy. For example, decision-makers who value political power should rank their personal political welfare over any other goal. A more individualistic view of political ambition emerges when we understand leaders in this way. They are held accountable not by the international system, but by the people who grant them political power. The way in which they maximize their welfare, however, requires a more precise examination of domestic institutions and their influence on leaders' behavior. To this argument I now turn.

NOTES

1. See Waltz (1979).
2. See Mearsheimer (2001)
3. See Samuels (2003).
4. For accounts of how Bismarck's personality influenced his policy see also see Pflanze (1972).
5. The philosophy of *realpolitik* grew out of a reaction against Hegel's idealism and metaphysical conception of the state. Leopold Von Ranke, a contemporary of Bismarck, became the academic spokesperson for *realpolitik*; he produced empirical hypothesis about the nature of the state and argued that the origin of any state had to be thought of in the context of preexisting relations among states (Aho, 1975, p. 35).
6. Some scholars argue that psychological factors routinely lead to a misunderstanding of the international environment as decision-makers are dependent on beliefs, images, and perception of the intentions of others in the decision-making process thereby limiting their rationality. See Jervis (1976).
7. For example, neoclassical realists try to account for why states sometimes fail to live up to neorealist predictions, such as when they do not recognize and react to clear and present threats or have "underbalanced" by responding to threats either imprudently or halfheartedly (Schweller, 2004, pp. 159–201).
8. Scholars have examined the independent role of leaders to explain institutional change, see March and Olsen (1984) Leaders can also practice the art of political manipulation and change their environments through the use of "heresthetics" in order to win, see Riker (1986).
9. See Glaser and Kaufman (1998).
10. Game theory is a decision-making approach based on the assumption of actor rationality in a situation of competition. Each actor tries to maximize gains or minimize losses under conditions of uncertainty and incomplete information, which requires each actor to rank order preferences, estimate probabilities, and try to discern what the other actor is going to do. For an explanation of game theory in international relations see Lake and Powell (1999).
11. See Mortgenthau (1978).

2. The strategic perspective of leadership: ambition as political survival

> And it should be considered that nothing is more difficult to handle, more doubtful of success, nor more dangerous to manage, than to put oneself at the head of introducing new orders.
> **Machiavelli**, *The Prince*

In Chapter 1, I criticized defensive and offensive realism on the grounds that both theories derive leaders' political ambition from the incentives and constraints of the international structure. I also argued that whereas defensive realism understates the role of ambition, offensive realism overstates it. According to both these realist theories, leaders' ambition and behavior are tightly coupled to the demands imposed by international anarchy.

This chapter examines a theory of strategic interaction and its relationship to transformative ambition. Unlike realism, this theory examines how leaders respond to domestic incentives and constraints as well as international circumstances. I concentrate my attention on *The Logic of Political Survival*, an ambitious theoretical and empirical study conducted by Bruce Bueno de Mesquita, Alastair Smith, Randolph Siverson, and James D. Morrow (2003) in which they explain how leaders make domestic and foreign policy decisions that are compatible with national incentives.[1] Although leaders are aware of international circumstances when they form foreign policy goals, their aims primarily reflect the interests of the groups that help keep them in power.

Their work is a tome that combines an original theory of politics and leadership, statistical analyses, mathematical models, and many illustrative case studies. First, the authors propose a theory of institutional incentives: democratic and autocratic institutions impact both the selection of leaders and the decisions they make. Second, they demonstrate how these decisions affect leader tenure and at the same time influence key dimensions of governance, such as taxing and spending, public welfare, civil liberties, trade, war, and regime change.

At the heart of the theory is an assumption about leaders' foremost political ambition: they seek political office and find ways to ensure survival in office. This belief improves on realism because it examines leaders rather than states as the essential unit of analysis. Leaders act according to their self-interest: "since the earliest polities, leaders have worried about their hold on power" (Mesquita et al., 2003, p. 15). Their choices "are motivated by the interest politicians have in holding on to office."

The authors base their theory of strategic interaction on "this belief in the desire to hold power," which raises some interesting implications concerning the relationship between regime politics and political survival (Mesquita et al., 2003, p. 16).[2] Leaders' interests are separate from the general population; they do not rule for the common good. There is no public-spirited leadership that is divorced from self-interest. Whether leaders are democrats or autocrats, they advance policies that enhance their hold on power.

In this chapter, I argue that the strategic perspective's assumption about ambition fails to account for political ambition that sets its sights beyond office.[3] Mesquita et al.'s narrowing of ambition begins in their failure to distinguish between political ambition and interests, as they define all interests as self-interest. When political ambition is understood as furthering one's interest, which can only be accomplished through political office, the result is that ambition is reduced to the sole desire for office, which the authors assume is uniformly shared by all leaders. When defined precisely as a drive that varies among individuals, political ambition is something that disposes leaders toward different objects (and some more strongly than others), such as power, political accomplishments, greater prestige, fame, and honorable distinction.

Whereas offensive and defensive realism offer two distinct views of leaders' international ambition (cautious security maximizers and dangerous revisionists), the strategic perspective offers one.[4] I critique the notion of strategic ambition from the inside out by examining the thought of Machiavelli. In the next section, I discuss how the Florentine philosopher accepts the premise that political survival may be a leader's only tenable goal, yet he still differentiates ordinary from great ambition. I pay specific attention to his discussion of the greats: political founders whose politics were not tied to any particular institutions. Following the analysis of Machiavelli's ideas, I compare the strategic perspective's explanation of why the American founders chose republican government to Douglass Adair's interpretation, which is that they transformed their parochial self-interest into a desire for grand fame.

The reason that the authors of the strategic perspective circumscribe political ambition is that they think the intense competition for office induces the politics of political survival at the expense of other goals. Successful leaders create and maintain a winning coalition within a regime's electorate. This faction is a smaller part of the general polity that has a say in choosing and supporting the leadership. Leaders who desire to survive in office, if rational, will adopt policies that are compatible with the preferences of their most important supporters (the winning coalition).

Since ambition among political leaders does not vary, the authors explain that the coalition's size makes a profound difference for the way leaders govern. Winning coalitions are large in democracies and small in autocracies. The former induce leaders to promote the public good, while in autocracies leaders distribute private goods to shore up the support of the few. Strategic leaders use their power and the state's economic resources to both vitiate rivals' challenges and keep their supporters satisfied. They maintain the loyalty of the groups that are instrumental in choosing and promoting the leadership by satisfying their preferences. In short, ruling is the satisfaction of the winning coalition's preferences.

Mesquita et al. argue that in democracies the majority of the population and even the disenfranchised are better off than in autocracies, as goods are more equitably distributed. However, they also find that leaders fare better in autocracies. Autocrats have longer tenures and their supporters tend to be more constant, while democratic citizens' allegiance is lukewarm. For the authors, loyalty is not a moral phenomenon; it is the product of political calculus among supporters. For example, it is more often the case in autocracies that supporters have more to lose from leader turnover or regime change, so they tend to remain faithful to an incumbent.

I challenge the strategic perspective's interpretation of leadership by comparing examples of democratic and autocratic leaders. I show the effects of transformative ambition in both types of government and also how the different ambition and character of leaders in similar autocracies sometimes supported or undermine their political survival.

This chapter also emphasizes how the strategic perspective departs radically from realism. Realists conceive of a division of high from low politics, which means that leaders decide matters of national security without worrying about their political fates. The authors of the strategic perspective suggest otherwise. Politics does not stop at the water's edge. Leaders' foreign policy decisions do not flow from the imperatives of national security but from the strategic interaction of leaders who respond to domestic incentives and international circumstances. Leaders in democracies try to avoid war, but when they do fight, they usually try hard to win. Autocrats tend to be more belligerent yet are less willing to expend precious resources toward a war effort.

MACHIAVELLI: FROM STRATEGIC AMBITION TO THE TRANSFORMATIVE AMBITION OF POLITICAL FOUNDERS

Strategic leaders are self-interested and the actions they choose are intended to redound to their own benefit (Mesquita et al., 2003, p. 21). Self-aware leaders should enhance their supporters' welfare, which implies that public-spirited leadership has selfish motives. Once in power, leaders gain authority over public resources and can use them in either of two ways: "they can promulgate general public policies that satisfy the desires of their supporters and perhaps the desires of others among the citizens of the state, and they can dole out private benefits to purchase the continued support of their critical backers" (Mesquita et al., 2003, p. 29).[5]

While many leaders are motivated by run-of-the-mill self-interest and the desire for office, political office is a small prize for those with transformative ambition. The latter may have a thirst for distinction, lust for fame, and a passion to rule over others (this entails office but has a greater scope). These motives can catalyze them to change the political landscape through bold and significant actions. They thrust themselves into grand enterprises, which manifest in various forms: wars of conquest or independence, imperial domination, and constitutional building that introduce new modes and orders. The first two actions may overturn existing governments and have a revolutionary character that can have a disorderly effect. The last goal is decisively transformative because it is motivated by the desire to found a state, which shapes a polity's way of life; it represents a grand political achievement and a paradigmatic shift in citizens' lives.

Only leaders with greater ambition and a superior awareness for what is possible can found a state and perpetuate its survival. To explain this phenomenon, I must turn to a model of political ambition that has a larger range than the one provided by the strategic perspective, which presumes a structured political environment. Machiavelli's thought prepares the way for a particularly powerful view of the ambition of founders and political virtue.

Machiavelli's advice to princes closely resembles what strategic leaders already know: to gain and keep power, they must heed circumstances and necessity. Machiavelli warns princes to avoid standards of moral virtue that do not aid in acquiring and retaining political power. He instructs them to answer to necessity, which calls them to follow what is truly in their hearts: personal aggrandizement at the expense of others. For Machiavelli, princes must use moral virtue for the sake of their selfish ambitions. Thus, a prince's virtue artfully blends vices and virtues, and he uses it to bond people to him. For leaders, politics is an arena where they can hold onto their power through controlling and managing individuals and their desires for acquisition. On some level, the politics of survival is Machiavelli's central theme.

The Prince speaks to a general audience of existing and prospective leaders. Yet, Machiavelli tells us that his lessons are not derived from his study of ordinary leaders, but from the behavior of the greats (Mansfield translation of 1998, p. 3). He explicitly differentiates between the ambition and actions of great men and all others who should emulate them. Machiavelli does not just prescribe rules that leaders should follow to survive, Machiavelli's advice is animated by inspiring examples of those whose supreme achievement ensured political survival through ambitious aggrandizement:

> I bring up the greatest examples. For since men almost always walk on paths beaten by others and proceed in their action by imitation, unable either to stay on the paths of others altogether or attain the virtue of those whom you imitate, a prudent man should always enter upon the paths beaten by great men, so that if his own virtue does not reach that far, it is at least in the odor of it. (1998, p. 22)

The great men Machiavelli speaks of, such as Moses, Cyrus, Romulus, and Theseus, were founders. Although these are an unlikely grouping of leaders, they established entirely "new orders" by responding strategically to incentives, which Machiavelli describes as the ability to seize opportunities (1998, p. 23). Machiavelli says, "[I]t was necessary for

Moses to find the people of Israel in Egypt, enslaved and oppressed by the Egyptians, so that they would be disposed to follow him so as to get out of their servitude" (1998, p. 23). Although Machiavelli makes a nod to a higher power, he actually attributes virtue to Moses in his ability to introduce a new order. At some level, Moses practiced the politics of political survival and the Jews took a calculated risk in following him. They had to believe that they would be better off in a new regime and under different leadership.

But how do a people become persuaded to leave behind an accustomed way for a novel order? For Machiavelli, the ambitious must understand necessity and command it: "such opportunities, therefore, made these men happy, and their excellent virtue enabled the opportunity to be recognized" (1998, p. 23). Machiavelli implies that Moses took advantage of the Jews' misery. They were in the grip of necessity, which he adroitly recognized as an opportunity. It was also helpful that the Jews perceived that behind Moses stood a powerful punishing God, who would not only punish Egypt but also reminded the Jews of their faith. Moses understood human necessity and how to manage it; as a founder he introduced "any form as he pleased" and created a regime with an altogether new polity and national creed (1998, p. 22). Thus, he surmounted one the greatest obstacles that a founder faces, which is the incredulity of men, "who do not truly believe in new things unless they come to have a firm experience of them" (1998, p. 23).

For Machiavelli, it is sensible for leaders to engage in political survival; but selfish ambition needs a vigorous expression. Since Machiavelli is a realist, he would agree that the prize of princely virtue is political power. However, princes with small ambition do not endure and those who engage in petty politics without seizing visionary opportunities are bound to be overcome by fortune. Although all leaders answer to necessity (political survival), they must aim for unnecessary glory. Thus, even when assuming that politics is a game of strategic decisions, Machiavelli's does not think that the actors are all that rational.[6] People and states are mostly irrational; and leaders tend to blur power politics with moral considerations. For optimal success, a prince's pre-rational disposition should be for great ambition, which is the only secure platform for political survival. For Machiavelli, there is no competing goal, personal or communal, which should compete with the prince's and, by extension, his principality's security.

This is an argument for the predominance of power seeking, which edges aside other considerations like justice and nobility. It has a tyrannical impulse behind it and can narrow a leader's concern for politics toward superiority and domination. When not tempered by other characteristics, this ambition exhibits aggressiveness and victory seeking in leaders. Great ambition, even for power, can evolve, however, as the experience and political thought of a leader changes. In Chapter 5, through an examination of Aristotle's magnanimous man, I present leaders with grand transformative ambition whose self-awareness and personal characters allow them to stand outside of the political desires that are product of more spirited natures. In essence, transformative ambition is best described as a deliberate desire.

To illustrate how this conception of transformative ambition is possible, I turn to the strategic perspective explanation of the ambition of the American founders, in which Mesquita et al. (2003) argue that the forefathers acted in their interests and were presented with fortuitous circumstances that favored republican government. In contrast, I present Adair's more powerful explanation of the Founding Fathers' self-conscious ambition for fame, which led them to channel their combined efforts in order to establish popular self-government.

CONTENDING EXPLANATIONS OF THE AMERICAN FOUNDING FATHERS' POLITICAL AMBITION

Besides worrying about their political survival, leaders face the additional problem that political regimes do not last forever. A government's decline is bad for incumbents and good for rivals. Regimes are threatened when "they are no longer able to provide sufficient resources to sustain political support" (Mesquita et al. 2003, p. 26). When a regime faces an existential crisis, it creates an opportunity for rivals to think of ways to ensure their own political survival. In some cases, elites with strategic ambition will band together "with a shared mindset or collective new belief system" and remake political institutions (2003, p. 27). Moments of crisis that were followed by this particular kind of regime change include the Glorious Revolution as well as the American, French, Russian, and Chinese Revolutions (2003, p. 27).

These states of emergency were unique because elites cooperated with each other to bring in new institutions, but even under such circumstances, strategic ambition was still in play. Elites will band together to design and select political institutions because "their incentive to cooperate at a moment of crisis exceeds their divergent interests" (2003, p. 27).

The extraordinary circumstances of the American Revolution postponed the politics of political survival, but elites were selecting institutions and thinking forward to a time when political competition would be no less intense.

Mesquita et al. (2003, p. 27) acknowledge that the leaders of the Glorious Revolution and the American Revolution formed a consensus, which fostered "lasting changes that channel[ed] future competition in socially productive directions." Yet this result is puzzling because, as the authors note, at other times "the solutions adopted in response to the momentary crisis fail to remove the incentives for destructive competition in the future."

All revolutionaries, they claim, "are motivated by the intention to overthrow the existing political order so that the excluded (that is, revolutionaries and their followers) become the included" (2003, p. 368). The authors argue that these uncharacteristic political situations arise during times of crisis, and under uncertainty leaders have more to gain by momentarily putting their divergent interests aside. As ambitious for power as the leaders of the American Revolution were, they created institutions that did not necessarily secure their hold on it.

Mesquita et al. (2003) fail to acknowledge the particular kind of ambition that is responsible for the promotion of the public good. The founders were motivated toward a deliberate desire for something grander than political power. Basing himself on Bacon's five-stage classification of the highest fame and honors, Adair (1974) offers an alternative explanation of the American founders' ambition in his influential essay, "Fame and the Founding Fathers." His take not only reconsiders the scope of ambition but also shows how self-interest can promote public-spiritedness in nonstrategic ways. He quotes Bacon's peak of honor and fame: "in the first place are *conditores imperiorum*, founders of states and commonwealths; such were Romulus, Cyrus, Ottoman, 'and significantly' Julius Caesar" (p. 15).[7] Adair acknowledges that most leaders are self-interested, but the founders manifested a much more powerful desire for fame:

> Fame, in contrast to honor, is more public, more inclusive, and looks to the largest possible human audience, horizontally in space and vertically in time. Fame is "celebrity, renown," it is the action or behavior of a "great man," who stands out, who towers above his fellows in some spectacular way. To be famous or renowned means to be widely spoken of by a man's contemporaries and also to act in such a way that posterity also remembers his name and his actions. The desire for fame is thus a dynamic element in the histor-

ical process; it rejects the static complacent urge in the human heart to merely be and invites a strenuous effort to become – to become a person and force in history larger than the ordinary. The love of fame encourages a man to make history, to leave the mark of his deeds and his ideals on the world; it incites a man to refuse to be the victim of events and to become an "event-making" personality – a being never to be forgotten by those later generations that will be born into a world his action helped to shape. (1974, pp. 10–11)

The strategic perspective attributes the American Revolution to a rapid and large change in the incentive structure. Adair argues that it also presented fortuitous and extraordinary circumstances that spurred the love of fame, which was "a noble passion because it can transform ambition and self-interest into dedicated effort for the community, because it can spur individuals to spend themselves to provide for the common defense" (1974, p. 12). Adair admits that the founders "were no angels but passionately selfish and self-interested men" (1974, p. 24). Yet, they became highly conscious of their desires, which led to a "redefinition in their own minds of their ambitions and the choice of new heroes to model themselves on," as well as their evolving situations as they "became fantastically concerned with posterity's judgment of their behavior" (1974, p. 7).

Adair sketches out each main figure. Alexander Hamilton modeled himself on Caesar. Thomas Jefferson sought immortal fame through the modern scientific project, and so he founded a scientific regime. James Madison identified with classical lawgivers and wanted to be remembered as the American Lycurgus. George Washington was obsessed with his honor and reputation; he feared that political office might tarnish it. Benjamin Franklin, who wrote in his autobiography that one should "imitate Jesus and Socrates," was the only founder who had achieved world renown before 1776.

The desire for fame, which Adair understands as the hope for immortality, directed the founders toward the great intellectual and political project of their time, which was the cause of enlightened progress. Adair argues that the politico-scientific project they settled on was to found "a national system dedicated to liberty, to justice, and to the general welfare" (1974, p. 24).

The American founders certainly had strategic ambition. They effectively ruled the new regime. Yet, to secure fame, they geared their efforts to the thoughtful and deliberate establishment of democratic republicanism and constitutional government. Thus, their audience extended beyond the coalition of supporters that would keep them in power to the entire world and, as Adair argues, to us as well, the unborn who would judge their lasting contribution and political greatness.

STRATEGIC AMBITION AND STRATEGIC LEADERSHIP

The loss of political power is always more dangerous for autocrats since leader turnover can be violent. Thus, to gain political power in autocracies, leaders should not shy away from using violence and unscrupulous methods. Despite the inherent dangers leaders face, there are no fewer contenders vying for control in autocratic regimes. Political survival is a high-stakes game, and a tactical approach is needed to win. Leaders may very well lack strategic ambition and not want to doggedly pursue office, but the authors note that leaders who have meeker dispositions are likely to be few and do not stay in power for long (Mesquita et al., 2003, p. 23).

In democracies, the size of the group that selects leaders is relatively large. On account of the vast membership in a leader's coalition, it is difficult for him to retain supporters' loyalty, which is why a democratic public may seem fickle and unforgiving of mistakes. Citizens in democracies are always ready to oust incumbents in the wake of setbacks and when public opinion turns against them. On the other hand, autocrats rely on a small coalition of supporters that must be personally rewarded for its loyalty through the distribution of private goods. Autocrats have a disincentive to distribute public goods, and, as a result, their states tend to be less prosperous. Autocrats also put less emphasis on national security.

For autocrats, loyalty is more important than prosperity and security. Their supporters' faith in the leadership is based on the fear that if a new leader comes to power, their private goods and privileges could disappear (Mesquita et al., 2003, pp. 65–7). From a realist perspective, an autocrat should benefit greatly by increasing the state's economic growth, power, and safety. He may need to satisfy the preferences of cronies, but shouldn't he act like a realist too, especially when national security is threatened? State security and power should be a primary concern even for a self-interested leader with strategic ambition. When power is maximized, it redounds to the leader's benefit as the state is in a better position to fend off international challengers.

The strategic perspective reverses the realist conventional wisdom and also the common opinions we hold about this sort of politics: "for autocrats, what appears to be bad policy often is good politics" (Mesquita et al., 2003, p. 19). When the number of people who keep autocrats in power relative to a country's population is very small, corruption, cronyism, and doling out special privileges to the members of those groups is the most efficient way of maintaining their continued support. Strategic leaders' ambitions are not tied to the motivation of the state under anarchy; they prefer to further their own interests. These leaders with strategic ambition want political power, they compete for office, and they prefer to hold power for as long as possible.

The political institutions that create and sustain positions of leadership dictate the scope of leaders' political ambition. That scope is quite narrow. Even if leaders have policy objectives not tied to office-seeking, political institutions across regimes create very strong incentives for them to focus on survival. Since all institutions in some way subject leaders to competition, survival becomes the primary and most palpable ambition. The incessant competition for office has a way of narrowing leaders' menu of policy choices to those that help them to perpetuate their tenure.

BRINGING AMBITION BACK IN: A COMPARISON OF LATIN AMERICA'S DICTATORS

The strategic perspective introduces the idea of competence, which assumes that differences among leaders' ability to run government vary, which influences their success in securing power. Mesquita et al. define competence as "the leader's ability to induce the government to run efficiently" (2003, p. 280). More specifically, it is the ability to produce and distribute public and private goods more effectively from the same pool of resources. Here, I argue that a more comprehensive view of leadership requires an understanding of the dynamic relationship between leaders, institutions, and supporters without dismissing the idea that institutions influence interests and strategies.

An enlarged definition of competence entails a leader's personal characteristics, goals, and ability to deal with constraints, defy these limits, and, in the vein of Machiavelli, take advantage of opportunities. These factors also contribute to a leader's ability to induce government to run productively, but inducing efficiency is only one element of what leadership can accomplish. A more extensive view of leader competence includes both the efficient management of institutions and the ability to confront fundamental organizational dilemmas.

In this section, I expand the strategic perspective's concept of competence by comparing political ambition and transformative leadership across autocratic regimes. I first examine Fidel Castro, who possessed transformative ambition as he altered the Cuban regime domestic and foreign policy to meet his vision. Initially, Castro was a revolutionary and founder of the current Cuban state that is undergirded by Fidelismo, a socialist experiment that is the product of his political agility, imagination, and stubborn grip on power. Since 1959, Castro has cast a spell on political leaders, intellectuals, and people across the developing world. As Tad Szulc (2000), one of his biographers, observed: "Since 1959, I have been impressed by his erudition, his sense of history, and his political agility and imagination" (p. 88).

I then contrast Cuba with an examination of autocratic regimes with leaders who lack the qualities of Fidel Castro. Alfredo Stroessner of Paraguay is an example of how personal characteristics can foster strategic ambition for power and limit any greater ambition. Conversely, an earlier predecessor of Stroessner, Francisco Solano Lopez's greater ambition for glory clouded his strategic concern for survival and led to his ruin. Lopez was heir to his father's (Carlos Lopez) authoritarian reign over Paraguay. While his father had no great ambition beyond kleptocratic rule, Francisco Lopez modeled himself after Napoleon Bonaparte and was obsessed with national security. He became intent on adding distinction to his name and launched an offensive war against Argentina, Brazil, and Uruguay, which proved disastrous to the Paraguayan state and to Lopez.

Castro created a regime that encroached completely on every aspect of Cuban life: "no autonomous groups or non-regulated counter-revolutionary forms of behavior exist independent of Castro" (Sondrol, 1991, p. 606). As early as 1961, he began to squeeze out potential rivals when he fired and exiled Anibal Escalante, who was the most powerful of the older Communists in Cuba. During his tenure, Castro regularly engaged in "moral rectification campaigns," which punished unscrupulous public officials but were really designed to help him avoid criticism and pulverize rivals (Sondrol, 1991, p. 611).

Without a doubt, Castro's regime was repressive, and his tactics for political survival flowed from the incentives presented in his autocratic regime. Yet, his political success and behavior cannot be understood solely on the basis of strategic ambition. Although he behaved strategically, Castro was a founder who transformed the Cuban regime. The spring of the Cuban revolution was change: a new society, organized on principles that were diametrically opposed to the Batista regime (Fagen, 1969, p. 3). He astonished citizens and captured their loyalty through his heroic acts, manly authority, and moralizing rhetoric. There was an enigmatic relationship between Castro and Cuba's masses that cannot just be described by the provision of private goods, fear of repression, or even the idea that his charisma overawed his followers.[8]

In fact, Castro was the regime on a political, historical, and moral level. He was both its founding memory and its reality. As the mythical hero who created a government on the principle of moral rebellion, he transformed domestic society by blending socialism with his personal vision of *la Revolución*. Castro's overarching revolutionary goal was to create a new "Socialist Man" at the expense of personal and political freedoms (Szulc, 1988, p. 50). As such, he embarked on a sweeping transformation of both the political and economic organization which destroyed Cuba's old political culture and allowed him to introduce new beliefs, habits, and sentiments.

To help materialize his vision of Cuba he traded an open society for social, educational, and health programs:

> Public education became accessible to the entire population, allowing older generations of illiterate peasants to watch their children and grandchildren become doctors and scientists; by 1979, Cuba's literacy rates had risen above 90 percent. Life expectancy went from under 60 years at the time of the revolution to almost 80 today ... the revolutionary government's public vaccinations programs completely eliminated polio, diphtheria, tetanus, meningitis, and measles. In these ways, the Cuban state truly has served the poor underclass rather than catering to the domestic elite and its American allies. (Sweig 2007, p. 44)

In Castro's purview the idea of a just regime was included; yet, it was a perverted one as he retained all moral and political authority in his person. He embodied the great man, *el caudillo*, the ideal man of Latin American society who represents the morally superior attributes that men should possess, but only a few do.[9] Castro's rule clearly aimed for political survival, and his repressive tactics and backward economic policies were in the spirit of a strategic leader. But his greater ambition was to make his revolution and rule legitimate, perpetual, and historically significant.

The last of these goals might be in reach, as Castro has used foreign policy for decades as a symbolic act of defiance against his perception of America's imperial aggression. Castro made Cuba a geopolitical player for decades as he severed links with the United States and declared fealty to the Soviet Union: "he foresaw that his regime would gain at home and in the eyes of much of the world if the Eisenhower administration (and later President Kennedy) reacted with hostility to his actions and rhetoric" (Szulc, 1988, p. 56). At the same time, Castro used the Soviets for money and weapons. Castro's transformative ambition, however, seems to have lacked the American founders' lust for fame insofar as the latter was directed toward building a lasting monument in the form of republican government. The Cuban revolution and regime are so tightly coupled to Castro that it remains to be seen whether the regime will outlive him.

Stroessner's long tenure, 1954–89, was built on his firm control of the winning coalition, which included members of the unified Colorado political party, military, and state bureaucracy. A civil war in 1947 left rival factions unable to assert their political hegemony, which resulted in a power vacuum. Stroessner was a ruthless general who had distinguished himself in the Chaco War against Bolivia. He came to power in a coup and was the eighth president in seven years and inherited a wildly unstable system that was characterized by factionalism (Lambert and Nickson, 1997, p. 125).[10] Stroessner did not plunge Paraguay into war as his predecessor Francisco Lopez had done, nor did he restructure national politics or reshape society like Castro. Yet, he transformed the unstable political system into a strong personalist dictatorship – the *stronato* (1997, p. 125). The basis for Stroessner's power was the organized Colorado Party, on which he held a tight grip. Yet, the party was simply an extended system of patronage that he used strategically by rewarding loyalty and excusing vice. In his regime, party affiliation brought sinecure office. Public employees, teachers, doctors, and students had to affiliate with the party (Cockcroft, 1992, p. 339). In addition, as the military's supreme commander, he made all decisions regarding the promotion of military officers. Loyalty, of course, trumped merit.

Stroessner induced loyalty by allowing corruption in the military and state bureaucracy. In contrast to Castro, he had no illusions about the aim of political power beyond cementing his rule and did not make use of the moralizing rhetoric of his Latin American counterpart. Stroessner limited his desire for office; it can be argued that he appropriated

Machiavelli's advice to princes and also understood the important use of the loyalty norm for political survival. In a striking quote, Stroessner allegedly said, "it is necessary to foment criminality, because criminality produces complicity and complicity produces loyalty" (Alexander, 1977, pp. 16–17).

Stroessner's ambition for power led him to drape himself and the Colorado Party in nationalistic imagery. History was rewritten to heighten Paragauyan nationalism and heroic symbols of Stroessner were erected throughout Paraguay. Loyalty to Paraguay meant loyalty to Stroessner: the nationalist regime was made to seem autochthonous, "the assumption was then that all opposition to the regime, could only be, by default *exótico*, in other words, antinationalist, anti-Paraguayan, and foreign inspired" (Lambert and Nickson, 1997, p. 128).

As power was centralized in Stroessner, he encouraged a cult of personality to develop around him. His name was omnipresent. An entire city bore his name: *Puerto Stroessner,* as well as schools and airports. He placed an emphasis on the ceremonial aspect of his rule, by always being present at events and openings of public facilities and works. He had a giant blinking neon sign erected in Asuncion's central plaza that read "Stroessner: Peace, Work and Well-being." He trumpeted himself as *El Excelentisimo* and received a constant stream of praise from the press, party members, businessmen, and the public, which showered him with the accolades: *el Gran Líder*, *el benefactor*, *el Único Líder*, and *el abanderado de la Paz y el Progreso* (Lambert and Nickson, 1997, p. 129). While to his enemies he was known as *el Tiranosauro* (Cockcroft 1992, p. 335).[11]

Unlike Castro, Stroesnner was a staunch anti-communist who supported the United States throughout the Cold War. He offered assistance to the United States by sending troops to Vietnam and to the Dominican Republic in 1965, which was occupied by 44 000 American soldiers after a coup was launched by Dominican revolutionaries. American administrations, up until Jimmy Carter's in 1977, lent their support to Stroesnner's regimes because he punctiliously observed Paraguay's democratic constitution, which was based on regular multiparty elections. As stipulated by the constitution, elections were held every five years: "in eight elections held between 1958 and 1988, Stroessner gained over 90 percent of the vote on five occasions" (Lambert and Nickson, 1997, p. 131).

Stroesnner lacked the international ambition of his belligerent predecessor, Lopez, known as *el mariscal* (the marshall), whose warped sense of glory and honor corrupted his ability to behave as a strategic leader should.[12] By the age of 20, with no military experience at all, López was promoted by his father to the rank of general in the Paraguayan army. In 1862, Lopez succeeded his father to the presidency: "he possessed personal gifts that enabled him to run his father's government efficiently, to seize power for himself on his father's death, to retain it for eight years, and to persuade the people of Paraguay to make endless sacrifices in pursuit of his policies" (Saeger 2007, p. 5). Two years into his tenure he declared war on Brazil, after he had issued an ultimatum to Brazil, which had invaded Uruguay, that its actions constituted "a violation of the principle of equilibrium among the states in the Rio de la Plata region" (Abente, 1987, p. 48). Lopez believed that Brazil threatened Paraguay's security and honor. After being denied access to Argentine territory to mobilize the Parguayan Army, Lopez declared war on Argentina.

Although the putative cause of the war was the balance of power, Lopez did not simply respond to the strategic environment nor did he require war to cement his dictatorial rule. Paraguay was militarily and economically a negligible power, which lacked the resources to wage a war against a much more powerful Brazil, not to mention Argentina and Uruguay. Much of Lopez's decisions were based on the self-image he had constructed. He was a voracious reader who wished to emulate the warrior-statesman Napoleon, but he had no military experience beyond his study of it in books.

Lopez showed desires for honor and expansion as he waged war against Brazil. Yet, his imprudence dragged Argentina and Uruguay into the war as they formed a Triple Alliance (Argentina, Brazil, and Uruguay). It was a total war that engulfed South America and lasted from 1840–70. Although Lopez saw initial success he made many subsequent errors and entertained false hopes. He believed that he could foster rebellions in Brazil and Argentina; he staked his hopes on an unfulfilled promise from the Bolivian Manuel Mariano Melgarejo for 100 000 men to defend *Asunción*; and he dreamed that America would intervene in the war in his favor by manipulating the image of a small republic being oppressed by Brazilian monarchy (Vieyra, 2004, p. 261).

Meanwhile, Lopez had no strategy for victory, and his only explicit goal was to win glory for himself. His military strategy and behavior was non-Napoleonic and downright ignoble. Lopez did not give his field generals any discretion on the battlefield, so the Paraguayan army's strategy was set even as circumstances changed. Although Lopez was in firm command of his forces' movement, he could not change battle tactics either. A natural coward, he always advanced at the rear of his army and retreated to safety at the first sight of battle. During the war, Lopez bestowed many honors on himself for his bravery. In addition, he had Congress orchestrate scripted supplications to Lopez to keep himself out of harm's way during combat. Since Lopez could not manage orderly retreats, the Paraguayan soldiers were known for their notorious courage as they assaulted Allied positions while suffering massive casualties (Centeno, 2002). The outcome of the war proved a disaster for Paraguay, as 72 percent of the prewar population was gone; the country had to cede a vast part of its territory, and a liberal constitution was imposed upon the people (Whigham and Potthast, 1999, p. 181). The war ended when Brazilian troops killed Lopez in 1870.

CONCLUSION

The examples in this chapter highlight the important role that personal characteristics have in directing leaders' ambition and statecraft. The strategic perspective's uniform definition of political ambition as a strategic and narrow explanation of leadership as competence do not do justice to the full exercise of leadership. The theory clearly fails to understand the range of political ambition and the varied personal attributes that make a difference in leadership. If the only thing that separated America's founders from the Latin American autocrats examined here was structural incentives, then all leadership is reduced to the most tangible political motives: securing office and holding on to it. Such a view does little to explain why leaders, even under structural similarities, behave so differently in office. Why did Castro try to transform and reinvent Cuba rather than simply preside over a party and the military, like Stroessner? I argue that the difference in ambition is responsible for guiding leaders in such contrary directions. The problem for political scientists of the strategic theoretical ilk is why do they not pay more attention not only to individual differences but to the difference in leadership itself?

Personality scholars have tried to fill this void by addressing the differences among leaders' personalities. Dissatisfied over the lack of emphasis on individuals in international relations studies, these scholars prioritize the complex influence of psychological motivations and personal characteristics. However, the study of personality and politics raises a question about such an approach. Which traits are pertinent to leaders' political behavior and to what degree do their personalities help or hinder their political goals? The scholarship and use of psychological terminology are both rich and diverse in this area. Next I examine the main advocates of this approach, and I also turn to an example that has become a classic in the personality and politics scholarship: Woodrow Wilson and the ratification of League of Nations Covenant.

NOTES

1. For similar examples of theories that link domestic politics, domestic institutional structures, and leader incentives to foreign affairs, see Acemoglu and Robinson (2005), Debs and Goemans (2010), and Fearon (1994).
2. Mesquita et al. (2003, p. 16) explicitly note that the examination of institutions and their relationship to political survival is a unique theory that has received limited attention in the literature on political institutions.
3. I refer to Mesquita et al. (2003) as the authors of the strategic perspective throughout this chapter.
4. Randall Schweller (1996) is a realist who argues that the neorealist theorist should distinguish between different state goals. He argues that neorealism suffers from a "status quo bias" (state security is the only goal) in the explanation of international relations, which makes the theory unable to comprehend the outcomes produced by a state with revisionist goals.
5. Decision-making authority and the distribution of resources are not always centralized in one person, but the authors' model requires that they make an assumption that the decision to tax and spend is centralized in the leadership and that leaders must have some control over public resources (Mesquita et al., 2003, p. 74).
6. Steven Forde (1995, p. 145) makes an incisive observation about Thucydides' and Machiavelli's view of rationality in politics: "Rather, irrationality in the real world of international politics is carefully integrated into their reflections on the status and purpose of realist theory ... the interplay between rationality and irrationality plays an important role in their evaluations of the status and significance of realist science altogether. Machiavelli's awareness that most states of his day fall short of the ideal of rational policy shapes his whole intellectual project."
7. Douglass Adair changes Francis Bacon's ordering by placing Julius Caesar last, and by excluding Ismael (the founder of the Safavid dynasty) to emphasize Alexander Hamilton's statement that "he considered Caesar 'the greatest man that ever lived'" (1974, p. 15).
8. A famous example of Castro's unconventional leadership style was the open-air discussion he held with 1000 prisoners arrested after the Bay of Pigs. After the end of a marathon interrogation, Castro debated the prisoners in a 5-hour televised free-for all discussion (Halperin, 1972, p. 111). The prisoners were ransomed for approximately $53 million worth of food and medicine, which was paid by private donors in the United States.
9. *Caudillo* is a generic term with its roots in the Latin word *caput*, which means head. It, however, has a special resonance in Spanish America, and has been applied as both praise and blame. For a comprehensive study of Latin America's *caudillos*, see Hamill (1995).

10. Between 1900 and 1954, Paraguay cycled through 34 different presidents. The instability was largely due to the devastating defeat of the war against the Triple Alliance between 1865 and 1870 and because it engaged in another costly war between 1932 and 1935 against Bolivia, which was known as the Chaco War.
11. *Líder* (Leader), *el benefactor* (the benefactor), *el Único Líder* (the sole leader), and *el abanderado de la Paz y el Progreso* (the flag bearer of peace and progress), *Tiranosauro* (Tyrannosaurus).
12. See Saeger (2007).

3. Personality and political ambition

I would rather fail in a cause that will ultimately triumph than to triumph in
a cause that will ultimately fail.
Woodrow Wilson

Realism and the strategic perspective explain leaders' political ambition
as something predetermined by the nature of international anarchy (realism) or by the requirements for political survival in democracies and
autocracies (strategic perspective). These theories are not interested in
the traditional view of leadership, in which individuals can have a
greater degree of superior qualities such as courage, moderation,
prudence, justice, and patriotism. In addition, some leaders have a much
greater store of political ambition than others. This traditional perspective attaches critical importance to the character traits that are requisite
for leadership, and the variation in these qualities has important consequences for politics.

Realism and the strategic perspective emphasize the instrumental
decisions that leaders should make when faced with different circumstances. Theories of statesmanship seek to explain how the correct
assemblage of character traits fosters its practice, or how an incomplete
or flawed character can lead to failure.

Realism and the strategic perspective do not properly link the practice of statesmanship to leaders' behavior. While rational leaders are
mindful of constraints and incentives, leaders' ambition and behavior are
not predetermined by the circumstances leaders inhabit. In fact, transformative leaders can work around constraints because they seek accomplishments with lasting power that are not necessarily tied to
institutional incentives, such as political office.

A more comprehensive understanding of statesmanship does
acknowledge that leaders' behavior is in large part a response to circumstances. However, amid the flux of international challenges and dangers
to peace statesmanship requires judgment and definition to understand a
situation and know whether to use diplomacy, alliances, force, or persua-

sion. The practice of leadership involves more than the application of resources. It requires gaining insight about reality, including an overarching knowledge about politics, what motivates others, and what a leader should motivate others toward, as well as a grasp of one's own ambition and capacities.

Using this more comprehensive view, scholars must not only examine the constraints leaders work under but also illuminate which traits make statesmanship possible. I single out transformative ambition as a unique quality of statesmanship that inspires some leaders to make substantial differences in the organization of the international world and in the lives of their fellow citizens. This chapter focuses on scholars who examine the same unit of analysis and phenomena that I do: leaders and the various motives that inform their political ambition. These scholars study leaders' personalities and how the full spectrum of human passions, inner motives, and personality traits influences their political behavior.

Personality scholars begin from the premise that personal characteristics and psychological motives are the most influential determinants of leader perceptions and behavior. They reverse the assumption of realism and the strategic perspective. For example, leaders behave like realists when they view the world of politics in terms of anarchy, distrust, and realpolitik and not because anarchic conditions make leaders behave like defensive or offensive realists. Likewise, the strategic behavior observed in autocracies is the product of a power-motivated individual who has a disposition for authoritarianism, and not because autocratic institutions incentivize despotic rule.

The personality approach focuses our attention back on the individual and shares common ground with this project by relating political action in international relations to a leader's independent character, thus broadening our understanding of foreign policy choices beyond the confines of realist or strategic perspective explanations. However, this focus is the only thing my approach shares with personality theories. I am interested in carving out a sphere of autonomy for statesmen in which transformative leaders not only rise above constraints but also change the rules of the game. Such high acts of statesmanship depend on the redefinition of ordinary political ambition into great ambition, which is a process that a leader can be self-conscious of as his experience and beliefs about politics evolve.

The personality approach is blind to the idea that leaders can act freely or that they can act from political reflection because it conceives of leaders as driven by psychological needs and subterranean compulsions; politics is the public display of deep-seated motives. Ironically, the idea of leadership is turned on its head through the study of leaders' personalities. Leaders lack the superior qualities I mentioned at the outset of this chapter. Instead, they are attributed the worst set of traits and problems related to egocentric drives.

THE PERSONALITY APPROACH: LEADERS AS DRIVE-DRIVEN

The problem with the personality approach is one that can be traced back to the ideas of the father of modern political psychology. Harold Lasswell (1948) makes the obvious observation that most political actors are power seekers. And why? For Lasswell, a political personality is characterized by "low self-esteem," which is the proximate cause of political ambition (pp. 40–41).

The personality approach skews our perception of leaders and political ambition toward the idea that politics is an expression of subterranean psyches. We cannot take a leader's words and actions at face value because the psychologist knows the leader better than he knows himself. Political ambition masks deeper needs. In the final analysis, politics is the manifestation of a leader's underlying and unconscious motives, which result from chance events in childhood. A real, and very problematic, effect of the study of personality on politics is that it minimizes the importance of statesmanship. As a consequence, we cannot take either leadership or politics seriously; and there is no real alternative to realist and strategic theories of leadership.

The mistake of personality theories is the explanation of the origin of political ambition and leadership and the inability to distinguish between differences in kind. Personality is an immature prepolitical development of an individual. Thus, the source of political ambition is squarely the product of an individual's desires and unalterable idiosyncrasies, what Lasswell calls private motives. Personality scholars have expanded beyond Lasswell's power-seeking personality, but they continue to conceive of motives as drives that are developed in the unconscious, especially the need for power, achievement, and affiliation.[1]

The leader's dominant motivation not only defines his distinct political personality, but it is also the most influential factor in his approach to politics. The primary drives fall on a continuum, where each point expresses the level of relative isolation or interpersonal relationships that the personality demands. The desire for power ends in isolation, achievement is in the middle, and affiliation at the other end is defined by a strong need for interpersonal relationships. Next, I will examine two of these motives, power and achievement, and show how each one reveals an incomplete truth about leaders' ambition; but, ultimately, all of the categories are too simplistic and fail to recognize that individual ambition (motives) can exceed mere desire by being transformed by a leader's beliefs and experiences.

Power-motivated individuals have a problem adapting to political contexts that demand flexibility. Margaret Hermann (2003) argues that when the desire for power is high, a leader in a nondemocratic setting is prone to manipulate his context to stay in power (p. 379). In her view, leaders who have this underlying motivation tend to have authoritarian personalities and create the conditions for autocratic rule. In their relationships they seek to dominate others, which reinforces and produces the hierarchical political environment that they prefer in the first place. For example, Hermann identifies Saddam Hussein's various needs: a high need for power and control and the need to influence other persons and groups. Hussein exemplifies the autocratic leader who chooses autocratic rule for private reasons but will act according to the logic of political survival. Strategic behavior (institutional behavior) is epiphenomenal: what really drives behavior is psychological motivation. To sustain their power, says Hermann, "such leaders work to manipulate the environment to stay in power and to appear a winner" (2003, p. 379).

Whereas the strategic perspective sees autocratic rule as a result of autocratic institutions, the personality approach views autocratic institutions as the product of the practices of a leader who is psychologically primed for power. When he has the desire and ability to increase dominion over others, sometimes over an entire population, autocratic rule can be established. Without a doubt, many political regimes reflect an individual's lust for power and need to dominate. However, the personality approach crudely examines these basic drives and dispositions. Not all leaders who have the will to dominate others actually do, for an ambitious individual can judge other goods in life as superior to mere power. Moreover, according to the personality approach's logic, the power seeker is never disinclined to take power as long as an opportunity is present, but the exercise of power can be a conduit to greater achievements, esteem from one's equals, and the pursuit of noble purposes, among other things.

Leaders who have a need for achievement lust after distinction. Much like power-driven leaders, they want to be on top but are willing to fulfill their needs through competition among equals. Those with a desire for high achievement want peer recognition, but they compete for esteem in the hope that they will be judged as better than their rivals and competitors.

As I will explain in Chapter 5, the achievement motive bears a striking resemblance to Aristotle's examination of the lover of honor, which I refer to as ordinary political ambition. For Aristotle, the complex desire for honor in politics depends on socially recognized traits and virtues on the one hand, but also on an appropriate (nonrelativistic) attitude toward honors, which also prepares one for the practice of great leadership. Yet, personality scholars ground the need for achievement and esteem in a defect of the human character. This need for admiration is fostered by a "grandiose self" (Popper, 2005), and for the more "famished selves," a continuous flow of adulation is required (Post, 2004). High needs for either power or achievement pull leaders in opposite directions. As David Winter argues, in contrast to an overwhelming desire for power, a balance in the need for power and achievement can develop into a "more pragmatic and (in a democratic context, at least) effective approach to politics" (Winter, 2003, p. 373).

Is pragmatism good for the leader's psychology or for the health of a democracy? Winter is not precise on this issue, which leaves some unresolved questions about his view of ambition. Specifically, does the balanced leader satisfy his needs for power and achievement through his pragmatism, or does a leader's pragmatism benefit a democracy because he neither craves too much power nor is too deeply in need of admiration? Winter implicitly assumes that as long as a leader's needs are balanced, then his fulfillment of them can bear positively on political life. However, balance is an accident of personality development. Winter does not conceive that balance can be the product of a leader's political moderation, a characteristic that is maturely and consciously developed by an individual. Winter's error, and the general flaw in the personality approach, is that, in an attempt to present the psychology of political actors, he drains leaders' characteristics of their vitality, especially their ambition. As a result, he and other personality theorists underestimate the complexity of ambition, particularly great ambition.

PERSONALITY AND IDIOSYNCRATIC FOREIGN POLICY

So far, I have focused on personality and motives, but motives are one variable among others that comprise personality and affect behavior. Personality scholars think about leaders' political personas as a more dynamic and integrated whole. I deliberately focus on motivation and political ambition because the idea of ambition in domestic and international politics is the unifying theme that I have discerned across theories of leadership in international relations. And it is the main idea that I revisit in the next two chapters through an in-depth discussion of Aristotle's examination of magnanimity and political ambition, Pericles' transformative ambition, and the latter's effect on Greek international relations. Although it is sufficient, for our purposes, to show that political motives take root in an individual's psyche, the remainder of this section discusses factors that combine to produce complex personality orientations that have varied effects on leaders' foreign policy. No one has contributed more to the study of leaders' personality and foreign policy decision-making than Hermann, who has devised an elaborate series of foreign policy outcomes based on a wide range of personality orientations.[2]

Of the rich range of orientations and foreign policy approaches, I will only concentrate on the most basic levels. Hermann (1980) has argued that the two basic and overarching personality types exist, aggressive and conciliatory. Each personality maps on to two patterns of foreign policy behavior; aggressive leaders tend to have a war disposition, while conciliatory leaders look to peace. Naturally, a war disposition leads to the outbreak of conflict, but it also disposes a leader toward advocating force or hostility, perceiving an enemy as a threat, and maintaining an independent foreign policy. A peace disposition is conducive to cooperation, arms limitation, and interdependent foreign policy.

Hermann's more complex personality orientation relies on four key characteristics, and different combinations allow her to predict a series of behaviors:

> Aggressive leaders are high in need for power, low in conceptual complexity, distrustful of others, nationalistic, and likely to believe that they have some control over the events in which they are involved. In contrast, the data suggest that conciliatory leaders are high in need for affiliation, high in conceptual complexity, trusting of others, low in nationalism, and likely to

exhibit little belief in their own ability to control the events in which they are involved. (1980, p. 8)

Although political motivation can underlie a leaders' behavior, other key characteristics are quite influential as well. Beliefs reflect a leader's self-conception and worldview. One who is war prone and aggressive is likely to have a need for power. For Hermann, it is likely that this leader will believe that national sovereignty is supremely important. For realists, leaders do not need to be aggressive in order to have this view as they are bound to protect sovereignty and ensure their state's survival.

Hermann differs from realists who argue that miscalculation leads to conflict, she argues that states are more prone to conflict when a leader shows an independent leadership style that entertains nationalistic beliefs and is competitive and distrustful of outsiders. Hermann's theory is not compatible with neoclassical realism because she argues that leaders define constraints (filtered by their personalities). International politics is completely open to interpretation. Hermann's thesis puts too much emphasis on psychological dispositions and leaders' interpretations of reality. As a result, she actually hinders the study of leadership because her theory sharpens the dualism between subjective psychological states and objective realities. Transformative leaders, I argue, are fully aware of constraints and challenge existing rules and political orders because they are ambitious, so they take advantage of opportunities and are willing to commit good to some and injury to others. However, they may lack a sense of measure and are loath to circumscribe their ambition, much like Alcibiades. This lack of restraint is not because the world is simply a projection of their personalities, these leaders want to go beyond the very real limits imposed on them and must do so to see their ambition succeed.

Hermann's personality types also lead her to circular conclusions. She claims that aggressive leaders are predisposed to think the world offers few alternatives: they initiate action, want to enhance state sovereignty, urge independence by limiting cooperation, and usually attempt to negotiate on their own terms. When crises escalate into conflict, Hermann concludes that one or both leaders involved was an aggressive leader whose personality projects threats and insecurity onto the world. For the sake of argument, if a leader with a nonaggressive personality (my term), found himself in a situation where his state was challenged by another state, and decided to risk war, wouldn't he have to take on an aggressive leader's personality and learn to be aggressive? Depending on the context, any leader can and should act aggressively when war can advance his goals. However, Hermann's leaders' personalities are static. They neither evolve nor learn; they just bring their psychic states to bear on politics.

A need for affiliation entails the desire to associate, cooperate, and build trusting interpersonal relations. A leader with this motivation should be able to show trust and have optimistic beliefs. Hermann expects that conciliatory leaders will seek internationalist goals. They see the international arena no differently than the proximate political arena, as a place where mediation and conflict resolution can take place. While the conciliatory leader's foreign policy is also intended to help country, he does this by encouraging the assistance of other countries and international organizations.

These typologies might be perspicuous observations about some kinds of behavior in international relations, but they are very poor tools to understand statesmanship. I am interested in self-conscious leaders who are more acutely aware of the complexity of things, especially the more involved situation in which a leader's actions serve greater ends, either for himself or a body politic. In each case, leaders with transformative ambition seek political means to supersede ordinary constraints. Thus, they rise above ordinary citizens, and despite their personal defects, they must know themselves and define themselves politically and not just psychically.

THE PERSONALITY APPROACH AND WOODROW WILSON: MISUNDERSTANDING GREAT AMBITION

To fully examine the misdirection of the personality approach's study of leadership, I turn to its classic application in Alexander George and Juliet George's (1964) psychobiography, *Woodrow Wilson and Colonel House: A Personality Study*.[3] The authors construct a model of Woodrow Wilson's personality through a psychological interpretation of his early childhood. Their characterization is an exact match of Lasswell's profile of a power seeker, an individual who compensates for low self-esteem by assuming leadership. The authors find confirmation of Wilson's political personality in key decisions and episodes in which he proved intractable.

Wilson's troubled behavior surfaced when he confronted monumental opposition, both as President of Princeton and of the United States, which roused his strongest emotions and revealed his deep-seated motives. Wilson manifested a political personality by his inability to make political compromises, which were psychologically injurious to him. He could not share power, consult, or take advice from others. Instead, he tried to impose "orderly systems" on others. I believe that what George and George mean is that Wilson had an independent streak, which got the best of him; he was responsible for the architecture of his greatest project, the League of Nations, and selfishly guarded its form. He tried, but failed, to implement it with as little interference as possible.

Before I examine the intricacies of Wilson's personality and political behavior, I discuss the main events that interest Wilson personality scholars, the Paris Peace Conference as well as the ratification of the Treaty of Versailles and League of Nations Covenant in the United States Senate.

Wilson took America to war in 1917, after the country had maintained a policy of neutrality for much of World War I. When the war broke out, it was Wilson who had declared that the United States should seek neutrality.[4] For three years, Wilson vehemently tried to avoid war and even campaigned for reelection on the slogan, "He kept us out of war." It is important not to misconstrue this idea, since Wilson was not calling for isolationism but seeking to present the United States as a party outside of, but still politically engaged in, the European war (Clements, 1987, p. 163). Wilson thought that as a neutral state, the United States could act as a mediator and bring the warring states to a peace agreement. Yet, he found it difficult to maintain neutrality as Germany abandoned accepted international rules regarding naval warfare. On account of Germany's diplomatic brinkmanship, which culminated in its decision to wage unrestricted submarine warfare, and Wilson's desire that the United States would have a significant role at the peace table at the war's conclusion, Wilson decided to take the country to war (Saunders, 1998, pp. 90–91).[5]

America's effort tipped the war in the Allies' favor, and in November 1918 Germany signed an armistice. That same month, Wilson led the American delegation in Paris, where he hoped to build an enduring peace and establish a new international architecture. His aim at the Paris Peace Conference in 1918–19 was principled, a desire that cannot be said of any other statesman at the time. Just a year earlier, he had issued his Fourteen Points and views on self-determination, which not only revealed his terms for peace but also his blueprint for a new international order.

Wilson's goals were fundamentally transformative as he sought to erect a moral and legal governing institution for relations among states. Prior to World War I, as Kendrick Clements states, Wilson "really believed that he alone had a clear vision of a world organized for justice and democracy" (1997, p. 197). Wilson wanted a lasting peace, one that did not vindictively or harshly punish Germany. For a true peace, Wilson believed statesmen would have to redefine the international order and traditional statecraft. The reliance on power and interest, which he derided as products of jealousy and greed, would give way to principle and law.

Two factors worked in favor of Wilson's plan. The shared experience of destruction and loss of life produced by a total war would push nations toward the accepting the League of Nations, which promised to put an end to major wars. In addition, each state gained a clear benefit from the League: individual acts of aggression could be thwarted through the enforcement of collective security, thereby increasing each state's security. But before states could reap any of these advantages, they would first need to commit to the League. Wilson's strategy depended on showing how it provided a transparent and effective mechanism for peace over the unreliable and immoral balance of power.

Henry Kissinger underscores how momentous Wilson's plan to resolve crises without war actually was; it "had never been put forward by any nation, let alone implemented" (1994, p. 52). Wilson's political goals were as breathtakingly ambitious as they were unconventional. He sought to substitute Europe's long-standing diplomatic practices, the balance of power and *realpolitik*, which he deemed immoral, with self-determination and collective security.[6]

Wilson believed that international conflict was not caused by a breakdown in the international balance of power. Leaders invoked balance-of-power politics to legitimize and satisfy their selfish and illiberal ambitions. Aggressive leaders in nondemocratic nations made war more likely. In Wilson's mind, he sought to introduce order into what he thought was international disorder. As a consequence of Europe's diplomatic relations, states had routinely imposed force or other tactics to gain advantage over others. For Wilson, the former was fundamentally unjust. A true international order depended on fairness; he believed that the world needed a forum where a union of nations could address grievances, collectively stem individual acts of aggression, and increase states' prosperity.

Wilson also disliked how the balance of power nullified the exercise of leadership in international politics; it was a tool to limit the discretion of leaders who might overreach and begin to dominate other states. Leaders used the balance of power as a constraining device – in other words, as preventative statecraft – to check the most powerful states and ascending powers. Wilson wanted to proactively engage nations in international politics, which could only be done by assuming political and moral leadership. In short, he saw the need for statesmanship at the international level, a means for a leader to act freely above particular national interests. The statesman's responsibility was to set down principles of international conduct and keep nations from straying from them. This responsibility, Wilson felt, fell on the United States and him, which explains why he was compelled to attend the talks. He was the only leader with the clarity and desire to bring about peace and end the balance-of-power system forever (Lang, 1995).

Throughout his academic and political life, Wilson was a proponent of the art of statesmanship. His early thoughts on the topic stressed the need for freer public leadership in the American political system; he "celebrated the transformative power of leaders such as William Gladstone, his boyhood hero" (Stid, 1998, p. 31). Wilson believed that in a democracy the statesman acts as the linchpin between political life and political ideals. The former is carried on by the public, which can either represent democratic ideals or can deviate from them. Not only is it a leader's responsibility to guide the public toward existing principles, but he must also know the public mind and reform long-standing political practice when change is needed. Wilson understood the transformative power of democratic leadership as interpretive statesmanship, the practice of circumspection that a leader uses to gauge the pulse of the nation and prepare it for political change. Thus, he thought that independent leadership was possible through rhetoric that could capture the hearts and minds of the public.

Naturally, Wilson supported the notion that conflict and wars grew out of the failures of national leadership. The conflict in Europe stemmed from the gulf between leaders with aggressive ambitions and a beneficent public that longed for justice (Saunders, 1998, p. 165). The outbreak of war not only represented the illiberal interests of autocratic rulers and nations but also the failure of European statecraft. If the 27 nations represented at the peace talks accepted Wilson's international governing principle, embodied by the League of Nations, then the international community could avert future conflict. Collective security reduces nations' uncertainty about other states' intentions and decreases the inherent dangers in international politics. An aggressor calculates the prospects of facing the strength and will of many states in armed conflict and most likely backs down. As League members, states would no longer need to enter alliances, conduct diplomacy in secret, and build up arms because states would redefine their interests on moral and legal grounds.

Wilson's plan for the League was not just a lofty proposal. The new international order promised that laws and principles would govern international relations through the unprecedented security the League would offer to individual states. The balance of power lacked guaranteed security because it left smaller states exposed to the ambitions of stronger ones or excluded from alliances. Wilson laid out his conception for a new international politics in a speech to the United States Senate in 1917:

> There must be not a balance of power but a community of power. I am therefore proposing that all nations henceforth avoid entangling alliances that draw them into competitions of power, catch them in a net of intrigue and selfish rivalry, and disturb their own affairs with influences intruded from without. There is no entangling alliance in a concert of power. When all unite to act in the same sense and with the same purpose, all act in the common interest and are free to live their own lives under a common protection. (Craig and George, 1995)

Wilson's ideas were unfamiliar to Europe's leaders, who were accustomed to conducting diplomatic relations with an eye to pragmatic results (Kissinger, 1994). Traditionally, victorious powers established a government in the vanquished state with which they could have relations, redrew territorial boundaries, and defined spheres of influence. The Congress of Vienna, which was convened in 1815, exemplifies this type of balance-of-power diplomacy. For European leaders its stable outcome was committed to Europe's historical memory as a blueprint and evidence of how the successful construction of a new balance of power led to peace. The status of France was the crux of the negotiations. Its redrawn boundaries deprived it of all territory conquered by Napoleon Bonaparte. To buffer another attempt at expansion, France was encircled by 39 German states. France, represented by Talleyrand, was part of the Congress, so the proceedings were not punitive but did ward off the potential for renewed French aggression. The settlement led to 40 years of peace. However, true to the balance-of-power spirit, each state still pursued its own interest, either to gain advantage or make up for some loss, all in the name of stability. Kissinger describes the essential difference between the traditional and Wilson's new liberal system:

> The preservation of peace would no longer spring from the traditional calcu-
> lus of power but from worldwide consensus backed up by a policing mecha-
> nism. A universal grouping of largely democratic nations would act as the
> trustee of peace, and replace the old balance-of-power and alliance systems.
> (1994, p. 52)

Wilson went to Paris supremely confident about his ability to dictate the peace terms, since the armistice between Germany and the Allied Powers was a product of the United States' negotiations with Germany. Moreover, Britain and France had agreed to the Fourteen Points as the framework for peace. Wilson spent more than six months in Paris, which broke a long-standing precedent that American presidents rarely travel abroad. His overriding goal was to make the League proposal an integral part of the conference, and compromises, if necessary, were to be made with an eye to getting states to accept the League (Saunders, 1998, p. 137).

Wilson's visit and goals in Europe might have set a trend for the American presidency, but the leaders of the battered Allies, Georges Clemenceau, the Premier of France, and David Lloyd George, the Prime Minister of Great Britain, were still simply interested in getting the best deal for their countries. To act otherwise could prove costly to their nations and to their political fates.

The British were determined to protect their command of the seas, and the French were especially concerned with future German aggression (Clements, 1987, p. 200). The fear of electoral reprisals at home certainly influenced Lloyd George's opinion. In Britain, for example, the *Daily Mail* carried a box on its first page that read, "The Huns will cheat you yet!" David Lloyd George's 1918 election slogan responded to this sentiment, "We will squeeze the orange till the pips squeak" (Craig and George, 1995, p. 45), and he secured reelection on the promise to make Germany pay war reparations. The French response to Wilson's aims was sardonic; the 78-year-old Clemenceau, known as "the Tiger," remarked that where God had only Ten Commandments, Wilson had now come with his Fourteen Points (Boller, 1996).

As the conference began, Wilson found that he could not just dictate terms to the Allies. The first issue taken up by the Allies, the disposition of the German colonies, required resolution through compromise. The Allies wanted an outright partition of the colonies, and Wilson sought an anti-imperialist mandate. The Allies eventually agreed to give the colonies to the major powers under a mandate system (Clements, 1987, p. 200).

Throughout the proceedings, Wilson was drawn into a debate over procedural details. Starting the conference itself was an ordeal; thus, he accomplished little in his first month at Paris. The peace talks also revealed that Wilson was not much of a negotiator; rather he saw himself as a judge, "applying the yardstick of his principles to the proposals which the various foreign statesman made" (George and George, 1964, p. 231). The colonial issue proved to Wilson that he would have to sacrifice greatly to get what he wanted. As a consequence, he devoted his strongest efforts to ensuring an agreement about the League's creation in the treatise, rather than have a two-stage conference with two concluding documents.

While Wilson succeeded in making the League a priority, the longer the peace talks lasted, the greater his sense of urgency to close matters became, overriding his desire to create a new international order (Kissinger, 1994, p. 230). More experienced and clever diplomats stifled Wilson and America's voice during the talks. Much of this was Wilson's fault since he left his aides in the dark about his ideas and did not have systematic plan to work through the conference beyond his Fourteen Points. The American diplomats tended to play passive roles on various commissions, ceding the initiative to their French and British counterparts.

In mid-February, after being abroad for two months, Wilson had to return to Washington. Upon his return, Republican senators and the media met his aims and accomplishments in Paris with strong criticism and skepticism. Wilson was prepared to fight back: "immediately upon his arrival in the United States he had thrown down the gauntlet to his critics" (George and George, 1964, p. 235). He landed in Boston, home of his nemesis, Senator Henry Cabot Lodge. Wilson quickly took the high ground, expressed the League "as the hope of the world," and stated that American rejection of the treaty would have tragic consequences for international politics (Saunders, 1998, p. 163).

Largely due to partisanship, the Senate's hesitancy also grew out of a genuine fear that the League would weaken national security and reduce America's influence in the western hemisphere. Critical senators also felt that the League's mandate to quell conflict supplanted Congress' war-making power. Following the advice of his closest counselor, Colonel Edward House, Wilson extended an olive branch by hosting a White House dinner with the Foreign Relations Committee, an overture that had no effect on the opposing senators.

Resistance stiffened when Lodge read a round-robin resolution in the Senate, signed by 39 Republicans. The proposal explicitly declared the

Covenant unacceptable in its present form and called for the separation of the League from the peace treaty. It "was intended to serve notice on Wilson and on all the negotiators in Paris that more than a third of the Senate was opposed to the Covenant in its current form" (George and George, 1964, p. 238). Wilson reacted forcefully by criticizing the League's opponents as "contemptible," "ignorant," and "provincial" (Saunders, 1998, p. 165).

Domestic opposition to Wilson and the League was not just the work of contrarian politicians looking to gain the upper hand. Their claims were rooted in a fundamental disagreement about the source and direction of US foreign policy. Although Wilson's alternative to the balance of power and American aloofness was gaining steady support from the media and the public, he had not convinced a strident group of Republican senators who felt that Congress' power was being usurped. Wilson vociferously defended the League's moral advantages, but he had a very difficult time explaining exactly how the League would actually function. The main reason that Wilson lacked these details is because the peace conference was consumed with practical matters that grew out of each participant's self-interest, making it hard to build the architecture for the League.

Wilson returned to Paris with his domestic support clearly weakened. Aware of the widely publicized Senate criticism of the League, the Allies made a concerted effort to chip away at Wilson's Fourteen Points. They knew fully well that Wilson's desire to create the League took precedence over anything else and that he would sacrifice many of the peace aims in order to push amendments that would address domestic concerns, including recognizing the Monroe Doctrine, excluding national or internal questions from the League's jurisdictions, and providing for the possibility of withdrawal from the body (George and George, 1964, p. 250). With his attention turned to the problem of Senate ratification of the treaty, Wilson's Fourteen Points were whittled down "to a barely recognizable state in the final draft of the treaty" (Hagedorn, 2007, p. 357).

As the peace talks came closer to an end, Wilson's image and standing had changed drastically. Throngs of cheering crowds greeted him when he first set foot in Paris; he was seen as a triumphant leader of great celebrity who would edify and save Europe. Once the conference began, he was pitted against more experienced diplomats and plucked from the soaring heights. Upon his return to Paris, he sacrificed his Fourteen Points to retain the League of Nations and was aware that the

Senate might reject the League if he was not willing to compromise on major issues. Near the end he became an embattled negotiator, who took it upon himself to keep the League alive.[7]

In which ways did Wilson stray from his Fourteen Points? There is no better place to start than the first point, which stated that the process of creating the Covenant would be an open and public procedure. During the entire conference, only the delegations were privy to its progress. Wilson also made major accommodations to other leaders, who were pressing their national security concerns. As a result, harsher terms were inflicted on Germany that limited its economic and military strength. These concessions were a cause for concern for Wilson because Germany could have refused to sign the treaty and fighting might resume (Saunders, 1998, p. 195). Although he started with high hopes for a more humane peace settlement, Wilson sacrificed many of his principles in order to create the League.

By mid-June, the parties had finished the key negotiations, and signing the treaty was just a matter of time. For Wilson, the possibility of Germany's refusal was now a moot point. Around this time Wilson turned his attention toward the Senate's approval. The possibility that collective security would be institutionalized through the League of Nations led to political upheaval in the Senate. Wilson was very vocal about the need for the League to go beyond agreements between nations. He envisioned a robust organization that would act as a political force; and American strength would be wielded to enhance its common strength. Moreover, Wilson's international goals were without precedent. Historically, American foreign policy rested on two pillars: the inviolability of sovereignty and a long-standing view of America's guarded isolation from Europe's entangling alliances.

Besides its radical departure from the tenets of US foreign policy, many senators fumed at Wilson's go-it-alone diplomacy. He drew up the League's framework entirely on his own. By not consulting the Senate's Foreign Relations Committee, he sidestepped the chamber's constitutional role in treaty-making, one that counsels the executive branch and therefore shares this power.

It did not help Wilson that in 1918 the Republicans retook the Senate. The constraints on him and the ratification of the League were clear, yet he was adamant about approving the treaty without reservations and hoped to avoid the concessions being asked of him by reservationist Republicans. Senate opinion was divided among loyal Democratic supporters, mild reservationists who sincerely supported the treaty, stronger reservationists, and irreconcilables who completely disapproved of the League.

The major divide in the Senate revolved around Article X – one that Wilson wrote himself – which could potentially commit the United States' economic and military power to the collective security of member nations. Article X states: "the Members of the League undertake to respect and preserve as against external aggression the territorial integrity and existing political independence of all Members of the League. In case of any such aggression or in case of any threat or danger of such aggression the Council shall advise upon the means by which this obligation shall be fulfilled." Lodge was the strident leader of the reservationist camp. He was genuinely anti-League of Nations because he thought that it posed a dangerous contradiction between the nation's sovereignty and the United States' obligation to the body. He was also fervently anti-Wilson, a sentiment based on personal differences as well as his dismay over what looked like Wilson's riding roughshod over the constitution, specifically Congress's power to declare war.

Lodge made it his priority to absolve the United States of any of the obligations in Article X. For Wilson, adherence to it was the only mechanism to make the League effective; if the United States extricated itself from this rule, it would render the organization quite powerless in the face of international aggression. Unlike the irreconcilables, many senators in the reservationist camp sincerely favored the treaty, but wanted it modified to protect vital American interests (Seymour, 1957).

To counter the opposition, Wilson took the offensive and defended Article X, while trying to mollify the objections of reservationists. He warned of the consequences of removing or weakening Article X, arguing that the Covenant provided the proper mechanisms to preserve the United States' security and interests. First, as a veto player, the United States could avoid hazardous foreign ventures. Second, the United States was not legally bound to any of the League's dictates. Yet, Wilson's rhetoric firmly expressed the view that even though the League did not constrain the United States in any legal way, it was morally obligated to respect and follow through on its decisions. Wilson never backed down from his position on Article X; he stated many times that it "was the very backbone of the Covenant" (Stromberg, 1963, p. 28). Thus, for Wilson, a moral obligation was infinitely superior to merely a legal one (Clements, 1987, p. 219).

Wilson's handling of the reservations was critical, since 79 out of 96 senators were in favor of approving the treaty and entering the League with some reasonable modifications (Stromberg, 1963). Wilson acknowledged the reservations but distinguished between substantive and interpretive ones. Substantive reservations, he argued, would require cumbersome and protracted process in which all countries would have to renegotiate the treaty's terms (Saunders, 1998, p. 216). Wilson accepted interpretive reservations as long as such understandings did not "form part of the formal ratification itself" (Clements, 1987, p. 218).

However, reservationist Republicans were intent on pushing beyond interpretive changes. Lodge held multiple hearings in the Foreign Relations Committee during July and August in an attempt to curb, radically reshape, and even defeat the treaty (Clements, 1987, p. 214). On 19 August, Wilson invited committee members to a three-hour question-and-answer lunch at the White House. However, Wilson still refused to entertain the idea of significant amendments. Given the impasse, Wilson came out of the meeting believing that opposition was partisan in nature and might be overcome with an appeal to the American people (1987, p. 218).

Wilson embarked on a nationwide series of speaking engagements on 3 September. On his tour, he "avoided making derogatory remarks about the mild reservations and concentrated his verbal salvos on the irreconcilables" (Kraig, 2004, p. 167). Wilson's rhetorical strategy was to paint ratification in stark moral terms and gave the impression that reservations were tantamount to rejecting the Covenant. Moreover, he made it seem that only two choices were available, accepting it as it stood or rejecting it.

Wilson masterfully weaved great moral promise and ominous portents into his speeches. While the League would render aggressive actions, such as Germany's, obsolete, rejection would plunge the world back into conflict. He was also keen to stress that the League's invocation of Article X did not automatically lead to the use of force. The organization would first use arbitration and diplomacy to deter aggressors and force as a last resort.

On his tour, Wilson made sure that his rhetoric transcended partisanship and turned ratification into a question of national greatness, which he defined "as that ability to develop a vision that penetrates to the heart of its duty and mission among the nations of the world" (Saunders, 1998, p. 223). His approach put aside the quibbling over details by reminding people that the League of Nations represented a great dream (Clements, 1987, p. 215).

Wilson's stirring oratory spoke to the moral sentiments that he held dear, and it also touched the hearts of his audiences as they greeted his speeches with cheers and applause. If he could not change the Senate's opinion, he would transform, steward, and rally that of the public toward this highest of causes. Wilson's approach had a political purpose. Wilson sought to exercise prerogative from the beginning of the peace process, but the Senate debate constrained him. On the speaking tour, Wilson could stand both outside of the debate and above the fray. As a result, he shied away from responding to criticisms and failed to suggest possible compromises (Cooper, 2009, p. 523). However, Wilson's omissions could have worked to his advantage. If he eventually compromised, such an act would be a necessary sacrifice for principle, while his opponents would never be able to position themselves as morally superior. But Wilson never capitalized on this advantage because he refused any reservations even when its defeat was certain.

By the time he reached Colorado, Wilson had traveled almost 10 000 miles and "was attracting enormous, enthusiastic crowds and a groundswell of support for the treaty seemed to be building" (Clements, 1987, p. 215). But he had to cut his trip short after delivering what turned out to be his last speech, in Pueblo, CO. Thoroughly exhausted, he could not continue his rigorous schedule; he was forced to return to Washington. A few days later he suffered a debilitating stroke.

In the end, Wilson's strategy failed. He resisted Lodge's reservations to the bitter end though he knew that most senators wanted some included in the treaty. He directed Democratic senators to vote down the treaty with reservations. The Senate rejected the treaty with, and then without, reservations. The first vote, on whether to ratify with Lodge's 14 reservations, was defeated by a vote of 39 to 55. However, the outcome did not bring reservationists who still desired the League over to Wilson's side. The second vote, for approval without any reservations, was defeated by a vote of 38 to 53.

THE FAILED RATIFICATION OF THE LEAGUE OF NATIONS: THE PERSONALITY STUDY

Which factors best explain the defeat of the League of Nations? From the perspective of political analysis, Wilson failed to have the Treaty of Versailles ratified in the Senate because he could not execute the complex balancing act that is required between international diplomacy and domestic politics, what international relations scholars refer to as "two level games" (Putnam, 1988).[8] Wilson made decisions and compromises with the Allies at the international level to preserve the League, yet he did not go far enough to satisfy the central decision-makers (the Senate) in the United States. Even as he faced a Republican Senate, he openly defied his opponents, was unbending in his belief that the treaty's rejection was unthinkable, and was adamantly opposed to reservations since such a change, in his mind, nullified the treaty.

Wilson made political miscalculations both internationally and domestically that someone more strategically competent might not have made. In fact, just by attending the Paris Peace talks, he allowed domestic opposition to form in the Senate. His presence also negated the formidable bargaining power he would have enjoyed as the major veto player, which was contingent on his remaining in Washington during the conference (Keynes, 1920; Lloyd George, 1938).

Are Wilson's strategic blunders attributable to errors that he could have corrected at the time? As circumstances played out, why did he not adjust his strategy? Why would a distinguished scholar of executive-congressional relations and an experienced President of the United States take actions that would likely reduce the prospects for ratification when other, more reasonable, alternatives were clearly available (Walker, 1995, p. 698)? This puzzle intrigues personality scholars. They interpret the ratification process as Wilson's refusal to accept reservations that would have ensured ratification without altering the treaty's terms in other than a cosmetic fashion (Bailey, 1945; George and George, 1964; Freud and Bullitt, 1967). Based on this interpretation of his behavior, personality scholars have surmised that Wilson's personality – his inner drives – led him to this crucial political mistake.

I argue differently. While the ratification process made particular traits, such as his anger and stubbornness, more pronounced and visible, his fight with the Senate is attributable to his ambition to erect the League and the mode he used to attain it: prerogative and rhetorical statesmanship. His actions more likely reflected his own beliefs about the power of his statesmanship: that it must be an independent force, which guides political practice and that rhetoric can edify and sway the nation toward correct principles.

WOODROW WILSON'S PERSONALITY: THE DESIRE FOR POWER AND ACHIEVEMENT

Winter (2003) argues that Wilson's personality affected three key components of his political behavior: his inept negotiation, his confusion of rhetoric with substance, and his refusal to compromise. Despite Wilson's principled advocacy of the League and his supreme confidence in its success, he showed a "consistent pattern in which he seemed to undercut his remarkable leadership skills and defeat or undo his considerable accomplishments" (Winter, 2003, p. 15). These patterns reveal that what was truly behind his lofty political and moral goals was a desire to impose his psychological needs on others. Wilson's particular personality made him increasingly stubborn as the challenges to the League's ratification mounted. As a result, he countered his opponents with lengthy and exhausting speech campaigns (2003, p. 15).

There is a problem with this interpretation however. Wilson was a determined and high-minded statesman; his academic and political career was guided by a conscious attempt to unite political thought and practice. As such, he put his ambition toward noble purposes and poured his energy into the art of statesmanship. However, psychobiographers overlook Wilson's deliberate choices and conscious political understanding in favor of the underlying psychological ambitions that produced the failed ratification. Rather than try to explain the nature of Wilson's political character and how it led to his attempt to overcome constraints on the domestic and international level, personality scholars divorce Wilson the individual from political practice and concentrate on his underlying compulsions. The latter surely exist, but they are mistakenly understood as both causes of individual behavior and political outcomes in general.

George and George (1981) plumb the depths of Wilson's life and argue that his personality orientation derailed his visionary goals as it led to "a ruinously self-defeating refusal to compromise with his opponents on certain issues that had become emotionally charged for him" (p. 642). Thus, their argument hinges on Wilson's inability to compromise, which was only a symptom of his underlying ambition: "an unconscious interest in imposing orderly systems upon others as a means of achieving a sense of power" (George and George, 1981, p. 38).

George and George are of the opinion that the desire for power guided Wilson's behavior throughout his life. It remained an unconscious motive because it was in tension with his moral code. Eventually, this desire for power overrode his explicit political aims. While Wilson thought that he took the high road as the proponent of the League, he found it impossible to compromise with the Senate for the sake of saving it. For George and George, "the substance of his program, although sustained by a variety of personal needs and intellectual conviction which sincerely committed him to it, was in the last analysis the external vehicle of his need to dominate" (1964, p. 208).

However, this is an odd theoretical understanding of Wilson's political ambition. On the one hand, the authors admit that Wilson's political program grew out of his mature political thought. On the other hand, his program was produced by an unconscious need to dominate others and served to satisfy his underlying ambitions. How would it have been possible for someone like Wilson, with a wealth of life experience and a thoughtful approach to politics and statesmanship, to be completely blind to his genuine desire, which was, apparently, to seek power? Here is the main problem with the examination of leadership character and ambition from a personality perspective. The personality is forged through conflict; so positive expressions of statesmanship such as Wilson's transformative, international goals are judged as latent expressions of inner turmoil. As a result of this poor theory of statesmanship, we are left with the low standards of the personality structure to judge Wilson's high, yet flawed, leadership.

Wilson's desire to achieve power was built on inner doubts and the low self-esteem that the authors attribute to his conflicted relationship with his father, Joseph Ruggles Wilson, a Presbyterian minister who made perfectionist demands on those around him and instilled Calvinistic doctrine into his family.[9] Thus, "the boy Wilson was steeped in a tradition which extolled moral achievement above all else" (George and George 1964, pp. 4–5). Joseph Wilson also played a very active role in his son's education, but mysteriously, even though his father was punctilious about the use of the English language, the young Wilson did not learn to read well until he was 11 (1964, p. 7). The authors suggest that "failing – refusing – to learn was the one way in which the boy dared to express his resentment against his father" (1964, p. 7).

The paternal demands exacted on the young Wilson were the origin of his motives and inner turmoil. He was a late reader and poor student but fully aware that individuals in his family sharpened their intellect and were expected to succeed in public life. The authors maintain that the gap between his father's demands and his own achievement created anxiety and resentment in him. However, Wilson never openly rebelled against his father. Not only did he repress his negative feelings, but he also adopted his father's standards as his own. As a boy, he could reduce his anxiety by pleasing his father through showing a strong desire for high achievement. Wilson's political personality pivoted on two distinct motives, the need for power and achievement. George and George's description of his complex relationship with his father is worth reproducing here.

> Dr. Wilson was noted for his caustic wit. This he directed not only at his contemporaries but at his young son as well. Tommy never retorted and he never rebelled. Instead, he accepted his father's demands for perfection, tried to emulate him, and interpreted his stinging criticisms as humiliating evidence that, try as he might, he was inadequate. He felt eternally inferior to his father in appearance as well as in accomplishment. He once remarked: "If I had my father's face and figure, it wouldn't make any difference what I said." (1964, p. 6)

Forged in his childhood, Wilson's power and high-achievement motives directed his behavior throughout his life via a compulsive striving for perfection (1964, p. 8). The timing and development of inner motives is critical to the personality approach because it suggests that psychological motivation is independent of a leader's maturing thought and political experience. If a leader's political personality is formed in his childhood and early adolescence, then inner motives are largely borne out of unconscious development and emotional turmoil. Political ambition emerges from this development; and its expression is interpreted as a displacement of these core needs.

The authors argue that Wilson rationalized his political behavior, actions that primarily satisfied his inner needs, by always appealing to a great moral purpose. Wilson's aims at the peace talks easily fulfilled his desires because he could vindicate himself as the architect of a moral peace settlement. However, even in grayer areas, Wilson's rationalization was at work, such as when he brought the United States into the war:

> His only means of justifying to himself his excruciating decision to go to war was to devote every last ounce of his strength to ensuring that out of the holocaust would emerge a moral peace settlement which would ensure that this would be indeed the war to end wars. The realization of such a sublime ideal was the only coin which could purchase peace of mind for him. To this compelling motivation were wedded others, perhaps even more basic, which sprang from Wilson's urgent inner needs. He had always wanted – *needed* –

to do immortal work. Devising a peace settlement which would prevent future wars was a task which appealed to everything within him which strove for self-vindication through accomplishment. (1964, p. 197)

George and George (1964) reduce Wilson's great ambition, which was the desire to do a great and immortal work and pursue such a sublime ideal, to something that is not exalted at all but also morally illegitimate – the desire to dominate. By using a personality approach, we can only conclude that Wilson had a tyrannical character and was only limited by a combination of inner repression and the constraints of democratic government:

> He had always wanted – *needed* – to dominate. The greatness of his cause provided justification for imposing his moral purpose on the whole world. In service of such an ideal, he could allow himself to seek control of the peace conference and to impose his will ruthlessly upon those at home who dared question the wisdom of his ideas about the peace settlement. (1964, pp. 197–8)

Wilson's competing needs lead George and George to conclude "that temperamental defects contributed to the President's tragic failure both in negotiating the Treaty and later in attempting to secure its ratification" (1964, p. 197). In activities in which Wilson invested emotional effort, he did not like to be challenged by anybody. During his early presidency, these problems went unnoticed. Wilson had a Democratic majority in Congress and gained party unanimity by "making unprecedented use of a traditional party institution: the caucus" (1964, p. 135). The authors also do not properly render Wilson's personality because they fail to examine his overall statesmanship. For example, early in his presidency, he galvanized Congress and used the office of the executive to produce more significant domestic legislation than any previous time in American history (Dimock, 1957, p. 6).

Wilson certainly had personality flaws; he angered quickly and was impolitic with his rivals. Without a doubt his flaws contributed to conflict with Lodge and with the Senate. However, he also harnessed the drives of his personality; he developed a strong will and incessant work ethic. He spent most of his adult life thinking about the problem of statesmanship as it related to the American regime and then later to world politics. Far from being a tyrant, Wilson advocated and tried to practice elevated leadership through a blend of moral wisdom, oratorical persuasion, and coercive politics. The basis of Wilson political character was his highly conscious attempt to discern the enlightened interests of the public and the international world. However, we are supposed to believe that his irrationality blinded him to his political interests during the League's ratification.

Scholars of American politics and American political thought have also criticized the personality approach's interpretation of Wilson on grounds that it fails to distinguish the rhetorical demands placed on Wilson from his psychological impulses. According to Jeffrey Tulis (1987), Wilson's rhetoric was defiant in the face of reservations because he was trying to stave off an equivocal acceptance of the League: "Wilson was preoccupied with the *problematic* character of the League of Nations. The League rested on nothing more than good-will and the ability of each of its member nations to transcend national interests" (1987, p. 156). In addition, Wilson had to adjust to quite different rhetorical necessities: he needed to persuade senators to vote for the treaty and the citizenry to pressure senators to vote for it (1987, p. 158). From another perspective, Daniel Stid (1998) argues that Wilson's self-defeating tour and action in the Senate were attempts to resolve a contradiction in his program, namely: "his determination to exercise absolute control over the treaty-making power was inconsistent with his recognition that the Senate was in a position and often inclined to thwart such presidential control" (p. 161). Wilson proceeded with this approach because he thought that the League required America's unconditional support. Wilson's also believed that it was important and necessary for the President to control the treaty-making process, which he articulated much earlier in his work *Congressional Government*. World War I had taught Wilson that a League of Nations that could enforce collective security was paramount for peace. He would risk the treaty failing rather than have it issued with numerous reservations that would lead other member-states "to reduce their commitments, intangibly if not formally" (1998, p. 153). While his refusal to allow the Senate to modify the treaty seems to issue from his irrational need to dominate, his behavior was reasonable if viewed in light of his view of the role of the President in treaty-making, his judgment of the paramount importance of the League and Article X for world peace, and his belief that his exercise of prerogative was necessary for the success of his project (1998, p. 153).

CONCLUSION

The criticisms levied against the personality approach's psychobio-graphical interpretation of Wilson are well worth exploring in depth. However, I want to emphasize one crucial flaw in the personality theo-ries that serves as a bridge for the next two chapters, which discuss Aristotle's idea of statesmanship and magnanimity as great political ambition. The development of a leader's political personality is random in nature. A mostly unconscious development underlies leaders' political ambition and concomitant statecraft. There is no way to distinguish between the more important variations of ambition among leaders, espe-cially ordinary ambition from the greater transformative kind.

Wilson exhibited the latter kind of ambition; he directed it toward changing the rules of international politics, which in his mind benefited the world and the United States. Thus, he practiced statesmanship at both the domestic and international level. Conversely, the personality approach understands leaders' behavior as the product of idiosyncrasy that is devoid of both political prudence and a systematic way of under-standing the relationship between the leadership and political environ-ment he inhabits. Wilson is not an example of the idiosyncratic leader. He implemented novel diplomatic ideas, risked his and his party's pres-tige, gambled the League on the power of his rhetoric, and defied constraints and other individuals not because of his personality foibles, but on account of his greater ambitions, understanding of the American regime, and beliefs about the international order.

NOTES

1. Personality scholars use the terms "motives" and "political goals" interchangeably and tend to express the idea of motivation as needs.
2. The personality orientations include expansionist, active/independent, influential, mediator/integrator, opportunist, developmental, and each has a respective foreign-policy definition. In addition, each orientation is made up of component personality variables, of which the motivation for power or affiliation is one (see Hermann, 1980)
3. This text is a classic example of personality and biography, what is called the "psychobiographical method" – to assess political leaders' behavior. Since the publi-cation of their seminal work, the authors have answered their critics (1981) and updated their interpretation in light of new data (1998). However, the thesis they provide about Woodrow Wilson's personality and political behavior has not funda-mentally changed over time.
4. See Woodrow Wilson's message to Congress (1914).
5. Unrestricted submarine warfare meant that Germany's U-boats would sink without

warning merchant or passenger ships, armed or unarmed, neutral or enemy, sailing in the war zone around England. Restricted submarine warfare meant that one or another of these categories might be spared altogether, or that submarines before firing would surface, warn their victims, and give them time to abandon ship (Hull, 2004, p. 279).

6. The concept of self-determination assumes that a cohesive group of people, a nation, has the right to choose its own political organization, and, consequently, its own state. As a result, this principle presents a challenge to the territorial status quo and invites conflict. Wilson understood this problem and only committed to the restoration of Belgium with complete rights to self-determination. According to Robert M. Saunders, this action underscores Wilson's pragmatism over his ideological aspirations (1998, p. 105).

7. One of the important dramatic elements of Wilson's time in Paris was the way his relationship with his personal counsel, Colonel Edward House, deteriorated after he returned from Washington. The interesting and dynamic relationship is fully explored by Alexander and Juliet George (1964).

8. Robert D. Putnam defines two-level games as: "[A]t the national level, domestic groups pursue their interests by pressuring the government to adopt favorable policies, and politicians seek power by constructing coalitions among those groups. At the international level, national governments seek to maximize their own ability to satisfy domestic pressures, while minimizing the adverse consequences of foreign developments. Neither of the two games can be ignored by central decision-makers, so long as their countries remain interdependent, yet sovereign" (1988, p. 434).

9. There are two methods to study personality and leader behavior. First, to study a particular leader's personality, analysts can use psychobiography, while a more generalized study of personality and behavior examines general traits that an individual possesses to varying degrees. For psychobiographers, personality is determined by the emotional and environmental influences during the formative stages of childhood and adolescence. Thus, a leader's personality assessment requires reconstructing these developmental stages using biographical data. However, there is an inherent problem with the biographical approach. This information can be scarce, and there is no direct access to political leaders as there is to clinical patients. In a clinical practice, a patient's narrative answers provide the psychologist with accurate information with which a personality assessment can be made, the same analysis that the psychobiographer wishes to replicate. Some scholars are explicit that the assessment of leaders' personalities at a distance is construction of a representation of a leader's personality (Greenstein, 1969).

4. Transformational leadership: a theoretical critique

> The genius, in work and deed, is necessarily a squanderer: that he squanders himself, that is his greatness. The instinct of self-preservation suspended, as it were; the over-powering pressure of outflowing forbids him any such care or caution.
> **Fredrick Nietzsche**, *Twilight of the Idols*

Transformative political ambition offers an alternative to the political science theories examined in the last three chapters, which posit that constraints and incentives in the external environment, as well as imperious demands of the personality, are the fount of leader behavior. Transformative ambition is specifically observed in leaders who seek to infuse ordinary politics with a higher purpose and fundamentally change their political conditions in order bring about their goals. My attention to political leadership and change builds upon the work of contemporary scholarship that has examined the independent role of leaders to explain institutional change (see March and Olsen, 1984); leaders as educators and moral guides who are capable of transforming the preferences of followers (Burns, 1978); leaders who practice the art of political manipulation and change their environments through the use of "heresthetics" in order to win (Riker, 1986). In this chapter, I pay special attention to James MacGregor Burns' theory of transformational leadership because it shares in the view of this work that individual leaders can purposely change the moral lives and psychological dispositions of their polities.

Despite the similar approach, I argue that in his attempt to demonstrate the purposeful and moral dimension of leadership, Burns abstracts too much and misses the realities of regime politics and concrete expressions of political ambition. In addition, I identify a problem with Burns' notion that transformational leadership leads to ethical transformation: the transmission of broad values and the attainment of self-realization. I critique his argument by exposing the inherent relativism in his understanding of values, his narrow conception of self-realization, which neglects its Nietzschean philosophical origins, and his failure to understand the complexity of political ambition as it is mediated by both a leader's character virtues and the political regime that he inhabits.

Burns' theory does not explain why transformational leaders adopt one set of values over another. As a result, I argue that transformational leadership denies the possibility of virtuous leadership that can be measured by moral standards. I find the root of the theory's moral relativism in its reliance on the idea that values are simply means for self-actualization or self-fulfillment.[1] I expose the contradiction inherent in Burns' theory that transformational leadership always participates in collective self-actualization. Unlike Burns, I pay close attention to the Nietzschean philosophical underpinnings of this idea that reveal aristocratic forms of self-realization. These forms are exclusionary and, sometimes, intolerant of others. Since Burns does not acknowledge that Nietzsche's view that self-creation is radically individualistic, he cannot defend self-realization as a collective endeavor. Thus, he cannot account for modes of transformational leadership that are guided by Nietzsche's ideas and originate in political orders that depend upon strict hierarchies.

In this chapter, I provide a sustained criticism of Burns' proposition that transformational leadership is the ethical elevation of leaders and followers by comparing his understanding of values to Aristotle's classical conception of political and moral virtue. For Aristotle, good leadership requires durable character traits and is more demanding and difficult to attain. I show that Burns' explanations of leadership traits such as creativity, inspiration, and charisma embrace popular desires too easily and that this results in the transmission of ephemeral beliefs. Transformational leadership lacks the venerability, weight, and, as Lincoln observed, the genius that disdains the beaten path. The critique of Burns' theory offered here suggests a need to understand the complicated nature of ambition and transformation. In the end, Burns is too dismissive of ambition. I propose ways to reinvigorate the study of ambition through political philosophers' understandings of how political regimes solicit specific character traits in leaders while stoking some forms of ambition and suppressing others.

THE THEORY OF TRANSFORMATIONAL LEADERSHIP

In Burns' seminal book *Leadership* (1978), he coins the idea of transformational leadership, which is when leaders and followers engage each other and create a change in the morality of both groups. Burns contrasts transformational with transactional leadership, which occurs when one person seeks out others in order to exchange something valuable (1978, p. 19).[2] These exchanges can be political, economic, and psychological, such as when a politician exchanges favors or jobs with legislators and trades votes with citizens. For Burns, these contrasting ideas of leadership provide the bedrock for understanding leadership across a variety of organizational contexts, such as politics, business, and non-governmental institutions.[3]

Burns sees the need for such a theory because he finds the prevailing definition of leadership in the social sciences limiting: an individual in a position of authority that wields power. Identifying a leader as the person in charge may seem like common sense, but Burns explains how this narrows researchers' focus on raw power at the exclusion of psychological and moral factors. For Burns, a leader is "a particular kind of power holder," and "not all power holders are leaders" (1978, p. 18). His is an expansive view of leadership that includes personality characteristics and motives. At its best, leadership is purposeful activity that arouses and satisfies the motives of followers (1978, p. 18).[4]

According to Burns, transformational leadership is a process of engaging individuals' greatest capacities for motivation and morality; it raises the level of human conduct and ethical aspirations of both leader and led (1978, p. 20). Burns tests his theory by supplying examples of leaders who either meet the criteria of transformational leadership or who are bent on aggrandizement and domination. The latter demonstrate the pitfalls of power wielding and cannot be rightly called examples of leadership. There is a moral undertow in his work because Burns extols transformational leadership; it is distinct and higher than transactional leadership as it provides an alternative to power wielding. Such lofty leadership conduces to self-realization, which connotes the idea that the individual can discover the highest levels of human motivation. For Burns, this is a synthesis of individualism and leadership, which is shown in transformational leaders who enable followers. Mahatma Gandhi serves as his foremost example of transformational leadership. About Gandhi, he writes: "who aroused and elevated the hopes and demands of Indians and whose life and personality were enhanced in the process" (1978, p. 20).

Transformational leadership is singular in the way it elevates the moral life of leaders and followers. In other words, it takes the inward nature of self-fulfillment and makes it social. Yet Burns does not stipulate what, if any, public moral virtues and goals are required for transformational leadership. The only demand he places on transformational leadership is that it must satisfy the "true" needs of leaders and followers (1978, p. 36). The particular characteristics of transformational leadership come to sight when leaders acquire new values and change existing ones. It is the defining role of a leader to help articulate the values that followers can share in common. In order to bring these changes in valuations about, Burns' ideal leaders make use of charisma, a combination of intelligence and vision, and inspiration.

Although these are potent qualities that are definitely advantageous for any leader to hold, none of them are particularly moral. Character virtue and publicly defined virtues are not necessary for transformational leadership. What, then, is moral about transformational leadership? Burns writes, "leadership is a process of morality to the degree that leaders engage with followers on the basis of shared motives and values and goals" (1978, p. 36). Despite this definition's open-endedness, Burns uses examples of shared values that are particularly liberal: "persons are guided by near universal ethical principles of justice such as equality of human rights and respect for individual dignity" (1978, p. 42).

LIBERAL VALUES AND TRANSFORMATIONAL LEADERSHIP QUALITIES

Like many academic scholars in the social sciences, Burns has disposed of the natural rights teachings that inform liberalism. Instead he explains morality as the attribution of value through personal belief and views values as means to help individuals make choices that fulfill the individual's greatest needs and motives: self-actualization. When Burns discusses the values that leaders use toward self-fulfillment he is not talking about specific values issues that are perennially contested in democracies, such as religion, the sanctity of the family, abortion, and gay rights, among others, which require politicians to routinely clarify their positions. Instead, he is referring to broad values, such as equal dignity and autonomy. Transformational leadership is not about achieving the right political and moral order but about promoting individual and social identities. The construction of new and overlapping identities between leaders and followers is an exercise in collective self-actualization, an idea I will examine in depth shortly. Transmitting values are a way of reaching this goal.

Burns thinks that transformational leaders will incline toward liberal values because the idea of autonomy is fundamental to self-actualization.[5] As such, human life is not determined simply by external forces or internal subconscious forces. If autonomy is the conduit of self-actualization, then an enlightened society would likely encourage freedom. Liberal theorists such as John Locke and Charles de Montesquieu encouraged democratic forms of freedom as well. However they went to great pains to explain that liberty should not be confused with license, which is the belief that one may do whatever one wishes. Laws restrain individuals from infringing upon the liberty of others; where the law is silent, individuals enjoy the right to choose from among many of life's opportunities.

Burns emphasizes liberal values but does not supply any grounds for favoring liberal values over others. From the perspective of natural rights, Locke would argue that liberal societies are simply more just. The adoption or revaluation of values poses a problem for the theory of transformational leadership. What set of criteria do leaders rely upon to help tell the difference between good and bad, and true and false, values? Burns does not say that transformational leaders submit their values to a rational examination or even to distinctions between good and bad. What he denotes as higher values does not depend upon knowledge of good and bad. What makes a higher value higher is not the value itself but its effect. Values are an individual's vehicle for greater emotional and cognitive clarity that promote self-fulfillment.

Transformational leadership transmits values through the qualities of creativity, commitment, and inspiration. Charisma is of special importance because it does not coerce followers but dazzles them. In essence, transformational leadership derives its authority from charisma, "rather than obtaining the appraisal that one deserves" (Faulkner 2007, p. 4). However there is no inherent reason why charismatic authority excludes the possibility of using coercive means to achieve political ends.[6]

Burns excludes a fourth quality of leadership, but one that is surely necessary, particularly in the study of political leadership: the ability to use power. Leadership that intends change is inconceivable without force coming into play as new values come into conflict with prevailing ones. Burns describes the change in values as occurring innocuously: transformational leaders act upon existing values, exploit the contradictions among values, realign them, and reorganize institutions where necessary (1978, p. 43). Power is obviated by what Burns calls *engagé* (engagement with followers). It is a type of commitment on the part of followers that firms up their adherence to new values.[7]

As Machiavelli observed, profound changes in followers' commitment are brought about by morally audacious leaders who understand how to manage fear through the principle of necessity while keeping the people inspired. In other words, leaders must be inspirational and creative, but also understand the importance of power and its relationship to the psychology of people. Burns' transformational leaders transmit values and reorganize institutions, but somehow manage to avoid Machiavelli's understanding that such changes depend upon using leadership qualities to wield power prudently and to the leader's advantage.

However, there is something Machiavellian in the princely and entrepreneurial qualities of transformational leadership. For Machiavelli, leaders that introduce novel and powerful values that help define and bring order to their polity must know the pulse of the people. Machiavelli understands that a combination of virtues and vices and constant reminders of the peoples' need for the prince bind followers to a leader and help them introduce any mode that they wish. Burns' leaders have some of Machiavelli's princes' virtues but none of their vices; they have the luxury of being lofty and positively social.

TRANSFORMATIONAL VALUES VERSUS THE CLASSICAL CONCEPTION OF VIRTUE

Burns shies away from permanent moral standards that would impose limits on what values transformational leaders should hold. Self-actualization is not a lasting state of happiness but a constant desire for greater self-fulfillment. The values used to achieve this state are fleeting and subjective. Transformational leadership's path to self-fulfillment is less demanding than Aristotle's idea of human virtue and fulfillment. According to Aristotle, the final end of human being is happiness that is achieved by the flourishing of various human excellences. Essentially, Aristotle circumscribes human flourishing to the practice of moral and intellectual virtue. It is an endeavor that is difficult to attain and is steeped in an arduous moral education. In Aristotle's world, self-fulfillment is accessible only to a leisured class of aristocrats that can devote their lives to virtue. Conversely, no way of life is barred from transformational leadership's quest for self-actualization.

Burns does not equip his leaders with character excellence and Aristotelian traits like magnanimity, justice, and prudence. For Aristotle, the person of high character has a proper comportment toward pleasures, power, and honor, while he practices the virtues of courage, temperance, liberality, moderation, justice, and prudence, among others. Aristotle does not think that most people are capable of character excellence; an individual must be groomed to live virtuously. His moral teaching targets gentlemen who are predisposed to live virtuously and enjoy abundant resources. Such gentlemen are already habituated to moral excellence and possess an intuitive grasp of the moral good. There is an unbridgeable gap between Aristotelian gentlemen and ordinary people; each group heeds the calls of different ways of life. Burns seeks to bridge this gap. His leaders are not virtuous by Aristotle's standards and not essentially different from their followers. Rather they have the qualities mentioned in the last section and a sense of the pulse of values that people will embrace.

In light of Aristotle's view of virtue and self-fulfillment, Burns' theory distorts moral virtue by opening up morality to sundry ways of life and an infinite variety of values. Values are mere opinion for Aristotle, and only virtues that are also ends in themselves are worth pursuing. According to Burns, values can be perceived as ends when they are psychologically internalized. Only then do values seem to attain the power of an external force on individuals, and "they follow the dictates of those values in the absence of incentives, sanctions, or even witnesses" (1978, p. 75). Yet, this power is forged by a combination of individual belief and social norms. Burns understands that values do not exist independently of people's belief in them.[8]

Burns rejects the main principle of Aristotle's virtue ethics: there are durable moral characteristics and ends that must be learned through practice but, also, depend on the knowledge of ends. For Aristotle, reason participates with virtue. Knowledge of the good and the consistent practice of the moral life are inseparable from each other. Burns sees the formation of values as dependent upon political culture, the moral development of children, and being influenced by one's peers and others (1978, p. 77). Values are social constructions and a matter of belief; they are good as long as they are useful.

Aristotle understands that morality is shaped by custom, but he argues that rational grounds can be supplied for moral choices. Virtue acts according to right reason: a state of mind that allows the individual to be steadfast in the face of swaying passions and changing circumstances. For Burns, Aristotle's virtue ethics may incline too strongly toward moral certitude. In today's political and social climate, such certitude connotes arrogance and intolerance. The criticism levied against the moral certitude of virtue ethics is that it is blind to the quandaries and ambiguity of moral practice. For proponents of values, the presence of ambiguity invites disagreement about the objectivity of morality and usually leads to the conclusion that there cannot be any moral certainty about ends. There are only beliefs, which is what values represent. Any number of values and perspectives can apply in the same moral situation.

For Aristotle, moral knowledge is acquired through experience and individual's mediation of claims for justice and nobility. Each moral form tugs at the individual: justice concerns others while nobility involves an individualistic concern with self-perfection. The foundation of Aristotelian self-fulfillment is moral choice that is not only good for the individual but also done for its own sake. Virtues are distinct from values because they exist without the individual's consenting to their worth. Virtue has a reality of its own.

THE PHILOSOPHIC ORIGINS OF THE IDEA OF SELF-ACTUALIZATION

Transformational leaders intend to help followers reach self-actualization:

> Self-actualization ultimately means the ability *to lead by being led*. It is this kind of self-actualization that enables leaders to comprehend the needs of potential followers, to enter into their perspectives, and to act on popular needs such as those for material help and for security and esteem. Because leaders themselves are continually going through self-actualization processes, they are able to rise with their followers, usually one step ahead of them, to respond to their transformed needs and thus to help followers move into self-actualization processes. (Burns, 1978, p. 117)

Within psychology, Abraham Maslow's (1943) idea of self-actualization is viewed as an alternative to Sigmund Freud's pessimistic outlook: the study of the human psyche through dysfunctional types. Known as positive psychology, Maslow's theory focuses on the healthy individual and conceives of human beings as reservoirs of potential rather than wells of subconscious sexual and aggressive forces. The idea behind self-actualization is that psychological growth and well-being is witnessed when people ascend from lower to higher needs: from lowest to highest are physiological, safety, love and belonging, self-esteem, and self-actualization. Burns adopts positive psychology's mantra: self-actualization for leadership leads to greater potential and fuller being (1978, p. 117).

Maslow thinks of self-actualization as what he calls a positive need that once it is tapped into continues to encourage individuals toward more growth and higher forms of consciousness. Self-actualization is deeply personal and expressed idiosyncratically. It is governed by the creative will, which is what strives for growth. This view is very far from Friedrich Nietzsche's notion of the amoral will to power and self-overcoming, in which the will seeks to break violently with what Nietzsche diagnosed as the decline of modern humanity. Burns adopts the idea that self-actualizing is unequivocally desirable and good and, thus, neglects Nietzsche's more penetrating view: the individual who reevaluates existing values by stripping away illusions about their perceived worth is deepening their self. Burns' optimism about transformational leadership can only be maintained by obscuring alternative self-actualizing projects such as the desire for greatness or noble superiority because these aims cannot be shared broadly. Not everyone can be great. Burns blunts the possibility for transformative leaders with much larger appetites and lofty visions about their own destinies.

One radical alternative to Burns' theory is reflected in Friedrich Nietzsche's ideas of continual striving and self-creation, which are the philosophical roots of the idea of self-actualization. Nietzsche understands freedom as founded upon self-creation. In the *Genealogy of Morals,* Nietzsche examines the values of bad conscience and unegoistic actions and criticizes how modern day thinkers analyse these values without accounting for their historical origins. He also explains how these values contribute to modern decay through mob, herd, or slave mentality. Nietzsche thinks that a reliance on modern values does not offer a better rationale for living a meaningful existence, since these values rely on a fundamental faith in human freedom and reason. Faith in reason becomes one value among many.

Nietzsche turns to the Dionysian notion of excess, an idea that enables the (self) creator to value dominance and admire strength. Nietzsche prepares a political climate that can be characterized, by liberal standards, as intolerant and harsh. Daniel Conway (1997) points us to an illustrative passage of Nietzsche's Dionysian streak in the *Twilight of the Idols*:

> The genius, in work and deed, is necessarily a squanderer: that he squanders himself, that is his greatness. The instinct of self-preservation suspended, as

it were; the overpowering pressure of outflowing forbids him any such care or caution. (p. 125)

Nietzschean creators are not bound by convention, concerns for a healthy personality, or collective self-actualization. Their creative acts serve the problem of the present self, which is frustrated by the modern values of egoism, bad conscience, and slave morality. In order to free themselves from modern values, creators cannot hold out any hope that their actions will be praised or followed by others. Self-satisfaction, not the ethical elevation of others, is the measure of creativity's deeds. By adopting self-actualization as the end of leadership, Burns has unwittingly inherited Nietzsche's idea of self-creation. Thus, transformational leaders who exhibit humane and liberal values cannot defend these values by their merits. Although Burns claims that transformational leaders internalize universal values and exhort others to live up to these, they must do so in the absence of a binding universal morality.

Self-actualization lacks any definite meaning, since it is something that has yet to be realized.[9] In self-actualization, Burns has turned to a psychological idea that endorses human striving and growth, yet it is unmoored because it is agnostic about moral ends. In the end, self-realization leads to relativism and to an unresolvable ethical problem for transformational leadership. For Nietzsche, self-realization must move into unfamiliar territory, especially as the individual calls existing norms into question. Moreover, for Nietzsche there is no prohibition on self-actualizers who turn to pleasure-seeking, aesthetic, spiritual, and intellectual acts that transgress conventional moral opinion and sacred restraints.

Burns' disciples, Bernard M. Bass and Paul Steidlmeier (1999), detected the problem with the theory's moral relativism as they were unable to distinguish between moral and immoral transformational leaders. In order to resolve this they tried to draw an additional distinction between authentic and pseudo-transformational leadership; authentic transformational leadership means that the leader builds genuine trust with followers. Yet trust does not substitute for solid moral foundations. Authentic transformational leadership is just as limited a theory because it relies on the relativity of values and a romanticist hope that leaders will have a sentiment for the collective well-being.

The rationale of authentic transformational leadership is that authentic leaders are inspirational and have ideals, while pseudo-leaders are inspirational but either falsely hold ideals or arrive to them by accident.

Bass and Steidlmeier's analytical distinction does not help them objectively distinguish between true and false values, and moral and immoral leadership. Ultimately, what these scholars call authentic transformational leaders is determined by their own value judgments.

The most troubling aspect regarding transformational leadership is that it does not have the appropriate concepts to judge a leader's values as good or bad. The need to develop a theory of authentic leadership arose from transformational leadership's inability to make sense of Hitler. He was charismatic and realigned the values of his nation. In essence, he led the collective self-actualization of Germany and its people. Before World War II's denouement, according to transformational leadership, Hitler fulfilled the highest needs of his followers. Transformational leadership scholars can only excise Hitler from the classification of a transformational leader in hindsight, since it became obvious that he caused a great deal of harm. However, because the theory is founded on self-actualization aided by charisma, commitment, inspiration, and creativity, its scholars do not have the tools to tell the difference between a tyrant and a public-spirited leader, especially if the tyrant is charismatic and the public-spirited leader is reticent and moderate. The tyrant might inspire but the public-spirited leader can observe justice.

Interestingly, for Winston Churchill, a statesman of Aristotelian ilk, there was never any question about Hitler's evil nature and how National Socialism was itself a denial of politics (Pelinka, 1999, p. 123). Transformational leadership presupposes the relativism of values and ignores the idea that moral choice requires reasonable differences between good and bad. As a result, transformational leadership scholars will always face the danger of not being able to tell if a charismatic leader is masking unethical ends by propagating values for self-actualization.

POLITICAL REGIMES, LEADERSHIP, AND AMBITION

A serious examination of good and bad transformational leadership must begin at the level of the political regime. It is through the presentation of alternatives that it becomes possible for the scholar to judge between good and bad leadership by comparing regimes as well as leaders within and across regimes. Political regimes impart a moral education to individuals and potential leaders. In addition, the phenomenon that Burns calls followership also begins at the level of the regime and this is where the analysis of transformational leadership should begin.

In general, political regimes make claims on their citizens by providing them with laws and particular goods: security, well-being, honor, glory, liberty, and equality to name a few. The obligation of citizens is to obey and love it back without reason except that it is theirs. Such sentiment is the essence of patriotism and is the bedrock experience of ordinary citizens. Burns' theory defies this commonsense view because transformational leadership does not make any claims on followers and this leads to a tenuous association between leaders and followers. Why should a follower that aims strictly at self-realization attach himself to any one leader, community, or set of values? All things being equal, any charismatic leader will do as long as he can keep people inspired. Conversely, if citizens are no longer inspired they are free to jettison the leader and his values. Burns' leader characteristics, charisma, inspiration, and creativity, emphasize novelty. These leaders need celebrity in order to succeed. The problem with this view is that the transformational leader's changes are not considered in relation to the regime, and whether such changes are just.

Although the spirit of transformational leadership is positive, it invalidates the differences between traditional and liberal regimes. How can one tell whether regime change is good if the regime cannot be identified in the first place? In addition, the instinctual bonds and attachments of the political community to a way of life are eroded by the concentration on values and well-being. This is why Burns proffers the elevation of values in the most general sense. For example, transformational leaders can stand for equality. However, without the mention of democracy the scholar cannot observe whether the perversions and excesses from equality are taking place, such as when unbridled equality devolves into the tyranny of the majority – a problem observed by Plato, Aristotle, James Madison, Alexis de Tocqueville, and John Stuart Mill.

Transformational leadership cannot tell the difference between a just egalitarianism versus a despotic one. For example, take the case of Hugo Chavez of Venezuela. He was a charismatic democrat who has motivated his followers into fits of revolutionary zeal, but he also acted as an unjust demagogue who concentrated power. Chavez was charismatic, inspirational, and creative; the people, the poor majority who loved him, adopted his vague and general values. At the same time, his regime eroded freedom, political participation, and trust. Chavez used the majority and elections to consolidate his rule without having to wield power in drastic and violent ways. In light of the principles of republican rule, however, it is possible to declare Chavez culpable of demagoguery, censorship, political intimidation, infringement on the separation of powers, and perverse constitutional engineering. All the while, Chavez transformed Venezuela by maintaining a charismatic personality and enigmatic relationship with his large swathe of followers who believed in him and the values of the Bolivarian Revolution.

The contrast between leadership and the regime helps reveal the imperfections of either the regime's laws or the values of transformational leaders. Burns' focus on transformational leadership's goal to self-actualize makes it impossible to give a realistic assessment of how to judge between good and bad leadership. Leaders can only act within the particular context of their regimes, which define the moral possibilities for leadership. His analysis presupposes a democratic regime. However, what would a transformational leader look like in an aristocratic regime, in which order, status, and rank structure the regime and society? Nietzsche and Aristotle provide unique insights from fundamentally different perspectives into these ways of life.

For Nietzsche, democracy fails to provide the necessary social and psychological distance for a creative individual. Self-realization is best achieved where rank exists because the deepening of one's soul requires a social distance between profundity and ordinariness. Nietzschean self-realization is witnessed in aesthetic, political, and philosophical activity. From a different aristocratic perspective, Aristotle endorses the life of virtue and philosophy as the best for human beings, which is the only life one can seriously contemplate as self-fulfilling. For Aristotle, only those who are truly good and alike in virtue can become friends. Ideally, political communities should be ruled by the virtuous.

For aristocratic transformational leadership, either Aristotle's or Nietzsche's, self-realization is already embedded into a stable social hierarchy that allows only some individuals, who must take advantage of their station in life, to dedicate themselves to human flourishing. In a modern democratic society, self-actualization is filtered through the moral ideal of egalitarianism. Simultaneously, transformational leadership works to assure individuals of their identities while seeming to strengthen democratic norms such as free expression, individual rights, and pluralism.[10]

Burns presupposes a democratic ethos because he thinks an entire society can self-actualize. Yet he betrays his political inclinations at the expense of fully understanding the possibilities of self-actualization in ways that are patently illiberal, unsympathetic, and harmful to other people. Self-actualization is an indefinite state of being. Only in a regime does it have a concrete moral direction. Burns does not attend to Nietzschean leaders' desire for radical independence and willfulness that is anathema to collective self-actualization. I argue that a leader's desire to aim for political and moral change, in ways they have determined are good for themselves and their polities, cannot be reduced to the ideas of ethical elevation, *engagé*, and self-realization. The desire to transform the world, yet do justice to the members of one's polity, is a complex interplay of political ambition and regime politics.

Burns examines ambition by contrasting it with the long-term consequences of leader behavior. He offers three examples: "Hitler fulfilled his own ambition – until the apocalyptic ending – but pulled down the nation he promised to lead to glory. Gandhi's ambitions for India have not yet been realized. The instrument of Lenin's ambition – the disciplined party – has been used for purposes abhorrent to Leninism as a liberating force" (1978, p. 112). Burns compares the "spur of ambition" of these three figures (pp. 106–11).[11] In its healthy form (self-actualized) ambition is transformed into the higher motives of transformational leadership. When ambition is yearning for power, Burns relegates it to the crude desire to wield power. Burns concludes that Hitler was a raw power wielder, Gandhi was a leader, and Lenin began as a leader and became a power wielder.

In each case, Burns says that the ambitions of the individual crystalized early in his adult life. For Gandhi, it happened when his professional ambitions were spurned by the racism and discrimination he confronted in South Africa, "his ambition became an instrumental motive, a means to the end of destroying injustice" (1978, p. 107). Gandhi began to practice civil disobedience and came to the belief that he was the only person who could reform South Africa's unyielding racist society. In contrast, Hitler's ambitions were forged in the denouement of World War I. He came to gloomy realizations about Germany's defeat, and bearing witness to its political decline he resolved to become a political leader. The experience hardened his willful desire for dominance (1978, pp. 107–9). Lenin's self-discipline, studious nature, and Marxist indoctrination helped him subordinate everything to his steadfast pursuit of revolutionary leadership (1978, p. 110). Lenin revolutionized Marxism and Russian politics with the idea that the masses should be controlled by the party, the party of one man. After Lenin assumed control of the party he demanded obedience and became a brutal power wielder (1978, p. 111).

Burns deprecates ambition; he sees it as motive for power wielding. Self-actualization is good because it dims ambition. Burns' distinctions do not do justice to the phenomenon of ambition. Even individuals who are ambitious for power do not necessarily express a crude lust for domination. In addition, the ambition of transformational leaders is obscured by Burns' insistence that leadership is defined by helping followers to self-actualize.

For example, when discussing Hitler, Burns traces his failure to a fatal flaw in his personality: a self-deceiving ambition, which, according to Burns, led him to seek power "for the sake of his own dominance and was willing to destroy his people for the sake of his own power" (1978, p. 108). Transformational leaders are self-effacing; their ambition takes a back seat to satisfying followers' needs. Burns' distinctions offer over-simplified choices: the moral transformational leader versus the non-leader who seeks to wield naked power. These stark choices are not surprising, since the modern study of politics is highly influenced by the ideas of modern political philosophy, specifically Hobbesian rationalism. Hobbes supplies the modern ethos for leadership and citizenship that is based in amoral egoism.

Modern legislators, such as the founding fathers of the United States, gravitated toward Hobbes' view that political ambition is a dangerous and ubiquitous human passion. For Hobbes (1996), ambition foments vainglory pride: a destructive passion that threatens basic public goods such as security and order (p. 42). Hobbes argues that the desire for power, honor, and wealth are natural to man but are also the causes of political conflict. Hobbes sees a solution to this conflict. These passions to overpower others, he believes, can be trumped by the overwhelming power that the fear of death has over the individual. The fear of death, when tempered by the light of reason, can constrain the more dangerous passions.

Ultimately, the stable social order that Hobbes envisions is accomplished by what Burns calls transactional leadership: enforceable contracts that are upheld by a sovereign power. Hobbes' influence on the idea of modern political power and the limits of moral leadership cannot be underestimated. He eyes glory (political ambition) warily and places it first among diffidence and competition as the factor that contributed most to the war of all against all.

Burns' leadership theory can be understood as an implicit response to Hobbes' dour view of human nature and his sobering conception of leadership. Hobbes wanted to tame the ambitious so he articulated leadership as nothing other than a rational institution that maintains order through contracts and the creation of a sovereign power. Burns is interested in leaders that yearn for something greater than law and order. Yet by not distinguishing between the political contexts in which ambition is spurred on or frustrated, and specifying the distinct character traits necessary for political greatness in a particular regime, he risks talking in abstractions that fail to bridge leadership theory to reality.

I understand political regimes as having animating principles that solicit specific character traits in its citizens: ambition is wrought in specific ways in each. In *Spirit of the Laws,* Montesquieu (1989) explains how these principles function as the psychological springs of a regime. Virtue is indispensable to republics as honor is to monarchies; in democracies citizens spiritedly guard over equality and freedom (pp. 22–7). Each regime's way of life conditions the habits and mores of its citizens and, thus, influences the ambitions of its leaders. Montesquieu thinks that ambition is at home in a monarchy, because it gives life to the government and it is perpetuated by the tumult that is created by nobles (1989, p. 27). It is not dangerous in such a regime because the rough and tumble of honor-seeking nobles helps divide power. Conversely, honor is dangerous in a democracy because it threatens equality (1989, p. 27).

Ambition takes on a different form in a democracy. Although ambition as honor-seeking survives, it conceals itself because the egalitarian nature of a democracy disparages men and women with great ambition: this is a subject I discuss in the next chapter. Burns hints at the dynamics of ambition and regime politics: "we must gauge not only the projective thrust of ambition but the political response to it and the political controls over it" (1978, p. 115). However, Burns says nothing else on the subject, perhaps due to the fact that his concern is strictly limited to the most general notion of transformational leadership. I interpret his statement as an exhortation to examine this question attentively.

CONCLUSION

Burns does not distinguish domestic from international political consequences. For example, as I examine in Chapters 6 and 7, Pericles transformed Athens' material and moral life through democracy and empire, but the expansion of the city's power led to unjust practices in foreign affairs. It is likely that Burns would view Pericles as transformational leader in Athens, but he likely would have drawn the conclusion that his imperialist foreign policy was power-wielding behavior. Did Pericles' exacting foreign policy toward other Greek cities negate his transformational leadership at home? Burns' theory cannot find a solution to this problem, unless one supposes that leadership should aim for the unrealistic goal of universal self-actualization through a universal state. The stark difference between the moral claims in domestic and international affairs raises issues of moral complexity that have vexed leaders and philosophers throughout the ages. Unfortunately, transformational leadership does not give guidance to leaders in international situations that must balance national interests and international ethics.

For example, if Burns were to look at Gandhi more closely he might find fault with his extreme individual piety and policy of peace and conciliation. Due to his moral loftiness and political disinterestedness, Gandhi failed to deal with intractable social realities: the ethno-nationalistic identity and strategic claims of the newly independent Indian state and the religious claims of Pakistan's Islamic state. As a consequence, one could argue that since independence India has been engaged in an enduring and dangerous rivalry with Pakistan.

I argue that it is necessary to look closely at the particular allegiances, passions, and moral claims that are aroused when leaders and followers interact in a specific domain, such as politics. In political life, transformative changes that are good for the polity many times require grand ambition and leaders of high character to serve as the catalysts of such changes. Moreover, I argue that great stores of ambition are not necessarily the mark of egoistic power seekers. For example, leaders with transformative ambition might desire to win and triumph splendidly, but they may do so in order to succeed and do something good for their polity.

When examined properly through the fine lenses of particular political regimes transformative political ambition is irreducible to egoistic power-seeking or altruistic self-actualization. Transformative ambition is only partly idiosyncratic; it is also molded by the polity's belief in what constitutes legitimate motives for rule and the public expectations on how power will be wielded. It changes a political regime by working through existing moral and political channels.

Leaders that desire to do great things must deal with changing circumstances that thwart their ambitions. In the context of regime politics, astute leaders balance their passion to rule with others who feel they deserve equal dignity. For example, they may face contentious rivals that seek power and high honors. Or, they may sense that the people desire but, simultaneously, are suspicious of the rise of great citizens. Political ambition is not a mere drive; it evolves over time and is affected by an individual's assessment of their worth. Political leaders may consider their worth on the grounds of their experience, virtue, intelligence, or greatness. As such, political ambition is a complex mixture of political morality and personal satisfaction (Newell, 2000, p. 4). Transformative ambition is a heightened form of this complexity because of its intent to win renown by changing political conditions and moral perceptions. A political regime has a hand in shaping and reigning in transformational ambition by encouraging and honoring the qualities these leaders possess in great abundance.

NOTES

1. I use self-actualization, self-fulfillment, and self-realization as synonyms throughout this discussion. For a discussion of why these terms can be used synonymously, see Alan Gerwith (2009, pp. 6–8).
2. The transformational school of leadership has built on the work of Burns (Bass, 1985, 1998; Bass and Avolio, 1994; Hater and Bass, 1988). Others have promoted visionary and charismatic leadership theories (e.g., Bennis and Nanus, 1985; Conger and Kanungo, 1987). The most important figure, however, remains the founder, James Macgregor Burns.
3. Burns is an authority in the discipline of Leadership Studies, which is a multidisciplinary academic field that studies the role of leadership in organizations, the social science, and humanities. While many academic disciplines take an interest in leadership, Burns and his disciples are largely responsible for making leadership a legitimate and self-sustaining academic area of inquiry.
4. Abraham Maslow's (1943) famous hierarchy of needs is central to Burns' theory; Maslow's hierarchy of needs include: physiological, safety, love, esteem, and self-actualization.
5. According to Maslow (1950) autonomy is a necessary prerequisite of self-actualization as it allows individuals to resist cultural and environmental influences.
6. In Judaism and Christianity, charisma means renunciation: a covenant with God, in which worshipers deny their base passion and obey God's law. As such, charisma was shared by those who obey divine commands, especially prohibitive laws that restrain man's more destructive passions. Max Weber, by leaving the claims of religion behind, redefined charisma to mean exceptional powers or qualities of certain unique individuals. According to Philip Rieff (2007), the term has been sloppily used ever since and has lent itself to analytic neutrality, which simply masks the desire for celebrity and flashes of spectacular performances.
7. *Engagé* is a termed coined by French intellectuals, most notably Jean-Paul Sartre (1956), to describe the social responsibility of individuals in the context of existentialism, in which the being of human beings is defined by contingency. In others words, there is no rhyme or reason for the existence of individuals or the world.

Existence is absurd. The individual is simply caught in the circumstances of his time and place. Thus, political ideals are grounded in political commitments, which can result in the individual's gaining freedom from their social context, which is a freedom without transcendence.

8. Burns distinguishes among end values and modal values. End values are perceived as ends in themselves, while modal values may be choice-worthy in themselves but are usually means by which politics and other social enterprises should be conducted (1978, p. 75). Burns argues that if leaders can publicly command an array of both end-values and modal values, while actually believing in these values as well, "they can summon a wide support from followers with many different values; but to the degree that these actions are controversial, they can also arouse intense opposition and conflict" (1978, p. 75). Thus, the only difference between end- and modal values are how they are perceived.

9. Self-actualization promises some future development for humankind that cannot be conceived presently. Malsow articulated this understanding of self-actualization as a rarified human possibility, which would inaugurate new forms of the self: "it is possible already to start thinking about the transhuman, a psychology and a philosophy which transcends the human species itself. This is yet to come" (1987, XXI). As such, self-actualization assumes that human intelligence and vital energies are undergoing an evolutionary change and that progress underlies human history. As such, values will change radically as cognitive power and clarity are enhanced.

10. Charles Taylor (1991), despite being a proponent of authenticity, observes what critics have noted about the unchecked culture of self-fulfillment: people lose sight of issues that transcend them, self-actualization takes on trivialized and self-indulgent forms, and people insecure in their identities seek out all kinds of different so-called experts that shroud their ideas in scientific jargon or ersatz spirituality (p. 15).

11. Burns acknowledges the importance of structure; he explains how some avenues for leadership favor power; others esteem; and, still others, affiliation. The source of ambition is more complex than a leader's idiosyncrasies: "as springing from different cultures and different situations" (1978, p. 113). However, Burns does not explore the idea at any great length.

5. Aristotle's idea of magnanimity and transformative ambition

> Nothing great is done without great men, and they are what they are for having wanted it.
> **Charles de Gaulle**, *The Edge of the Sword*

For Aristotle, magnanimity is the peak and completion of virtue, attainable only by the morally serious individual. An abiding characteristic of magnanimity is that it pertains to "great things," such as great honors and great deeds (*Ethics*, 1123b, translated 2002). It is also defined by the right attitude toward the most valuable external good, honor. The magnanimous man's desire for honor is based on his self-worth; he believes he deserves not only great, but the greatest things. This certainty of what he merits is not a fiction but is based on the presence of something truly great within him.

Honor is a recognition of an individual's worth and the starting point for the analysis of magnanimity. Like money, this external good is a fickle thing, but it differs from other external goods because honor refers to an individual's intrinsic character. It points to the magnanimous man's virtue; while honor is a fickle thing, virtue is not. As such, the magnanimous man's view of himself is not empty self-esteem or narcissism. Aristotle argues that the magnanimous man must be the best human being, and it would be impossible for him not to be good (1123b27–8, 1123b36).

As the peak of virtue, magnanimity involves all the other virtues Aristotle examines in the *Ethics*: courage, temperance, moderation, liberality, magnificence, political ambition, gentleness, friendliness, truthfulness, justice, and prudence. This overarching virtue does not come to sight as an event in the way, for example, that courage is displayed by one's actions on the battlefield. Magnanimity is a proper self-awareness and knowledge of one's virtue. It is the virtuous individual's ability to delight in his own excellence of character. As such, the magnanimous man is concerned about receiving honors, but he is characterized by knowledge of his worth: "who considers himself worthy of great things, and is worthy of them, for one who does so not in accordance with his worth is foolish" (1123b4).

Magnanimous leaders are more acutely aware of the nature of their greater ambition. Magnanimity's self-awareness points to a serious political leader's ability to transform his ambition beyond the desire for power. With the aid of Aristotle, I improve on personality theories that reduce all ambition to unconscious desire. In addition, magnanimity serves to illustrate the possibility of leaders whose power to make decisions is free from political constraints; this kind of ambition leads politicians to take on great and necessary risks to transform their world.

For Aristotle, the magnanimous man acts rarely, only in the exceptional cases that are worthy of his greatness; there is an unbridgeable distance between him and others upon whom he looks down with particular disdain. The magnanimous man's knowledge of his worth and belief that he is owed great honor make him remiss to openly desire political office and honors. This is a depiction of extreme individualism in Aristotle's thought; the moral man who lives for his own sake and conceives of himself as the noble and superior. Aristotle describes an individual who must reject almost all political actions because they are beneath him. Magnanimity ironically produces an immobile being who sidelines himself from politics. Transformative ambition and this consequence of magnanimity are incompatible.

I am interested in exceptional leaders who desire to achieve greatness in politics through energetic statesmanship; their virtue does not lead them to stand outside of politics. Rather, their ambition is such that they look for genuine opportunities for leadership that are greater than political office. Transformative ambition is a more vigorous drive; it makes an individual challenge the rules of the day and can be revolutionary as leaders seek to make their mark on the world. Their ambition is profound. As such, these leaders' foreign policy is not defined by the structure of international relations, but by their view of how international politics serves their ends. They are not blind to constraints but want to shake them up and use their state's capabilities and the art of statesmanship to push others to accept their worldviews.

Aristotle's magnanimous man represents the peak of excellence; he is inextricably linked to political life. He is owed honor and cannot maintain his opinion of superiority without others' esteem. His greatness is activated in the exceptional circumstances, in which he needs political power and other resources. Since he possesses all the virtues, he is just and, thus, must nobly devote himself to others. Or because he exceeds all others in virtue, he may rule over them. Magnanimity has two opposed natures: a depoliticized and a politicized one. The subtleties of Aristotle's argument reveal these two sides, and I will illuminate the political and apolitical directions that the magnanimous man takes later in this chapter.

Unlike the theories of leadership examined thus far, Aristotle's magnanimous man helps explain historical outliers, whose ambition and political leadership are in a class of their own, such as Pericles, Washington, Lincoln, Churchill, and de Gaulle. Their statesmanship proves that it is still necessary to understand the constitution of such characters and how they impact politics and world events. For example, Churchill's aristocratic background, hunger for glory on the battlefield, and high ambition in politics were character traits that helped him lead Great Britain in its darkest hour. Through his wartime speeches he evoked the nation's greatness, grit, and fortitude. As a result, he not only galvanized his own countrymen but also helped strengthen the bonds between Britain and her vital allies. We heap admiration on Churchill not only because of his leadership during a time of great crisis, but also because we believe that he rose above the morass of office-seeking and political survival. Such principled behavior is what John F. Kennedy called courage in politics.

In this chapter, I first discuss how contemporary political theorists are applying Aristotelian ideas such as magnanimity, honor-seeking, and great political ambition to the study of leadership. I then address a legit-imate objection to their uses in studying leadership: Aristotle's context and moral perspective is too dissimilar from a modern one. Through a casual discussion of presidential character and ambition in the United States, I show the necessity for political scientists to pay closer attention to the role of great ambition in political life. Next, I discuss Aristotle's presentation of magnanimity as a virtue by considering how it achieves what is described in the *Ethics* as the mean, which describes a virtue in contrast to its vices. In this case, magnanimity is contrasted with vanity and smallness of soul.

I further reveal the problem that I stated at the outset of this chapter: the magnanimous man is the peak of excellence and the prize of the political community, yet not in the least bit a political animal. He desires to be of great service, but by believing he is owed great honors, he looks down on those whom he is supposed to serve. Despite these seeming contradictions in Aristotle's thought, an analysis of the vices, particularly smallness of soul, more clearly explicates the relationship between magnanimity and statesmanship: magnanimity is the capacity for statesmanship and the ability to wield power for the benefit of the political community. Later in the chapter, I also discuss what direction the magnanimous man's statesmanship takes by looking at magnanimity's relationship to justice. Although the magnanimous man may be dangerous to established governments, Aristotle points to an individual with a sober pride who prioritizes virtue over honor yet remains steadfastly superior by fully embracing politics from a position of independence. The magnanimous man's distance and disdain toward citizens can be transformed into a generous friendship toward the polity.

Lastly, with the connection of magnanimity and statesmanship in place, I turn to Charles de Gaulle. De Gaulle not only embodied the spirit of the magnanimous statesman, but he also exhibited transformative ambition in international relations as he tried to reshape the order among states during the Cold War.

ARISTOTLE AND THE STUDY OF STATESMANSHIP

Magnanimity and statesmanship connote something unusual, which makes it difficult to find many examples of leaders who deserve to be called magnanimous. I argue that those like Pericles and de Gaulle approach this ideal. However, are there other cases of leaders who embody magnanimity as Aristotle describes it? Robert Faulkner (2007) provides a terrific instance of how to apply this virtue to actual leaders in his excellently crafted book, *The Case for Greatness: Honorable Ambition and Its Critics*. By returning to the seminal accounts of ancient thinkers, he revives an understanding of honorable ambition and great political leadership. Examining Aristotle's "complicated treatment" (Faulkner's term) of the magnanimous man, he argues that scholars who interpret modern leaders' great political achievements as motivated by a lust for fame, poorly understand iconic figures such as George Washington. For Faulkner, not only does the idea of leaders as fame seekers limit our ability to truly understand the motives of Washington, Abraham Lincoln and Nelson Mandela, among others, but it also depreciates great leadership.

His purpose is to correctly explain Washington's political ambition and leadership, an endeavor made possible through the prism of

Aristotle's thought. As a soldier-statesman, Washington combined a desire for high honors with republican virtue, which were the qualities that led to his public-spirited statesmanship. Washington sought great esteem and was extremely cautious about tarnishing his reputation, which made him wary about holding political office. At the same time, his personal concern with honor was subordinate to a sense of duty that bound him to the young Republic's survival and success.

Washington's magnanimity allowed him to turn his ambition toward the service of justice, honor, and duty (Faulkner, 2007, p. 16). In this case, this quality produced a self-denial of personal ambition; he did not seek glorious victories and power. Rather, he "defended the democratic republic, accepted its limitations, and framed and settled its fundamental laws" (2007, p. 16). Washington had a gentlemanly attitude: he could have pride in his superior characteristics and virtues, on the basis of which he could claim exceptional opportunities. However, as Faulkner argues, Washington felt more concern for the common good of the common citizen (2007, p. 22). His magnanimity was neither superficial self-absorption nor was his contemporaries' recognition of his virtue a socially constructed category. Faulkner notes that thoughtful citizens recognized his superiority: "the Second Continental Congress chose Washington unanimously as commander in chief; the members of the Constitutional Convention chose him unanimously as president" (2007, p. 23). His exercise of power lent credibility and support to America's fledgling and untested institutions. Washington set the tone for the seamless and voluntary transition of executive power, even though he had attained mythic status during his lifetime and could have easily retained power.

Like Faulkner, I am interested in applying Aristotle's more complex and rarified notion of political ambition and statesmanship to pertinent historical cases. Faulkner's approach emphasizes the transcendent qualities of leadership and ambition. However, I am interested in a modified version of the Aristotelian ideal that I can use with latitude and in conjunction with current theories that stress the difference between the attributes of leaders' personalities and the more reflective and self-conscious practice of statesmanship. Fortunately, Waller Newell has already paved the way for this approach.

In Newell's book, *The Soul of a Leader: Character, Conviction, and Ten Lessons in Political Greatness* (2009), he shows how the traditional, but currently unpopular, idea of honor-seeking in public life can help us understand the difference between ordinary and great leadership.

Although Newell and Faulkner both think of leadership in this traditional sense, Newell shows how the traditional concept can be considered alongside an examination of leaders' personalities and psychological pathologies (2009, pp. 28–35).

For example, Newell observes that many revered leaders were afflicted with a serious psychological condition such as Winston Churchill's "black dog" (depression) and Lincoln's melancholy. However, these "traditional" men of character also drew on their personal hardship to help them reflect both on themselves and the magnitude of the political challenges that they faced. Newell writes, "[G]reatness may require a degree of depression, melancholy, a sense of one's own frailty, and the vicissitudes of fate. It is precisely in overcoming one's inner demons to achieve something for the benefit of one's country or mankind that many men have risen to nobility and grandeur" (2009, p. 46).

In his quest to understand how great leadership is possible, Newell keenly interweaves modern psychology and Aristotle's ideas. For example, Newell observes the Freudian bent about Churchill's immense desire for fame: he longed for his distant and aristocratic parents' approval and love. However, it was Churchill's deep-seated desire for achievement and recognition that helped him reach his greatness through statesmanship, a feat true of many great leaders:

> The exceptional leader finds only the gravest challenges of statecraft arduous enough to demand his fullest talents. Such men are often bored by the ordinary domestic politics of budgets and taxes, and perform poorly when politics is confined to such issues. Yet the threat of war or civil war, stimulated by struggles worthy of their inner sense of greatness, allows them finally to show their full capacities. (2009, p. 46)

Newell endorses political greatness but does not airbrush notable leaders. In fact, he argues that a leader's talents and defects underpin great leadership. For example, in discussing Lincoln's political ambition and statesmanship, he describes Lincoln's contradictory impulses and personal traits that included his awareness of the tension between his great ambition and the Republic's needs, his ruminations about achieving immortal glory, the severe bouts of depression that shaped his life and leadership, the simplicity and depth of his personal style and oration, and his lack of a gentlemanly upbringing, all of which Newell contrasts with Lincoln's goodness.

Through the civil war, Lincoln found the opportunity to direct these conflicted drives and energies toward fulfilling his great ambition, which was also in service of the common good. Newell argues that Lincoln's significant achievement was to reset the political and moral principles of the American Republic. Lincoln defined equality much further than the original founders might have intended, "pledging something like continual political action to work toward actual equality of condition" (2009, p. 183).

What I take from Newell's approach is that to understand a leader's politics and behavior, we need to know what makes him tick. However, we cannot understand the very personal dimension of a leader's ambition without a view of the leader and the regime. For example, Lincoln's admirable character was the product of his own inner motivation, composed nature, and maturing political thought, but these settled and became great in him through a confrontation with the challenges facing his party and country.

Newell contrasts Lincoln with his great antagonist, Robert E. Lee, the South's natural leader, as a man who embodied the Aristotelian gentleman in an outward form: "Lee was the perfect expression of a personally noble character and a stainless reputation for courage, honor, gallantry, love of family, and respect for higher learning. He was more balanced, more integrated, than Lincoln, aesthetically more pleasing" (2009, p. 192). However, Lee did not possess Lincoln's ability to choose principle over personal integrity. He lacked moral imagination. He thought slavery was a sin but owned slaves. He opposed Virginia's secession from the Union but chose loyalty to the state over command of Union forces. Lee had all the appurtenances of gentlemanly greatness but lacked Lincoln's justice. Lee's character was indelibly shaped by the Virginian way of life that demanded his fidelity. Though a gentleman warrior, he is not venerable because he was a prisoner of circumstances that he knew were immoral, while "the interaction between Lincoln's personality and his burdens as president gained in depth and intensity, fusing them into an increasingly legendary whole" (2009, p. 196).

Like Faulkner and Newell, I argue that Aristotle's account of ordinary and great political ambition, which culminates in his discussion of the magnanimous man, provides a model for publicly spirited leadership. I follow their application of Aristotle to leadership by showing how magnanimity also infused de Gaulle's approach with what the late statesman referred to as "grandeur." I discuss this example in the section "Magnanimity and statesmanship: Charles de Gaulle's politics of grandeur," which considers de Gaulle's professed grandeur as an expression of transformative ambition.

THE CHALLENGE: WHY ARISTOTLE?

Aristotle presents ancient Greek conduct and morality as the basis for his ethical teaching, which arguably limits the applicability of magnanimity to a contemporary context. In addition, his education toward virtue is highly exclusive and steeped in unbending moral standards that would be difficult for most individuals to follow to the letter. Aristotle's ethical teaching can be criticized on the grounds of a familiar adage: virtuous citizenship and leadership might be good in theory, but how does it stand in practice?

In practice, political ambition is usually in the service of personal gain, and we cannot count on an individual's virtue to limit his ambition. Classical philosophers understood that our self-centered and spirited natures were to blame for the fragility of the virtuous life and just politics. In light of human nature, modern political theorists neglected virtue in favor of the proper working of institutions that either checked or redirected the selfish interests of individuals. Of what use is Aristotle's lofty conception of virtue if it may be impossible to attain?

To address this concern, I begin with a discussion of how Aristotle's distinction between great and ordinary ambition is still relevant. Ambitious politicians are everywhere in the United States today, but virtue rarely makes an appearance in political life, not to mention that magnanimous statesmanship has no place in the political lexicon, as the term is loaded with unegalitarian and sexist implications. In the current political discourse, high-minded talk about virtue in politics gets a dubious reception. However, politics is filled with moral pretense since no politician could survive on a platform that appealed explicitly to calculating self-interest. Despite politicians' public vows of morality, many claim the moral high ground only later to become embroiled in private scandals that expose them as hypocrites. Yet, politicians cannot be blamed entirely for their conduct because the public is at odds with itself. Citizens hold political leaders to a higher standard and want them to show their moral credentials. Simultaneously, they are cynical of leaders who preach morality in politics.

While the public is ambivalent about morality and politics, it expresses its concern with political ambition negatively. Americans are wary of leaders who show too much political ambition, because it is commonly assumed that these people have selfish interests and will try to oppress others. Political ambition might be a necessary trait for an individual to succeed in politics, but it can also hurt his or her prospects for higher office. For example, in the 2008 American presidential nomination campaign, Hillary Clinton was dogged by the media's and public's perception of her "naked ambition." This characterization of her stuck, and little about Clinton's character, speeches, and campaign could persuade people otherwise.

Conversely, the media and public gave Barack Obama's soaring ambition a comfortable reception. Although Obama's message was vague, his rhetoric for hope and change appealed to voters because he seemed genuine and his language bespoke a cause both larger than him and strongly democratic. A younger generation of voters, enthusiastic about being part of a grassroots social movement, helped shape his image as a social leader before politician.

As election day neared, the interest in Obama began to shift from his inspirational message to a discussion of his leadership qualities. Talk centered on his presidential tone, coolness, and measured temperament in contradistinction to John McCain's gut decisions and infamous hot temper. The focus on each candidate's personal characteristics and style showed this important but less-talked-about factor. Voters were not only weighing who was fit for the job and where candidates stood on the issues, but they were also judging presidential character. Although the personality that citizens find desirable in a president is surely dictated by the times and there is no ideal type of American leader, Americans will always judge individuals with some universal traits favorably, as those deserving the highest office in the land: an admirable person who is recognizable as an ordinary citizen, yet concerned for all citizens' equality and liberty. The president must champion democracy at home and abroad, be self-assured and decisive during a crisis, have rhetorical skills that can inspire his fellow citizens yet such oratory cannot be overly flourishing. Ultimately, Americans look for a leading citizen, a first-rate character who carefully balances his political ambition within the limits of cherished institutions and long-standing practices.

Presidential elections have a way of sneaking virtue in through the back door as leaders must demonstrate individual moral excellence. In the 2008 election, Americans were especially sensitive to character and leadership potential, given the vacuum created by George Bush at home and abroad. John McCain received high marks for his character, he earned a solid reputation from his proven bipartisanship, long career in the Senate, heroism in war, and love of country. But it was Obama's inspiring rhetoric, remarkable background, cool execution, and deft organization, in the end, that showed more glimmers of presidential greatness.

Americans are democrats at heart and so will continue to be suspicious of political ambition, yet the 2008 presidential election showed that strong leadership qualities matter to citizens. Nonetheless, it will always be difficult to find good and powerful leaders who do not have a healthy dose of ambition. These contradictory desires point to a real phenomenon: there exists a range of ambition and leadership qualities. Oddly, while ordinary citizens show a fervent desire for great leadership, the theories of leadership we have examined thus far do not differentiate between the ambitions of ordinary and great leaders.

ORDINARY AMBITION AND MAGNANIMITY: THE FULL RANGE OF AMBITION

Aristotle's explicit purpose in the *Ethics* is to instruct individuals on how to become virtuous. A basic precondition is necessary to achieve this goal; an individual requires a qualitatively superior education in virtue. As a consequence, Aristotle's main audience is an exclusive group of aristocratic elites, one that he refers to in the *Rhetoric* as the "well born."[1] Despite its exclusive audience and stringent ethical goals, the *Ethics* describes a variety of lives and also the full range of political ambition, with ordinary political ambition following magnanimity in Book V. I do the reverse, describing ordinary political ambition first and then continuing with an examination of magnanimity.

Ordinary political ambition is witnessed in individuals who are filled with a love for honor. Recall that honor is the external good, unlike power and wealth, which is related to a human being's perception of his intrinsic worth. The ambitious pursue honor, and among them political office is a much sought-after prize. Early on in the *Ethics*, Aristotle makes an observation about ordinary politicians' ambition: it is common for politicians to seek honors to be convinced that they themselves are good (1095b27–28). In general, the honor lover seeks to fortify his sense of worth by adding achievements and accomplishments to his name, which is dependent on his political climb. Aristotle's discussion of political ambition resembles our modern conception of the politician who uses a self-interested political calculus to gain and retain office with the critical difference that Aristotle presents the moral conundrum that stalks ordinary politicians as they confuse ends with means.

The ordinary politician seeks honor, recognition, and power while pursuing a less venerable path. He uses office to add another achievement, another honor, and, ultimately, another office. Most politicians give into this ordinary desire, which is why scholars of the strategic perspective assume that all leaders are solely motivated by political survival. Aristotle might agree with some elements of this logic, but he views the ordinary politician's economy of honor as morally unstable. The pursuit of office for its own sake confuses the means to attain honor with honor itself. Racking up accomplishments and chasing after commendations, the honor lover must use his power and wealth. Although he believes he is attaining virtue, in reality this form of honorable ambition is compromised because power and wealth (the instruments to attain political honors) are truly what people come to respect (1124a24–25).

Magnanimity entails great political ambition and also concerns honor, but not just any kind of honor. It sets its possessor's sights on higher distinctions and fosters the desire to take part in great deeds. Yet, magnanimity is the peak of virtue and a collection of them all. As complete virtue, it necessarily involves justice and prudence, which connects it to statesmanship.

Aristotle says that the magnanimous man has a correct opinion of his worthiness. He deserves society's most prestigious tribute, and the highest political office is sometimes offered to the most deserving citizens. Political office is not just a reward since it entrusts an individual with political responsibility. Magnanimity has two sides: it is a virtue that is individualizing and rare but also one recognized by others and therefore subsists on a society that can properly acknowledge it. How else would citizens be able to bestow great honors if they could not recognize greatness? As such, magnanimity is the most individuating virtue, but its basis is social and political. While only the magnanimous man can experience full virtue, magnanimity must be discernable to those charged with distributing honors and selecting the leadership.

A magnanimous leader will accept higher office, because this honor satisfies his self-worth. However, his fellow citizens can offer him nothing else. Thus, the satisfaction he gains from high office is circumscribed by the fact that even honor, which he is especially concerned with, turns out to be a small thing (1124a15, 19). The honor of serving is depreciated, which fosters the magnanimous man's contempt for the city. His virtue is not devotional, and in his estimation, his good is of greater importance to him than service to the city, which only cares about its survival. It preserves the life of its members and contributes to their basic interests.

What is the character of the magnanimous man's ambition? Although he does not openly desire office, he believes that he is owed such things.

This assumption implies two distinct possibilities. First, individuals who hold such beliefs can be a danger to public life if the public does not recognize his worth and denies him his proper deserts. Second, magnanimity adds sobriety to the virtuous individual's expectations from politics, limiting his political ambition rather than fostering it. Aristotle directs us toward the second option, which is revealed more clearly through the relationship between magnanimity and justice. In addition, Aristotle subtly shows how such heightened self-awareness about one's virtue and depreciation of external goods contradicts the mechanisms that support magnanimity. In fact, external goods contribute to greatness of soul. An honor like political office is good fortune for the magnanimous man; a staging ground for the exercise of his virtue, it contributes toward "greatness of soul" (1124a22–23). Thus, the magnanimous man does not quite acknowledge that he needs external goods. Although his goodness is truly honorable, his posses-sion of power, wealth, and goodness is considered more worthy (1124a24–28).

MAGNANIMITY AS A VIRTUE

Magnanimity is distinct from the other virtues in the *Ethics*. It is a meta-virtue, a heightened awareness that combines the moral reasoning of the virtuous man with a sense of superiority, while the acquisition of the virtues is an ongoing project of perfecting the character. The exercise of these virtues depends on having a correct feeling and performing the proper action in a particular context. For example, one becomes coura-geous by forming the right disposition to fear. When confronted by something fearsome, too much courage leads to rashness, while too little makes one a coward. In practice, courage is the mean between extremes. The mean is not an average of rashness and timidity; rather, it is the abil-ity to face fear in a way that is just right. Aristotle says that the coura-geous sacrifice their lives for something noble, in defense of something greater and when the prospect of dying a beautiful death presents itself (1115b3–5). The most visceral virtue, courage points to the political nature of virtue itself. In Aristotle's context, political courage was martial courage, the bedrock of the Greek *polis*. It was born from polit-ical necessity, the defense of the city. However, if courage is a virtue, it must be noble and done for its own sake. When exercised in combat, it demands the greatest sacrifice, one's life. Yet, courage is also the most painful to those who long for nobility and the virtuous life because death robs them of the opportunity to continue the quest.

Other virtues demand less. For example, virtue is also practiced through the temperance of one's desires or generosity, and if one has great wealth, one can be magnificent. However, an individual's possession of only some of the virtues is not sufficient for him to live the moral life that Aristotle has in mind. He reserves magnanimity, the peak of the virtues that makes each one greater (1124a3–4), for the first discussion of the full moral life. Yet, in the fifth book of the *Ethics*, we learn that justice is a second peak. It puts complete virtue to use (1129b30–33). Thus, the magnanimous man is pulled in opposite directions: his greatness fosters his sense of superiority over others, while it also pushes him toward justice.

Magnanimity, like the other virtues, stands apart from its extremes or vices, vanity and smallness of soul. The vain believe that their worth is greater than it really is. However, vanity suggests that the problem concerns an incorrect assessment of one's worth. Specifically, the vain judge that more honors are owed to them than they actually deserve; some may be mistaken but not necessarily vain. In the context of magnanimity, however, Aristotle says that vain people are unworthy because they consider themselves worthy of great things (11232b7). Carson Holloway (2008) clearly articulates Aristotle's distinction between a mistaken self-worth and vanity. He says, "[V]anity implies not mere pretense to unmerited consideration, but more specifically pretense to unmerited *extraordinary* consideration" (p. 15).

Vanity's opposite, smallness of soul is characterized by an individual's inability to realize his true worth. It is the condition someone is in when they are actually worthy of great things but do not consider themselves worthy of them (1123b11) and so are deprived of the things they deserve (1125a20–21). For Aristotle, smallness of soul is worse than vanity. There is a baffling hesitancy with these people. They have what it takes to perform deeds on a grand scale, but they do not. As a result, they fail to take part in ennobling and virtuous actions, which are exactly the kind that they are meant for. Aristotle is clear about what they miss out on: great (beautiful) actions, worthy pursuits, and external goods (1125a20–33). At the same time, as he discusses these vices, Aristotle eases up on vanity, no longer calling it a vice and is harsher on smallness of soul.

Aristotle's explanation of these vices tells us something, admittedly in a very oblique way, about the political character of magnanimity. If smallness of soul is contemptible because it is the self-denial of virtue and honors through inactivity, then this points to the importance of action, specifically great political actions. On the one hand, political action must satisfy the magnanimous man's sense of worth and concern with virtue. On the other, political action is based on political necessity. In both cases, the magnanimous man's behavior depends on his role as a leader and relationship to the regime.

The order of Aristotle's examination of the virtues implies a relationship between magnanimity and justice. However, he does not say much about the relationship between magnanimity and political activity. Aristotle demands that we proceed cautiously when drawing inferences about magnanimity's political role because he offers two opposing portraits of the magnanimous man. There is a coolness and detachment that flows from him; "he seems to have a slow way of moving, a deep voice, and steady way of speaking" (1125a14–15). His outward characteristics show that he can easily postpone entry into politics as he is a slow starter and full of delay (1124b23–27). Moreover, he is not a business-as-usual politician and is not interested in things held in popular esteem: he does not ask for help, does not like to receive favors, and is indifferent to praise and blame. At the end of the day, the magnanimous man strives to be and becomes self-sufficient. His lack of interest to the concerns of ordinary politicians is the privilege of complete virtue.

Besides his reluctance to enter politics, Aristotle also implies that the magnanimous man has contempt for society. He looks down on others justly, is "not capable of leading his life to suit anyone else" (1125a1), and, ultimately, thinks that "nothing is great" (1125a5). This is the peak of human excellence! In the end, the magnanimous man does not think anything is worthwhile, which is a despairing view of the virtuous life that is supposed to lead to happiness. This separation between virtuous life and life itself is odd. The character excellences that overlap with statesmanship only serve to keep the magnanimous man at a distance from the morass of politics.

Magnanimity is characterized by self-reflection and a heightened awareness of one's virtue, which slows the magnanimous man down and keeps him out of political life. Political life will seem quite pointless as he is not capable of leading his life to suit anyone else and, ultimately, nothing is great to him. Unlike the inaction produced by smallness of soul, magnanimity is inactivity. How can the idea that the magnanimous man who points to the possibility of great ambition and leadership be reconciled with his view, which borders on flippancy, that nothing is great?

The problem with Aristotle's depiction of the magnanimous man is that it creates the impression that he is a finished product. Aristotle does not describe magnanimity's ascent toward greatness, but rather shows it at rest; greatness is self-sufficient. What Aristotle demonstrates, however, is the magnanimous man's misunderstanding of himself. His knowledge is not proper knowledge.[2] He artfully forgets that his state of self-sufficiency (of supposed inactivity) needs the equipment, money, and action, which make the virtuous life possible. Despite the distance, asymmetric relationship, and feeling of contempt the magnanimous man may have for society, again this virtue is conditional on society.

Poised to do great things, the magnanimous man is inclined to do so when a significant honor is there to claim (1124b27–30). Although politics is the natural arena for these deeds, Aristotle is not explicit about the way and to what degree the magnanimous man is involved in politics. In addition, Aristotle does not specify in which regimes we should see a magnanimous leader though his target audience is aristocratic.

One way to understand magnanimity's political character is by identifying the political things that the magnanimous man does not pursue. He is not single-mindedly bent on acquiring power and its attendant wealth. Unsurprisingly, many individuals believe that magnanimity is associated with power and riches, so many consider themselves worthy unjustly (1124a22–28). Honor is the only external good that the magnanimous man values; yet, the magnanimous man looks down upon external goods, including honor, which is why he is perceived as arrogant (1124a20–21). However, it would be a great pain to him to be dishonored or ruled by someone unworthy.

The magnanimous man is well fit for political leadership but is reluctant to enter into politics. While political leaders around him covet and pursue power, he stands aside. What sort of political action befits a man of his talents and desires? Few things are truly honorable: he takes few great risks, avoids having favors done for him, and is effusive when doing them for others (1124b5–6). Moreover, he assists others eagerly and will finally enter the fray when a great honor is at stake and not because of the opinion of others. The magnanimous man's politics transcends everyday politicking and partisanship, but he cannot transcend politics altogether. The ascendancy of virtue reaches its peak in magnanimity, yet the magnanimous man is brought back to earth because great honors and great deeds must be politicized.

The political direction of magnanimity is made explicit in Aristotle's *Eudemian Ethics*. Here he notes that magnanimity attaches importance

to great offices (1232b20–25, translated 1935 [1992]). The most important honor society confers is its highest political office, "for by investing
a citizen with its supreme authority, the community entrusts him with its
most precious interests" (Holloway, 2008, p. 1). As a magnanimous
statesman, he can use virtue and take part in great deeds. Magnanimity
synthesizes virtue and practical political activity: there is no statesmanship without magnanimity and no magnanimity without statesmanship.

MAGNANIMITY AND JUSTICE

Magnanimous statesmanship connotes such high-mindedness that it is
easy to overlook the question of justice. We might even assume that
justice flows naturally from this kind of leadership, but Aristotle
reserves the discussion of justice as the second peak of virtue. Thus, we
must examine what is only an implicit relationship between magnanimity and justice. In the discussion of justice, we learn that magnanimity
must involve a consideration of the requirements of justice, such as law
abidingness. Does the magnanimous leader accept the regime's rules?
The laws that matter most for leadership are the ones that define and
circumscribe his office. Of course, as regimes vary, so do leaders'
responsibilities and discretionary powers.

The magnanimous man's law abidingness is implied by his disposition
toward external goods and changes in fortune. When in power, he does not
bask in it or find it troubling if he loses it, since he is "neither overjoyed
when in good fortune nor overtly distressed when in bad fortune"
(1124a18–19). He practices political moderation. In the end, virtue is
more significant to him than any worldly possession, so the magnanimous
leader is disinclined to act unjustly to seize political power.

However, if the magnanimous man is capable of greatness and seeks
grandeur, what discourages him from pursuing worldly achievements
that fulfill his understanding of greatness but spill over into tyranny and
conquest? He may not covet political power for its own sake, but power
is the conduit for such a soul to act and make its mark in political affairs
and history. Aristotle says that the magnanimous man holds few things
in high honor and is prone to great risks and to be unsparing of his life
(1124b5–6). If the opportunity for great and noble deeds does not arise,
what keeps him from becoming the catalyst of his own opportunities?

Although the magnanimous man is self-sufficient, there is something
unsatisfactory about complete virtue remaining idle. It would be tragic

for the magnanimous man to wait in the wings but never be called on for lack of opportunity. Just think, if not for the "fortunate" crisis in Algiers, de Gaulle might have never returned to public life. Truly a misfortune for de Gaulle, but was it a misfortune for France?

Susan Collins (2006) points to this specific problem with Aristotle's account of magnanimity. She says, "[I]n the absence of the necessary 'resources' the longing for noble action that distinguishes the morally serious human being requires him either to remain idle or to acquire the means to exercise his virtue" (p. 64). We have no reason to assume that a cozy arrangement is reached between the magnanimous man's great ambition and the regime. Law abidingness can dampen greatness and the more individualistic virtues.

Collins directs us to two passages in Aristotle's *Politics* where he is more explicit about the tension between noble pursuits and justice. Aristotle says, for "having authority over all is best, for in this way one would have authority over the greatest number and noblest of actions" (1325a3–37). In addition, if political greatness is a leader's prerogative, then it requires that he forgo the obligations of justice, and even of family and friendship, in order to rule over others (1325a36–41). This might be especially tempting to leaders with ambition in the realm of international politics, where custom sometimes dictates behavior but no real laws prohibit international action, particularly in war. Previously, we observed that the magnanimous man was a reluctant political particip-ant, but we now realize that he might also be a dangerous one.

Aristotle's progression of the virtues, specifically magnanimity and justice, poses a complex scenario: a life of moral virtue with two opposed peaks. At one end, the magnanimous man cannot live for anyone else and is self-sufficient. At the other end, full virtue depends on the regard for others.

What should keep a magnanimous leader from becoming a danger is the strength of his settled virtue. His concern for virtue leads him to constrain his behavior; he must voluntarily be just. He is not consumed solely by his honor-seeking motive because he measures all his practi-cal activity by appealing to the standards of virtue. Justice is the virtue that is related to someone else and for this reason is believed to be the greatest one (1129b30). The magnanimous man can potentially pursue self-perfection and bring about the good of others simultaneously. While magnanimity is full virtue because all the individual virtues are made greater by it, justice puts full virtue to use and satisfies the magnanimous man's continued longing for nobility and goodness.

Yet, even if the magnanimous man's self-limitation makes citizens sanguine that their leader's intentions are benign, a problem persists. Why would his regard for others, which is good for his fellow citizens, also be good for him? On average, individuals care more about living untroubled domestic lives that guarantee security, freedom, and well-being. These very basic needs are a far cry from great honors and deeds. As this discussion has shown, basic external goods, except honor, do not motivate a magnanimous leader. Aristotle says, "[H]e is someone who takes great risks, and when he does take a risk he is without regard for his life, on the ground that it is not on just any terms that life is worth living" (1124b6–9). If being just requires the magnanimous man to live for others, then, at some level, he must care about the basic needs that he not only neglects but also disdains.

How is the relationship that we established between magnanimity and society brought into balance? Does the magnanimous man lower his standards and treat the ignoble desires of the community as noble? Or does he elevate the political community's conception of itself? Although he observes justice, there is room for him to exercise his virtue when he practices statesmanship.

Justice reconciles his desire for greatness with the common good. The nature of his justice depends on a conditional relationship. First, one component is law abidingness, and as a just person, the magnanimous statesman recognizes the regime as the authoritative power in citizens' affairs. In particular, he accepts the political order and the duties of his office, believing that such an order is just. Law abidingness implies that an established consensus exists, but the political participants of a specific regime came to it for the common benefit of a select group. They also develop the leader's role, which indicates that external political constraints apply to leaders no matter how virtuous they might be.

However, the idea of great ambition and a politics of grandeur do not befit a coerced leader who chafes under the regime's laws. His justice flows from obedience to law, but it must also come from within. Aristotle's magnanimous leader already has an ingrained sense of justice, which may show itself as a prerational patriotism; and like all things magnanimous, this is a high patriotism. As a patriot, the magnanimous man is a friend to the regime and able to see beyond its particular order since crisis and political discord can push a regime into less desirable forms. For example, the Vichy government's acceptance of fascism shocked de Gaulle. Although he rebelled against the regime, he did not abandon democratic and republican principles altogether. Upon his return to France, he sought to strengthen these tenets and elevate French citizens to see beyond their mere material interests.

Political ambition matched with public spiritedness can amplify a statesman's range of action. Much like Churchill and de Gaulle, great statesmen and statesmanship are summoned during crises, when a political community shows the greatest need and insecurity. Ironically, when these nations were in peril and their institutions were not robust, these two twentieth-century leaders tried to transform their fellow citizens' political and moral understanding by instilling a sense of greatness and common purpose.

MAGNANIMITY AND STATESMANSHIP: CHARLES DE GAULLE'S POLITICS OF GRANDEUR

Aristotle's discussion of magnificence precedes his dissection of magnanimity. He describes the grandeur of magnificence as anything "related to the common love of honor, for instance where people believe that one ought to equip a dramatic chorus, or fit out a warship, or even give a civic feast, in a splendid way" (1122b22–24). The magnificent possess great wealth and the ability to spend lavishly, in ways that not only fit an occasion but also evoke a sense of grandeur. Magnificence is only available to those with means, but the grandeur of magnificence does not result from spending money; it is the production of something beautiful and great, which inspires wonder: "and the excellence of a work, its magnificence, is in its grandeur" (1122b15–18).

The magnanimous man can also produce grandeur, but he has an alternative means at his disposal: the possession of all the virtues that are animated by great ambition. Political leadership is the vehicle for grandeur, and grandeur is the prism through which the magnanimous man sees politics. A sense of grandeur in politics is partly the product of something concrete: an existing regime, its citizens, the concern for survival, and the values and way of life they believe are worth defending. Even a leader who calls his country to greatness must be dedicated to its survival. While public spiritedness is necessary for leadership, a politics of grandeur calls for a productive vision and desire to create a lasting work. This vision originates from a leader's ambition, creative impulse, and energetic statecraft. A politics of grandeur is tied to his character; evocative in nature, it abstracts from the constraints on action without forgetting political reality.

The desire to practice politics on a grand scale resides within the "soul of a leader" – to borrow a term from Newell's study of greatness in leadership – and he must work to bring his sense of grandeur to bear on politics. Aristotle offers two examples of magnanimity, Zeus and the Athenians, but it is difficult to know what to make of them because neither example reflects an individual leader. I illustrate the concept of grandeur by examining de Gaulle, whose political leadership depended entirely on his idea of French grandeur.

I argue that de Gaulle's idea of grandeur is an example of transformative ambition because he tied his national goals to his moral vision of France and turned to foreign policy to achieve them. He sought to transform the perceptions and behavior of French citizens through the promotion of French unity. He believed this could be achieved by asking his countrymen to live up to France's historical greatness. He turned deliberately to foreign policy to increase the nation's rank in the world and to create a shared sense of national purpose.

De Gaulle did not accept the Cold War's structural constraints, in which France had relatively weak material capabilities in comparison to the United States and the Soviet Union. De Gaulle's ambition to recapture French grandeur for the sake of unity led him to increase France's international role by transforming the global order at the margins: he attacked the Cold War status quo, made inroads in the Third World, and sought to maximize France's influence and freedom of maneuver despite the fact that its relative power did not warrant such a forceful foreign policy.

De Gaulle is a national hero in France and has ascended the ranks of great twentieth-century statesmen. He demonstrated many magnanimous qualities as he was dually committed to outstanding statesmanship and grandeur for France. De Gaulle (1960) publicly announced his philosophy of military and political leadership in *The Edge of the Sword*, which he wrote when he was 40 as the General Secretariat of the Supreme Council of National Defense. In his book, he endorses a heroic and transcendent leadership. In some ways, this abstract silhouette points to the future, to General de Gaulle (Lacouture, 1966). De Gaulle's vision of a great leader, writes Lacouture, "is an animal of great power, over himself and others, a man whose vision is so uncluttered by thought of God that action alone can raise him to 'the divine game of heroes'" (1966, p. 38). De Gaulle believed that there was a necessity for men of character who instinctively prefer action and gain their authority through personal leadership: "when faced with the challenge of events, the man of character has recourse to himself. His instinctive response is to leave his mark on action, to take responsibility for it, to make it *his own business*" (1960, p. 41).

De Gaulle's man of character is radically individualistic, but like the magnanimous man, his initiative and actions are generous.[3] This man willingly and instinctively takes on the burdens of leadership: "the confidence of those under him give him a sense of obligation. It strengthens his determination but also increases his benevolence, for he is a born protector" (1960, p. 43). Unlike the magnanimous man who rejects politics and is openly disdainful, de Gaulle's exemplar reaches the summits as a highly politicized actor who seeks great distinction.

At the same time, de Gaulle's outward leadership character as a great risk taker contrasts interestingly with his privacy and remoteness from others. Like the magnanimous man, de Gaulle seemed completely independent, and, in politics, he never sought out the counsel of others, even his intimate advisers: "in the end all of de Gaulle's talking, as one adviser noted, was with himself; his advisers were mirrors in which he would examine his own ideas" (Jackson 2003, p. 54)

De Gaulle's endorsement of great leadership and active statesmanship worked in tandem with his conception of a politics of grandeur, French grandeur in particular. He routinely evoked these principles but never defined them because grandeur was not a policy with particular aims as much as it was "a self-conscious defense of the independence, honor, and rank of the nation" (Mahoney, 2000, p. 17). However the idea of grandeur is the key to unlocking de Gaulle's ambition. For many, de Gaulle was a galling personality, especially for those who perceived him as pompous and imperious, which was certainly Franklin D. Roosevelt's impression when he told Churchill that he found de Gaulle intolerable and as having a Messianic complex (Berthon, 2001, p. XII). Yet he was publicly self-conscious of his demanding and rude outward disposition.

His attitude matched his ambition, which he believed was a good trait insofar as it was always aligned with France's interests. In contrast, he viewed Napoleon's ambition as petty and vulgar. About him, de Gaulle said: "he conceived his destiny as that of an extraordinary individual. But an individual counts for little compared to a nation" (Jackson 2003, p. 58). De Gaulle's ambition was not self-effacing, however; he wanted to make his mark on the world, but it was through France and for it. The idea of grandeur played the essential role in fostering his ambition; it is itself a complex set of beliefs that became the cornerstone of his policies and political actions.

As Daniel Mahoney (2000) notes, the meaning of grandeur cannot be inferred from policies but only by "unpacking the implications of his hortatory rhetoric" (p. 16). De Gaulle gives voice to this view in his *Memoires de Guerre*:

> All my life I have had a certain idea of France. This is inspired by senti-
> ment as much as by reason. The emotional side of me naturally imagines
> France, like a princess in the fairy stories or the Madonna in the frescos, as
> dedicated to an exalted and exceptional destiny. Instinctively I have the
> feeling that Providence has created her either for complete successes or for
> exemplary misfortunes. If in spite of this, mediocrity shows in her acts and
> deeds, it strikes me as an absurd anomaly, to be imputed to the faults of
> Frenchmen, not to the genius of the land. But the positive side of my mind
> assures me that France is not really herself unless in front rank; that only
> vast enterprises are capable of counterbalancing the ferments of dispersal
> which are inherent in her people; that our country, as it is, surrounded by
> the others, as they are, must aim high and hold itself straight, on pain of
> mortal danger. In short, France cannot be France without greatness.
> (Mahoney, 2000, p. 16)

De Gaulle's language draws our attention to various distinctions. His idea of France is disclosed by reason and sentiment, it is epic and tragic, its interests and the interests of Frenchmen are not necessarily the same, and it is in constant danger of decline. France must always aim for greatness. This certain idea of France is what leads to de Gaulle's view that France has a unique identity that is shared by the French and is, at the same time, the glue of their social unity (Cerny, 1980, p. 85). France's history wavers between mediocrity and greatness; thus the nation-state is for de Gaulle and exalted vision it has a destiny and is defined by its moral direction. Unlike Bismarck's cold rationalism, who thought of the nation-state as one self-interested actor among many, de Gaulle invests the nation with a particularity of its own, which is forged by history, language, successes, failures, and ambitions (Gordon, 1993, p. 10).

De Gaulle's vision of France was based on his assumption that he felt no need to justify: "France had a special right and duty to play the role of a world power simply because it was France" (Gordon, 1993, p. 15). As such, grandeur required great projects and only a man with the ambition of de Gaulle could help France achieve its destined goals. From the view that France obtained its own historical legitimacy, de Gaulle integrated the French aspiration for grandeur with the realities of France's reduced power.

GAULLIST NATIONAL AND FOREIGN POLICY: FRANCE'S INDEPENDENCE AND WORLD STATUS

For de Gaulle, the pursuit of greatness was a means of promoting France's unity, which was necessary during World War II and the Cold War, because in reality the country was torn apart internally and in decline as a world power. Domestically, he sought a government and leadership free of partisanship; he cast himself as a nonpartisan patriot who proposed the prominence of the nonpartisan state (Codevilla, 1981, p. 222). However, in 1945, de Gaulle's advocacy for a strong executive was rejected by voters. He refused to run for president and retired from politics until he was called back by the French in 1958. Such an episode is not evidence of the incompatibility of de Gaulle's ambition and French politics. He coveted power, yet he simply believed that the Fourth Republic would prove ungovernable, which proved prescient. De Gaulle took a pragmatist view of the political system: "he took as his guiding principle Solon's reply when asked to define the best constitution: *for what people and what period?* [16 June 1946] (Jackson, 2003, p. 62).

His notion of France's "sacred unity" became genuinely achievable when he was called in 1958, after a decade of absence from public life, to take charge of the country. In 1958, France's stability was being threatened by an insurrection in Algiers. It was at this time that de Gaulle could try to make good on his goal for national unity because he was given special constitutional powers. The May 1958 crisis was the portal through which the country accepted de Gaulle's control of government policy through the presidency.

In 1958, de Gaulle viewed France in the following way: "France must fulfill her mission as a world power. We are everywhere in the world. There is no corner of the earth, where, at any given time, men do not look to us and ask what France has to say. It is a great responsibility to be France, the humanizing power par excellence" (Gordon 1993, p. 15). His Algerian plan, to give the colony its independence, was the first example of his belief that France's global role mixed power and grandeur.

At the same time, de Gaulle combined his ambitions for France's rank with sensitivity to changing circumstances. No example is as clear as his policy to give French colonies their independence; thus presiding over the transformation of the French empire into the sponsor of Algerian independence (Gordon 1993, p. 8). In anticipation of the post-colonial era and France's waning international influence, he sought to retain its "civilizing" influence in the Third World by becoming a broker between nation-states and the superpowers. Although a staunch French Nationalist, de Gaulle never allowed his ideological aspirations for France to truncate his political options. As Raymond Aron observed, "[de Gaulle] had the intelligence to renounce his conceptions when they were overcome by events" (1993, p. 8). He combined his belief of France's greatness with prudence, yet without allowing calculating reason to ever subsume his faith in France's eternal mission.

Did de Gaulle's notion of grandeur have its intended effect, or did the limits of France's real power hinder de Gaulle's vision of France's global role? The stark reality was that France was no longer a great but a diminished power, which begs the question, was de Gaulle simply stubborn, proud, and impossibly nationalistic? During the Cold War, France was not a player on the world stage like the United States or Soviet Union. Yet, de Gaulle, who had a nuanced view of the relationship between foreign and domestic policy, sought to prolong France's influence by the "subordination of that part of the domestic which is self-indulgent to that part of foreign policy which is responsible, that is, humanly virtuous" (Mahoney, 2000, p. 17). His awareness of France's enfeebled position is what led to his public pronouncement about France's need to sit atop the hierarchy of world powers and, at the same time, promote policies that were derived from the principle of France's independence. Moreover, independence would inspire pride in the French, which would mitigate the feeling of dependency that led to passivity and resentment (Gordon 1993, p. 21).

De Gaulle consciously turned to foreign policy as a moral choice, in an attempt to fulfill his vision while also supporting France's national interest. His diplomacy rested on the principle that it was France's imperative to maintain a forceful independence during the Cold War. This idea extended to his views about European integration, which he believed had to be executed by subordinating the mechanisms of integration to the primacy of nation-states.

True to his principles, de Gaulle withdrew France from NATO in 1966, and he insisted on France's need to develop an independent nuclear deterrent.[4] De Gaulle did not think that France could become a superpower on par with the United States and the Soviet Union; his statecraft aimed to reshape the rules of Cold War relations that the superpowers had imposed by sheer dominance and the vicious logic of nuclear annihilation. Forceful independence was a means to reconfigure the idea of the world divided in two opposing blocs; France would lead the reemergence of cooperation among nation-states, each with its distinctive characters and peoples.

De Gaulle's ambition to modify international relations was deliberately transformative; he linked foreign policy to France's national flourishing. He invested foreign policy with cultural and symbolic significance; such grandeur would deepen the public's convictions about France and help make the state's institutions more efficacious so that it could take on its international role. Such politics is a deliberate choice to put political office, wealth, and the state's power, among other concrete elements, to greater and noble purposes. De Gaulle sought grandeur through international politics; he was not motivated by power, but to make France a player on the world scene at a time when smaller powers' choices were constrained by the United States and the Soviet Union.

De Gaulle's ambition was above the mandates of – but not contrary to – survival; it resisted the status quo and needed far-sighted statecraft for it not to be destructive to the state. His ambition was transformative, but it did not destabilize the balance of power, seeking instead to modify it. He wanted to counter the hegemony of the two dominant superpowers by reconstituting the pattern of cooperation and interdependence among nation-states, which would be made possible by permitting France to assume a greater part in international leadership than should have been permitted given its inferior capabilities. France's rank would be recognized by its ability to fuse morality to power and by its historical position in international affairs.

CONCLUSION

This chapter has illuminated the relationship between the magnanimous man, the idea of a politics of grandeur, and the thesis I put forward in this work. Thus, the magnanimous man's ambition for a politics of grandeur is not simply self-serving or self-deluding, but something within the realm of possibility. It expresses a very ordinary and human desire to be a part of a totality greater than oneself. The magnanimous man will go through extraordinary lengths to achieve ambitious goals that depend on his ability for energetic and prudent statecraft, which correctly calibrates what passions need to be fostered in order to encourage the polity to greater moral heights.

Is transformative ambition always a prudent political program? Transformative ambition may lack the restraining influence of magnanimity. As I discuss in the next chapter, Alcibiades' desire for his grandeur sought to radically shift the pole of Greek power to Athens through an ill-conceived and grand imperial policy: he tapped into the national ambition of Athens for daring and dismantled the remnants of Periclean restraint. Pericles demonstrated a more reflective transformative ambition, more akin to de Gaulle's than Alcibiades'. Pericles sought grandeur but never took unnecessary risks to increase Athens' glory. I will show how Pericles' ambition for supreme achievement led him to spearhead a political and cultural transformation of Athens that was based on a foreign policy to make Athens the center of the Greek world.

In the next chapter, I use the model of transformative ambition infused with magnanimous qualities, to examine Pericles' rule of Athens. His rare intellectual gifts, prudence, moderation, and patriotism combined with his great political ambition so that he had a long tenure in politics and presided over the growth of the Athenian empire. Through imperial policies, he sought to bring unparalleled glory to Athens and its citizens. As such, he practiced transformational statecraft both domestically and internationally.

Although Pericles worked within the parameters of Athenian democracy, and also contributed to the further democratization of the city-state, his unprecedented authority in Athens inspired Thucydides' description of Athens as a democracy in name only, effectively the rule of one man. Thucydides invites us to think about Pericles' leadership and his political motivation in the way Aristotle has made us analyse the relationship of magnanimity to leadership. Did Pericles want to expand democracy out of principle or use the democratic base to attain political power? Was he loyal to his supporters, the laws of the city, divine laws, or to his own grand ambitions and pursuits? What role did the Athenian empire play in his plans, and why did he pursue his international policies? I now turn to these questions and a thorough examination of Pericles' leadership.

NOTES

1. In the *Rhetoric*, Aristotle says, "[A]n individual is well born on the male or female side if he is a legitimate citizen on each side and, as in the case of the city, if his earliest ancestors were renowned for their virtue or wealth or any other admired quality and if the family had many illustrious members, male and female, young and old" (1360b trans. 1954 [1984]).

2. The magnanimous man's penchant to reflect on his own virtue should not be confused with the life of contemplation, or philosophy, since he is not given to wonder (1125a4).
3. For an example of an interpretation of Charles de Gaulle through the lens of narcissist personality, see Post (2004, pp. 46–8).
4. See Jacques E. C. Hyman (2006) for an analysis of how a national leader's individual understanding of the nation's identity contributes to the state's nuclear policies, especially the decision for a state to go nuclear.

6. Pericles' transformative ambition (1): regime politics and character

> Pericles indeed, by his rank, ability, and know integrity, was enabled to exercise an independent control over the multitude – in short to lead them instead of being led by them.
> **Thucydides**

Pericles was Athens' premier democratic statesman at the height of its empire. He showed transformative ambition on three levels: in policy decisions that brought the city's democracy and empire to fulfillment, in his inspirational rhetoric to inspire citizens to live up to their greatest ambitions, and in a wartime strategy he implemented against Sparta that aimed to solidify Athens as Greece's preeminent power.

Pericles neither founded the democracy nor was he responsible for establishing the empire. He did, however, bring the democracy and empire to their peaks by inexorably linking domestic and foreign policy. His domestic agenda to increase democracy and embark on a grand building project relied on his reorganization of the Athenian Empire. Most significantly, he implemented a policy that siphoned off allied tribute for Athenian purposes. Pericles spearheaded a massive construction campaign that fortified Athens' defensive walls, beautified the city, and put the citizens under public pay. The use of these funds allowed Athens to blossom into an expansive democracy and cultural mecca, strengthening its position as the center of the Greek world.

While he was alive, Athenian democracy reflected Pericles' political ambition because of his masterful command over public opinion, known integrity, incorruptibility, and rank as the leading citizen. His ambition proved transformative as he had a driving desire to surpass in power and glory not only all of Athens' rivals but also the founders of the Athenian Empire. To accomplish these goals, he took the long view. His rhetoric not only persuaded Athenians to follow his policies, but Pericles also tried to inculcate a particular political understanding of Athens. Such an edifying feat was possible because he could both curb the Athenians' dangerous imperial impulses and rid them of their fears. This accomplishment is best witnessed in his *Funeral Oration* (Thucydides, 1996), which I examine in this chapter. In it, Pericles extols the Athenian way of life, focusing his audience's attention and energies toward a standard that it simultaneously embodies but must constantly renew, and, therefore, try to live up to. Pericles possessed a blend of personal qualities that enabled him to lead and inspire the Athenians in peace and war.

Lastly, this chapter analyses Pericles' statesmanship during the Peloponnesian War, which is the subject of much debate. He devised a rational defensive strategy that broke and radically reshaped the Hellenistic rules of war. Moreover, it was antithetical to the Athenian national character, and through the force of his character, he executed and made the Athenians stick to it. Ultimately, his plan failed. A plague decimated Athens' population and morale; it also killed him two years into the conflict. While the turn of fortune contributed to Pericles' failure to win the war, it also exhibited the major failures of the Periclean regime and his statecraft. Focusing on the precarious balance of the common good in an especially individualistic and wealthy democracy, his cautious and rationalist strategy strained the institutional power that made the empire successful, expansion. His death proved that in the absence of a great and prudent leader like Pericles, the imperial democracy produced selfish and dangerous politicians who took Athens down a disastrous path leading to its eventual defeat by Sparta.

My analysis of Pericles broaches scholarship in the subfields of political science and in history. I first analyse realist international relations scholars who investigate the outbreak of the Peloponnesian War. I critique their various theses because they abstract too much from the impact of actual decision-makers, especially Pericles. I then turn to the work of political philosophers who place a greater focus on Pericles and on the theme of statesmanship. The issue of Pericles' leadership and his importance for Athens' politics is only a subtheme of a more general interest in Thucydides' *History* and its relationship to political thought. In addition, I pay specific attention to various political theorists' interpretations of the *Funeral Oration*. These points serve to explain how Pericles used his oratory to confront two challenges that he thought were paramount to Athens' political situation, the difficulty that the democracy posed to the balance between self-interest and public duty as well as the moral justification for the Athenian Empire.

I contrast the theoretical interpretations of Pericles' actions with Donald Kagan's biography of Pericles, in which he portrays him as the champion of a stable and flourishing democracy. Kagan defends him against conservative accusations of demagoguery, flawed vision and policy inconsistency, and his dooming of Athens to war, civil strife, and loss of empire. Although I am indebted to Kagan's artful reconstruction of Pericles' life, I maintain a critical distance from his reading of the Athenian statesman's ambitions. I also examine Pericles' character to identify the unique qualities that shaped his ambition and leadership. I discuss these traits by distinguishing among pertinent categories of his experience as a citizen and statesman, including an aristocratic upbringing, sophistical education, and military experience. I also examine how his leadership was defined by his political rise in the rough and tumble of Athens' democratic politics.

In this endeavor, I have culled information from various ancient and modern sources. Among the ancients, I concentrate mainly on Thucydides, Plutarch, Plato, and Aristotle. These sources pose some difficultly as each thinker supplies both biographical information and political judgments about Pericles and his statesmanship, sometimes interweaving opinions with what each classifies as facts regarding Pericles. Thus, where applicable, I make explicit references to each commentator's overarching interpretation of Pericles' leadership.

INTERNATIONAL RELATIONS THEORY: THUCYDIDES AND THE PELOPONNESIAN WAR

The Peloponnesian War, fought between Athens and Sparta, began in 431 BC, engulfed the entire Greek world, and lasted 27 years. When the conflict broke out, each *polis* was at the height of its power. In Thucydides' estimation, it was "the greatest movement yet known in history" (1.1.2, translated 1847). On account of its intensity, duration, and the radical differences in political, military, and economic organization between Athens and Sparta, the war transformed the Greek world. The balance of power shifted to Sparta, Athens never regained the international vitality it had under its maritime empire, and civil strife, which unhinged the Greek *poleis* during the war, became commonplace in Greece.

Why did Athens and Sparta go to war? Thucydides provides an answer:

> To the question why they broke the treaty, I answer by placing first an account of their grounds of complaint and points of difference, that no one

may ever have to ask the immediate cause which plunged the Hellenes into war of such magnitude. The real cause, however, I consider to be the one which was formally most kept out of sight. The growth of the power of Athens, and the alarm which this inspired in Sparta, made the war inevitable. (1.23)

International relations scholars, who have duly noted Thucydides' distinction between the immediate cause and the real cause for the war, understand his *History* as an early expression of power politics and structural realism (Wight, 1978; Waltz, 1979; Keohane, 1986; Gilpin, 1988; Doyle, 1997). For these realists, Thucydides' statement about the war's inevitability implies a neorealist explanation. These scholars think that Thucydides vindicates the realist perspective for two reasons. His search for an underlying cause for the war ends in the discovery of power politics. In addition, Thucydides thinks of power in transhistorical terms. As a result, the role of events, leaders, and regime politics give way to the analysis of power operating at the system level. Two great powers struggled in an unstable balance of power; the uneven growth of one contributed to the fear of the other; mutual suspicion and distrust led the states' leaders into a series of decisions that culminated in the Great War.

Robert Gilpin (1988) has argued that Thucydides' explanation of the war in 1.23 offers an early attempt to provide a structural account of international politics, and, specifically, Thucydides proposes a theory of hegemonic war (p. 592). As such, Thucydides understood classical Greece as a system composed of two powers, in which the distribution of power defined the system and the hierarchy of power ordered and stabilized it.

Thucydides' theory of hegemonic war attributes the outbreak to the uneven growth of power in Athens over Sparta, which is explained by three factors: demographic and economic necessity, the mastery of naval power and the expansion of commerce, and the rise of the Athenian Empire after the Persian Wars (1988, pp. 597–8). Athens' commercial democracy and rule of the sea encircled and threatened Sparta, which was more conservative and austere. Up until the Persian Wars, Sparta was Greece's hegemon, thanks to its masterful command of land warfare. Its strength lay in its regimented warrior society, conservative constitution, and suppression of the Helots – a subjugated Greek people who lived as serfs to the state. However, the conclusion of the Persian Wars had an inverse effect on Sparta in comparison to Athens: "that war and its aftermath stimulated the growth of Athenian power at the same time that the war and its aftermath encouraged Sparta, the reigning hegemon and the leader of the Greeks in their war against the Persians, to retreat into isolation" (1988, p. 598).

Despite Thucydides' explicitness about the war's true cause, Michael Doyle (1997), in a careful reading of the narrative, urges us to pay closer attention to the Greek thinker's complex realism. Doyle argues that Thucydides' work "is a testament to the fact that he held that a state's ends, its means, and (therefore) its choices could not be adequately determined through an analysis of international structure" (1997, p. 73). For Doyle, the explanation for the conflict is more complex as Spartan fear, vulnerability, and pride contributed to its declaration of war. Thucydides rejected shallow interpretations of power (1997, p. 74).

Each city's political, economic, and cultural systems animated, and constrained, their foreign policies. From a neorealist perspective, Sparta should have balanced against the increase in Athens' power by investing in a fleet, a larger expeditionary force, and its own empire, but Sparta's social structure, "which was equivalent to a massive penal colony designed to control and exploit the oppressed Messenian helots, resisted innovation" (1997, p. 74). Conversely, Athens' wealth and power was supplied by a strong navy that could project the city's power throughout the Aegean Sea.

In addition, Doyle argues that Sparta's and Athens' interactions were not just based on rational assessments of each other's power. Their dealings were also laced with enmity, mistrust, and Spartan envy. Doyle agrees that Thucydides offers a structural explanation for the war in 1.23, but he emphasizes each city's appeals to security, honor, and self-interest as sources of its behavior. For example, Spartan fear and honor equally contributed to its declaration of war against Athens.

These realist scholars make room for leaders' perceptions, but they mostly interpret them as a series of miscalculations that brought the cities to war. I argue the opposite. The war was consistent with Pericles' ambition to supplant Sparta's influence. The root of many changes in Athenian society and Greek warfare were not just constructivist in nature. Although many social conventions are accidental, major shifts in Athenian politics were attributable to Pericles' domestic policies, farsighted foreign policies, and high-minded view of Athens. These new conditions were not accidental. His statesmanship was marked by various episodes in which he convinced his fellow Athenians to follow his policies and accept his beliefs.

In this chapter, I present evidence that demonstrates how Athens' domestic politics, which was relied heavily on Pericles' personal leadership, were the driving force behind the war. Athens was an imperial democracy; domestic and foreign policy were tightly bound. Moreover, the Athenians' worldview was fueled by their daring spirit (a phenomenon recognized by the Athenians as well as outsiders) and the combined efforts of its greatest leaders. Pericles' influence on international relations explains the many steps that the Greek world took toward the imbalance of power that Thucydides' observed and the realists concentrate on. If the realists want to understand the true cause of war (Athens' power), then they must understand Pericles' part in the historical drama.

POLITICAL PHILOSOPHY: EVALUATIONS OF PERICLES' AMBITION

As Clifford Orwin (1994) explains, Pericles' *Funeral Oration* defines one pole of the interpretation of Athenian imperialism: "it presents the empire as unextenuated by necessity" (p. 15). In the speech, Pericles praises the Athenians who enjoy many benefits from the empire but adds that they may relish in the fact that the empire is freely undertaken by them. He claims that Athens' citizens are not compelled to act in response to various necessities such as that of power politics or human nature. This view starkly contrasts with the amoral realism that Athenian ambassadors presented at the Spartan debate prior to the war's outbreak. In that blunt and inflammatory speech, discussed later in this chapter, the Athenians claimed that human nature and necessity compelled them to act out of fear, honor, and interest (1.75).[1]

Conversely, in Orwin's view, Pericles insists that imperial Athenian ambition rested on a supremely noble and original goal that had no precedent (1994, p. 16). Pericles' speech both describes and prescribes. On the one hand, he depicts the political culture that made Athens worthy of its empire. On the other hand, the speech exemplifies Pericles' power of rhetoric. He exhorts the Athenians to live up to his ideal, shaping their ambition and moreover disclosing his unusual ambition.

In the *Funeral Oration*, Pericles introduces novelty. Although Athenian tradition calls on its leading citizen to commemorate the fallen, Pericles does not praise the dead, he praises the living. He deprecates both custom and ancestral wisdom by acknowledging his compatriots for their particular civic virtues, courage, love of beauty, love of wisdom, and self-sufficiency (1994, p. 16). The prize of Athenian virtue is the undying glorious reputation that is only attainable through the city and demands self-sacrifice and the greatest risk, which is one's life. Women, on the other hand, can only gain renown by not attracting attention of any sort (1994, p. 19).[2] Pericles sets out to convince his countrymen that risking death for the city is the greatest good because imperial Athens is the worthiest pursuit.

The Athenians acquired their empire because of their unique character and do more with it than most states, which simply try to accumulate vast amounts of power and wealth. The latter regimes' aims are based on self-interest. However, the Athenians' sheer ambition points to their noble superiority above self-interest. For Pericles, Athenian determination gives the empire its direction. Thomas Pangle and Peter Ahrensdorf (1999) argue that this particular view of what is exalted provides Pericles with a position on which he can claim that imperial Athens is good despite its abuses: "Pericles argues that the Athenians are morally superior to their adversaries, not only because they are generous to others without calculation of profit or loss, but also because of the sheer grandeur of their ambition" (p. 25).

Pericles presupposes unlimited Athenian imperial ambition: "we have forced every sea and land to be the highway of our daring, and everywhere, whether for evil or good, have left imperishable monuments behind us" (2.41.4). He exaggerates to be sure, but the speech's plausibility in practice presupposes, according to Michael Palmer (1992), "a universal empire, which means a war like city, a city always in motion – power – is the ground of the glory that proves the virtue of the individual citizen" (p. 830).

Steven Forde (1986) highlights the particular importance that Pericles pays to the virtue of daring, Athenian individualism, and erotic passion as driving forces for the empire's origin and behavior. Forde argues that Pericles' homage to Athenian "individualism" and exhortation to the common good point to the leader's attempt to address "the problem of cohesion in the city" (1986, p. 439). For Forde, the oration is not so much a testament to Pericles' ambition, as it is his awareness of the difficulty in asking the Athenians to die for the city. He makes both a customary and a novel appeal to the Athenians, persuading them to fight for their traditional love of glory. Meanwhile, he calls on their erotic longings and tries to fuse eros with patriotism, which "circumvents or supplants those conventional mechanisms of community, and seeks to bind the Athenians directly or immediately to the city, depicted as a beloved object" (1986, p. 440).

Political philosophers acknowledge Pericles' transcendent tone in his speeches and the qualified praise that Thucydides bestows on him. As a leader of the democracy, Pericles could restrain the demos, but he did not limit the regime's imperial insatiability. The only time he practiced imperial restraint was during the war, and as a precautionary measure. During his tenure, whatever moderation Athens had was the product of his moderation. After his death, the Athenians launched an ill-planned conquest of Sicily, destroyed the small polis of Melos, executed many talented generals, and succumbed to civil strife. Thus, political philosophers criticize Pericles' moral leadership and political wisdom. He deftly led the democracy, but from a Platonic and Aristotelian perspective, why did he not use his powers to make the Athenians better? I examine these questions in more detail when I discuss the relationship between his leadership and persuasive rhetoric.

DONALD KAGAN'S PERICLES

My analysis of Pericles' transformative ambition builds on the former interpretations of the *Funeral Oration*. I emphasize his deliberate attempt to transcend traditional moral constraints and give Athens a suprapolitical character. However, this is not a universal ambition that genuinely seeks to foster Pan-Hellenism, which is Donald Kagan's (1991) thesis. He describes Pericles as both a rationalist and a visionary who faithfully served democratic principles; he wanted to give full power to the people, and, at the same time, "to educate his people to civic virtue" (p. 10). Kagan also argues that Pericles desired to coexist peacefully with Sparta.

Pericles' dovish foreign policy was shown in his restraint of Athenian imperial ambitions. He did not seek Athenian supremacy. Rather, he promoted Pan-Hellenism for the sake of gaining legitimacy for the empire, as evidenced by his founding of the colony Thurii, in Kagan's view. In 434–3 BC, Thurri's colonists were beset by civil discord. Both Sparta and Athens claimed the territory, yet Pericles allowed the oracle of Delphi, which favored Sparta, to mediate the dispute. Prudently, the oracle claimed that the colony belonged to the Greeks. Athens respected the decision and gave up its strategic holding in the west. I disagree with Kagan on three key issues.

First, Pericles' ambition for Athens was not at all compatible with Pan-Hellenism. In the *Funeral Oration*, he pays homage to the city and speaks to the rest of the Hellenic world, but his language is exclusionary. He contrasts the Athenians with the Spartans to highlight the former's political and moral superiority. I draw the opposite conclusion to Kagan. Pericles was devoted to the idea that the Athenians stood to gain glory and benefits from the empire, which depended on the subordination of other cities. What truly distinguished Pericles' ambition from all others was not his democratic spirit, but his belief that the imperial city could provide an "ageless life on each whose radiant virtue shines through it" (Orwin, 1994, p. 20).

Second, Kagan assumes that Thucydides and Plutarch were biased toward the aristocracy because they do not cast Pericles as an uncritical champion of democracy. As a consequence, those who learn about the historical Pericles from Kagan receive a one-sided reading of Thucydides' and Plutarch's Pericles. Kagan uses Pericles to defend Athenian democracy and in the process gives a misleading interpretation of his ambition. Here is Thucydides' assessment of Pericles' leadership: "Pericles indeed, by his rank, ability, and known integrity, was enabled to exercise an independent control over the multitude – in short to lead them instead of being led by them" (2.65.8). Plutarch divides Pericles' political career into two stages, which are marked by a watershed moment, the ostracism of his conservative opponent Thucydides. Afterward Pericles exercised aristocratic rule over Athens:

> After this he was no longer the same man he had been before, nor as tame and gentle and familiar as formerly with the populace, so as readily to yield to their pleasure and comply with the desire of the multitude, as a steersman shifts with the winds. Quitting that loose, remiss, and, in some cases, licentious court of the popular will, he turned those soft and flowery modulations to the austerity of aristocratic and real rule; and employing this uprightly and undeviatingly for the country's best interests, he was able generally to lead the people along, with their own wills and consents, by persuading and showing them what was to be done; and sometimes, too, urging them, whether they would or no, yield submission for their advantage. (translated by Dryden, 2001, p. 215)

Third, Pericles' policies prior to the war indicate that in his estimation the conflict was inevitable. He carefully steered Athens toward the war. A victory over Sparta was necessary for the empire's maximum security and would vindicate Athens' elevation of its daring and limitless ambition over the traditional restraints imposed on cities and individuals by

Greek morality. Pericles' transformative ambition reflects Athenian drives in general but is also an attempt to justify the empire by reshaping the Greek world in an Athenian mold. Kagan overlooks this dimension because he mistakes Pericles' prudence in diplomacy and war as signs of his being sated with Athens' gains.

However, Pericles fully endorsed the Athenians' love of glory, and he pursued it on the grandest scale. His drive for Athenian grandeur was international in scope. Yet, his internationalism lacked the concern with justice that the more pious and trusting Melians entertained. Although Pericles and the Athenians ignored considerations of justice, he still desired to justify the empire's, and his own, actions, which he openly admits produced both good and evil (2.41.4).

The remainder of this chapter proceeds in three parts. I first provide a background of the Athenian regime and the setting in which Pericles developed his leadership qualities. Athenian politics was not circumscribed by the formal political system, which was practiced in the democratic assembly and the law courts. It extended beyond official government structures and encompassed the family, tribal allegiances, friendship and followers, agonal competition for honors and power, religious practices, and military service. Thus, I examine all the factors that contributed to Pericles' character development.

I then turn to Pericles' domestic policies and argue that they were intertwined with his aim to transform Athens into the center of international influence. The last part of this chapter examines Pericles' foreign policies over the span of his 15-year leadership with particular attention to his handling of the diplomatic crisis that led to the war with Sparta and his wartime strategy.

FAMILY BACKGROUND AND OSTRACISM IN ATHENIAN POLITICS

Pericles' noble birth was most auspicious in his time. His renowned aristocratic lineage has no comparison in today's world. His father, Xanthippus, was the commanding general who defeated the Persians at Mycale and had a statue erected in his honor on the Acropolis (Pausanias, 1.25.1, translated 1918). As one of the men of Marathon, he won heroic acclaim, which gave him considerable political power. Through his mother, Agariste, Pericles was associated with the powerful Alcmaeonidae family. She was the great niece of Cleisthenes, an

Athenian aristocrat who ended the tyranny of Pisistratus' sons and laid the foundations for Athenian democracy.

The illustrious history of the Alcmaeonidae family is recounted in Herodotus' *Histories* (translated 2007, 6.121–31), which culminates in Pericles' birth. We learn of it in a famous passage in the *Histories*: "this Agariste married Xanthippus son of Ariphron, and during her pregnancy she had a vision in her sleep: she dreamed she saw herself giving birth to a lion, and a few days later, she gave birth to Pericles son of Xanthippus" (6.131.2). Plutarch continues where Herodotus leaves off: "in other respects perfectly formed, only his head was somewhat longish and out of proportion, for which reason almost all the images and statues that were made of him have the head covered with a helmet, the workmen apparently being willing not to expose him" (2001, p. 203).

Political liabilities were also attached to his noble birth. Thucydides tells us that Pericles inherited a family curse, the agos, because the head of the Alcmaeonidae household had killed suppliants after promising them their lives. "From this deed the men who killed them were called accursed and guilty against the goddess, they and their descendants" (1.126.11).[3] The Alcmaeonidae were expelled from Athens twice, once by the Athenians and then again by Cleomenes of Sparta with the aid of an Athenian faction (1.126.12). During the diplomatic escalation just prior to the Peloponnesian War, the Spartans used Pericles' family curse to no avail in an attempt to turn the Athenians against him.

Ambitious Athenian aristocrats who aspired to positions of leadership carefully timed and prepared their entry into politics. Plutarch describes how the political stigma that Pericles inherited affected the timing of his career:

> Pericles, while yet but a young man, stood in considerable apprehension of the people, as he was thought in face and figure to be very like the tyrant Pisistratus, and those of great age remarked upon the sweetness of his voice, and his volubility and rapidity in speaking, and were struck with amazement at the resemblance. Reflecting, too that he had a considerable estate, and was descended from a noble family, and had friends of great influence, he was fearful all this might bring him to be banished as a dangerous person, and for this reason did not meddle in state affairs. (2001, p. 206)

The ambitious had to contend with possible ostracism, which Pericles experienced first-hand when, in 484 BC, his father was banished and the family went into exile. Political rivals could well take advantage of any sign of ambitious behavior and seek his ostracism on the grounds that he was dangerous to the political order.

Cleisthenes introduced the practice of ostracism. Each year, the Athenian assembly voted on the question whether it should take place. If they agreed, the vote for ostracism would occur on some other date. On the day of the vote, each citizen could write the name of someone he wanted ostracized on a piece of broken pottery called an ostracon. If 6000 citizens voted for ostracism, the man with the majority of votes had to leave Attica for 10 years. Archeologists have found ostracons that identify Pericles' father, one of which states that he is "accursed" (Pomerory, 1996). The other says, "Xanthippus, son of Arriphron, is cursed for his rascality; too long he has abused our hospitality" (Broneer, 1948).

According to Kagan, the process effectively deterred hostile factions from starting coups to unseat popular leaders (1991, p. 17). Aristotle disagrees with Kagan's view that ostracism functioned as a corrective device: "for instead of looking to the advantage of their own regime, they used ostracism for factional purposes" (*Politics*, 1284b17). Aristotle argues that democrats unjustly used it to cling to power by banishing outstanding citizens. It may have been legal in the democracy, but it was wielded for private advantage and therefore "it is perhaps also manifest that it is not simply just" (1284b23–24).

During Pericles' tenure he successfully ostracized Cimon and Thucydides. There is no evidence that these conservative political rivals threatened to dissolve the democracy through a coup, as Kagan implies by his understanding of ostracism. Nonetheless, as a consequence of these actions, Pericles consolidated his power and ruled Athens without any serious opponents.

PERICLES' EDUCATION: RATIONALITY AND PERSUASIVE SPEECH

Pericles came of age at the beginning of one of Western civilization's most remarkable periods. Cutting-edge pre-Socratic philosophers and sophists were challenging traditional forms of instruction and turning religious ideas on their heads. Pericles' education was at the cusp of a monumental transition from orthodox Greek education in character formation to radical forms of rational demonstration and skepticism toward religion and tradition.

Through cosmology and speculative thinking, the pre-Socratic philosophers turned to nature to explain the underlying order of things. During Socrates' lifetime, the sophists came to be known as a particular class of professional educators who instructed young men in public displays of eloquence (Guthrie, 1971, p. 35). For a fee, they taught practical skills, and instruction was purposely geared toward the effective use of speech, which was becoming the critical skill sought by Athenian politicians.

In Plato's *Gorgias*, the eponymous character articulates the putative relationship between rhetoric and politics: "I for one say it is being able to persuade by speeches judges in the law court, councilors in the council, assemblymen in the assembly, and in every other gathering whatsoever, when there is a political gathering" (452e trans.1998). The difference between rhetoric and politics was almost indistinguishable, "the word 'rhetor', indeed, comes almost to mean politician" (Rhodes, 1986, p. 141). Owing to the expansion and ubiquitous use of rhetoric, Athenian citizens did not need a formal education in order to be exposed to the sophistical arguments of the day. For example, in the Mytilenian debate, Thucydides' Cleon criticizes the Athenians for letting clever points and sophistical arguments delude them (3.38.2).

Plutarch tells us that the pre-Socratic philosophers deeply influenced Pericles' education. He was a hearer of Zeno and kept close company with Anaxagoras, who first proposed the idea of an immaterial *nous* (mind). Early exposure to a philosophical education refined Pericles' thought and helped him perfect his use of speech. However, just as important, it provided him an understanding of the world that was "superior to that superstition with which the ignorant wonder at appearances" (2001, p. 205).

Kagan identifies Pericles' rationality as the key trait that guided his leadership, especially in developing the war strategy to fight Sparta, but Kagan does not see how Pericles' rationalism is in tension with his unorthodox morality. For example, in the *Funeral Oration*, Pericles denigrates tradition, shuns Homeric values, and makes no reference to Athens' religious beliefs. This outlook is consistent with his rationalism and shows strains of amoralism. However, Pericles' rationalism must balance his great aspirations for Athens, which are based on the notion that the city possesses moral superiority.

Notwithstanding his lack of piety, Pericles' ambition for Athens is suffused with a longing for nobility. Ultimately, his rationality is not opposed to belief. Yet, as noted before, such pursuit of nobility abstracts from considerations of international justice. For Pericles, the city's moral superiority rests on the Athenian choice to pursue goals that cannot be regarded simply as maximizing security: its unlimited ambition and quest for glory puts it at considerable risk. The Athenians transcend self-interest and are not compelled to act; rather, they freely choose empire.

Pericles was too intelligent to forget that conventional notions of justice made the empire a morally questionable project. Once the war was underway, he acknowledged that the Athenian Empire is like a tyranny (*History*, 2.63). We cannot say that Pericles' statesmanship was summed up by his rationalism. In fact, I identify a tension between it and his moralism. His rationalism gives rise to a frank amoralism in Athenian foreign policy, but he also prides himself on the city's nobility. I return to these themes in the sections "Pericles' transformation of citizen virtue" and "Athenian and Periclean realism: the debate at Sparta."

In addition to Pericles' rational disposition and ambition for nobility, the cornerstone of his education was persuasive speech. Plato attests to Pericles' prowess; the character of Socrates claims that Pericles was "the most accomplished of the rhetoricians" (*Phaedrus*, 269e translated 1995). Further, he says, "[T]his was, as I conceive, the quality which in addition to his natural gifts, Pericles acquired from his intercourse with Anaxagoras whom he happened to know. He was imbued with the higher philosophy, and attained the knowledge of the Mind and the negative Mind, which were favorite themes of Anaxagoras, and applied what suited his purpose to the art of speaking" (*Phaedrus*, 270a).

Pericles' speaking style, rhetorical ability, and preference for rational explanations became well settled in him on account of his great natural genius. His preference for reason over custom, omens, and divinations made its way into his policy proposals. As I will discuss later, his long-term strategy to fight Sparta was based entirely on a sophisticated rational policy that not only defined how the war was fought for many years but also changed the Hellenistic rules of war.

PERICLES' POLITICAL CHARACTER AND REGIME POLITICS

Plutarch considers that Pericles' aristocratic lineage combined with his education resulted in an elevation of purpose and dignity of language "raised far above the base and dishonest buffooneries of mob eloquence" (2001, p. 204). After Pericles' death, Cleon practiced just the opposite. Aristotle says the he "was the first person to use bawling and abuse on the platform, and to gird up his cloak before making a public speech, all other persons speaking in orderly fashion" (*Athenian Constitution*, 28.3). Pericles applied his talents and virtues with perfect comportment, and "upon which account, they say, he had his nickname given him, though some are of the opinion he was named the Olympian from the public buildings he adorned the city; and others again, from his great power in public affairs," says Plutarch (2001, p. 207). Plutarch's description of Pericles' Olympian loftiness and composure provides insight into how he derived authority through self-command and persuasive speech. But Pericles' political power was built on more than good speeches.

In Athens, aspiring politicians needed renown. While this was partly inherited from family stature, Pericles had to attract a following of close companions and distinguish himself in Athens' competitive society. With no political parties to speak of, political groupings were formed around the name of one person. Thus, Athens' prospective pool of leaders was drawn from the most ambitious individuals who had garnered public attention through various accomplishments, for example, in war, athletic contests, successful prosecutions, paying for civic feasts, and producing dramatic choruses.

Leading politicians surrounded themselves with a group of lesser men who worked on their behalf, "holding offices, appearing in the courts and proposing measures in the assembly" (Rhodes, 1986, p. 138). Thanks to his network of associates, Pericles crafted his public persona. Wary of appearing common, he was present at intervals, "not speaking to every business, nor at all times coming into the assembly, but ... reserving himself for great occasions" (Plutarch, 2001, p. 206).

Although Pericles naturally leaned toward aristocratic government, Cimon was the leading figure of the conservative faction. Pericles rose through the dissident democratic faction. During the early part of Pericles' career, Cimon was Athens' most powerful and popular leader. His father Miltiades "had won fame at Marathon and disgrace at Paros after losing a tyranny in the Chersonese" (Fornara and Samons, 1991, p. 60). Cimon was a highly regarded general whose many victories contributed to the growth and wealth of the Athenian Empire; he was the first to use the spoils of war to beautify the city (Plutarch, 2001, p. 654).

Known for his ease and social grace, Cimon also redistributed his wealth among the poor as a way to satisfy the common people without granting political authority: "[h]e pulled down all the enclosures of his gardens and grounds, that strangers, and the needy of his fellow-citizens, might gather of his fruits freely. At home he kept a table, plain, but sufficient for a considerable number; to which any poor townsman had free access" (2001, p. 650).

As the leader of Athens' aristocratic faction, Cimon supported the conservative Aeropagus council and was the key promoter of friendly diplomatic relations with Sparta, which was a divisive issue in Athens. As the empire became more successful, thanks to leaders like Cimon, the Athenians began to conceive of themselves as the greater peoples in the Hellenic world. Cimon admired Spartan society for its traditional way of life, adopted many Spartan habits, and named one of his sons Lacedaemonius. Yet, a pro-Spartan policy eventually led to his political downfall, which opened the way for Pericles' democratic faction.

A critical episode in 461 BC led to the deterioration of the Athenian and Spartan relationship. Still allies after the Persian Wars, Sparta called on Athens, which was experienced in siege warfare, to help subdue a Helot revolt. In the assembly, Cimon successfully argued that Athens should aid the Spartans, a hard-won diplomatic mission as many citizens hoped for Sparta's demise. Cimon led the expedition, but when the Athenians arrived, they were hastily dismissed on the grounds that they were no longer needed. Thucydides says, "[T]he Spartans were apprehensive of the enterprising and revolutionary character of the Athenians, and further looking upon them as of alien extraction, began to fear that if they remained, they might be persuaded by the besieged in Ithome to attempt some political changes" (1.102.4). Cimon returned to Athens disgraced and was ostracized soon after.

Cimon's banishment coincided with Ephialtes' attack on the Aeropagus, which controlled legislative matters in Athens. Pericles was Ephialtes' younger associate in the democratic coalition. Together they transferred judicial and political power to the Boule of the Five Hundred, the assembly, and the dicasteries. During this transition, Ephialtes became the victim of a political assassination, and Pericles, still in his early 30s, inherited the democratic leadership.

In democratic Athens, matters of religion, public festivals, finances, inheritance, ostracism, office, and all issues of foreign policy were decided by a popular assembly, the Ecclesia. There was no restriction on speech in the assembly. Here citizens met to try and persuade each other to vote on decrees that affected both private individuals and public life.

A simple majority decided an issue, and voting was mostly conducted by show of hands, sometimes by secret ballot.

The meeting drew at least 6000 of 30 000 eligible citizens (the number necessary for a quorum), and the assembly convened 40 times a year. The Boule was council of 500 citizens who were selected by lot, and they set the agenda for the assembly to vote on. The meeting was called to order by a lotteried president chosen on that day; he announced (through a herald) the first item on the agenda. After reading it, the president asked, "Who of the Athenians has advice to give? " (Ober, 1993, p. 483). As the herald's identity remained unknown prior to the meeting, no person could control the items on the agenda once debate began. Leaders relied strictly on their ability to sway public opinion.

Once ordinary matters were settled, the assembly debated controversial issues. Given the range of concerns, both public and private, discussed in the assembly, each citizen had the freedom to speak his mind, but speakers did not face a calm and welcoming environment. They could be met with *thorubus* (clamor or tumult), which signaled disapproval. It also acted as an informal mechanism to sanction members who seemed to lack proper qualifications to give an opinion on a given matter. Likewise, the constant banter, tumult, and shouting down of speakers deterred many from ever talking at all.

The chief and most prominent elected officials in Athens were the strategoi, ten generals serving one-year terms with no limit on reelection, who commanded the army and navy. The office did not carry formal powers, and when Pericles initiated policy in the assembly, he did so as a citizen. Unlike the demos-led assembly where he needed to be a leader of the people, "old attitudes may have lingered with regard to military affairs, and a general may have been elected (like Cimon on his return from ostracism) because their aristocratic birth was taken as a sign of their ability to lead" (Fornara and Samons, 1991, p. 33).

When acting as a general, Pericles was charged with military and diplomatic affairs. He was also scrutinized for each decision he made since the generals were subject to a yearly review, prosecution, impeachment, fines, exile, and even death. This position lent authority to Pericles, but the assembly is where his real power arose (1991, p. 31). Pericles was held in esteem by the people, and his overwhelming rhetorical skills gave him an advantage over them. Thucydides' Pericles says that he was "second to no man in knowledge of the proper policy, or in the ability to expound on it, and who is moreover not only a patriot but an honest one" (2.65.5). Pericles was conscious of his commendable qualities. What I find of special importance is his awareness that he could make his knowledge clear in exposition.

Pericles knew things about policy that most citizens did not. Thus, when they accepted his advice, they were being influenced in a Periclean manner. Pericles might expound on what he knew, but this does not mean that the demos could retain knowledge and, consequently, articulate it on its own. Pericles' rationalism was lost on the demos. Comprehending this, he affected and used the passions of demos to lead them, "making that use of hopes and fears, as his two chief rudders" (Plutarch, 2001, p. 215). As a master of political psychology, he could move the demos over to his position, and, as Thucydides says, "whenever he saw them unseasonably elated, he would with a word reduce them to alarm; on the other hand, if they fell victims to a panic, he could at once restore them to confidence" (2.65.9).

Pericles' rank, integrity, and power of persuasion ran so deep that he led the people instead of being led by them (2.65.8). Thucydides' claim is proven by Pericles' success in making the Athenians submit to a painful strategy of restraint during the war. From Plato's perspective, Pericles' absolute rule over the democracy was not praiseworthy because the democracy was imperfect. He tried to graft this form of self-discipline onto the democracy, but he never sought to make the citizens moderate. For Plato, Pericles' leadership did little to chasten the imperial democracy's desires, and he used his rhetoric to flatter the many. In Plato's *Gorgias*, the character of Socrates articulates the moral consequences of Pericles' statesmanship. In a response to a question by Callicles, Socrates says:

> Nothing but if the Athenians are said to have become better because of Pericles, or, quite the opposite, to have been corrupted by him. For I at any rate hear these things, that Pericles made the Athenians lazy, cowardly, babbling, and money lovers, when he first brought them into the state as mercenaries. (translated 1998, 515e)

As one of ten annually elected generals, Pericles was given the post 16 times. Owing to his unparalleled status and success in Athenian politics, Thucydides introduces him as "the first man of his time at Athens, ablest alike in counsel and in action" (1.139). During his political career, Pericles supported Athens' democracy, never usurped power, and was incorruptible. Was Pericles, who advocated the democracy's expansion – which for Plato and Aristotle, was the root of Athens' corruption – committed to the rule of popular sovereignty as Kagan argues?

Thucydides makes us ponder this question when he announces that on account of Pericles' authority, Athens was a democracy in name only and effectively the rule of one man (2.65). To better understand this statement, I now discuss Pericles' particular transformative ambition and its influence on Athens' domestic and international affairs.

NOTES

1. These are the reasons that the Athenian ambassadors to Sparta give at a Spartan assembly for Athens' acquisition and expansion of the empire.
2. Pericles addresses women at the end of the speech, specifically the newly widowed of the fallen men: "great will be your glory in not falling short of your natural character, and greatest will be hers who is least talked of among the men whether for good or for bad" (2.45.2).
3. Aristotle provides more background on events surrounding the Alcmaeonidae: "the Alcmaeonids were tried, on the prosecution of Myron, by jurymen solemnly sworn in, selected according to noble birth. The charge of sacrilege having been confirmed by the verdict, the bodies of the guilty men themselves were cast out of their tombs, and their family was sentenced to everlasting banishment. Thereupon Epimenides of Crete purified the city" (*Athenian Constitution*, 1935 [1992]

7. Pericles' transformative ambition (2): democracy, empire, and the Peloponnesian War

> Far from needing a Homer for our eulogist, or other of his craft whose verses might charm for the moment only for the impression which they gave to melt at the touch of fact, we have forced every sea and land to be the highway of our daring, and everywhere, whether for evil or for good, have left imperishable monuments behind us.
>
> **Thucydides**, *Pericles' Funeral Oration*

The Athenian and Spartan regimes shaped the character of their leadership; "the laws, the constitution, the mores, and way of life – fostered certain character traits to the exclusion of others" (Newell, 2009, p. 227). Athens promoted the rise of bold leaders who made foreign policy gambles, which more often than not helped expand the empire. Sparta's constitution produced moderate leaders who had an aversion to far-flung expeditions. They were reluctant to wage protracted military campaigns because Sparta feared a Helot uprising and the corruption of its generals.

In Athens it was common for individuals to gain prominence and establish a consistent program over many years. Before Pericles, some notable Athenians made great political strides. Themistocles laid the empire's foundation by persuading the Athenians to shift their military power to the navy. Ephialtes initiated the radical democratic reforms that Pericles fulfilled. Cimon won major battles against Persia; he diminished the Persian threat and heralded an era of magnificent civic benefaction. Yet as a visionary leader, Pericles surpassed them all (Hale, 2009, p. 126).

Pericles' tenure as a general was longer than any other Athenian. Unlike election to the advisory council (the Boule) and juries, the position of *strategos* had no term limits. As the authors of the strategic perspective observe, the ranks of the *strategos* grew in the fifth century and helped mitigated the perverse incentives created by term limits in the council (Mesquita et al., 2003, p. 318). The *strategoi's* political survival was coupled to policy performance. From this perspective, because Pericles faced yearly reelection and review, he had an incentive to shift his attention to effective public policy. Although Pericles practiced his share of political calculus, his ambition is not reducible to the desire to remain a strategos for the sake of retaining power. Instead, it lay in substantially reforming democratic Athens and reorganizing the empire to draw on its vast resources for the city's purposes.

Pericles' rise to power, in the decade 460–450 BC, was coeval with the implementation of *misthos*, state payment for public service. This disbursement gave poorer citizens a say in the city's affairs; their responsibility for Athens' naval power was now being represented in their share of the city's power. When Cimon returned from ostracism in 452 BC, his power had been supplanted through this political victory of the common people over the upper class.

Thanks to Pericles, the poor were paid to attend the assembly, and, as Aristotle observes, public pay meant that all citizens took part and exercised their citizenship because the poor enjoyed leisure by receiving pay (*Politics*, 1292b41). For Aristotle, Pericles' measures produced a public bad because the needy, not the laws, controlled political affairs. As a result, the desire for money replaced civic virtue as the requirement for political participation:

> The wickedness of human beings is insatiable. So to begin with an allowance of only two obols is enough, but as soon as this practice has become an ancestral tradition, the demand is always made for more, and so it goes on without limit. For it is the nature of desire to have no limit, and satisfying desire is what the many live for.[1] (Aristotle, trans. 1997, 1267b1–4)

Pericles' most radical measure instituted jury payment. Aristotle explains the reason behind this policy: "Pericles first made service in the jury courts a paid office, as a popular counter-measure against Cimon's wealth" (Aristotle, 1935 [1992], 27.2). Jury payment marked the turning point that brought city affairs into a radical new balance.

Pericles' domestic policies were predicated on a deliberate decision to rely on the permanent availability of imperial revenue. Aristotle, who disapproved of the dependence on payment for civic participation, described how Athens' public funds were divvied up at the height of the empire.

> They also established a plentiful food supply for the multitude, as Aristeides had proposed; for the combined proceeds of the tributes and the taxes of the allies served to feed more than twenty thousand men. For there were six thousand jurymen, one thousand six hundred archers and also one thousand two hundred cavalry, five hundred members of the Council, five hundred guardians of the docks, and also fifty watchmen in the city, as many as seven hundred officials at home and as many as seven hundred abroad; and in addition to these, when later they settled into the war, two thousand five hundred hoplites, twenty guard-ships and other ships conveying the guards to the number of two hundred elected by lot; and furthermore the prytaneum, orphans, and warders of prisoners – for all of these had their maintenance from public funds. (Aristotle, 1935 [1992], 24.3)

The decision was truly epochal. The state treasury was opened up to the community at large, and the possession of Athenian citizenship entitled its holder to payment for public service. Judicial and legislative matters would be entrusted to persons without education, qualification, or, "indeed even the serious expenditure of mental or physical energy – unless vicarious participation in oratorical display" (cf. *Plato Republic*, 1968 [1991], 492b; Fornara and Samons, 1991, p. 67).

The new and expanding empire brought unprecedented wealth to Athens. In 431 BC, Athens had an annual income of 1000 talents, of which 400 came from internal revenue and 600 from tribute; and it had 6000 talents of coined silver in the treasury (Kagan, 1991, p. 232). According to some sources, at one point there may once have been as much as 9700 talents in the treasury (Rhodes, 1986, p. 91). What was the value of this currency? Pericles set up a peacetime routine for the navy that launched 60 triremes each spring. One talent was the amount of silver needed to pay a trireme crew for one month, with tours of duty lasting eight months. The annual cost of Athens' peacetime navy of 60 ships was 480 talents (Hale, 2009, p. 127).

With Athens' largesse, Pericles spearheaded a massive building program. The Long Walls that connected Athens to the port of Piraeus were completed. Later, I will show how Pericles' strategic decisions during the war were contingent on the completion of a third Long Wall. In addition, the most famous architectural works were built on the Acropolis: the Parthenon, Erechtheion, Propylaea, and temple of Athena Nike. Pericles oversaw the conception and construction of many of these buildings and temples. Politically, the initiative functioned as a public works program. Laborers, architects, craftsman, traders, and merchants could be of service, and as a result, "it put the whole city, in a manner, into state pay" (Plutarch, 2001, p. 212).

Pericles supervised the construction of the Parthenon, the crown of the campaign. Built atop the Acropolis, it was "meant to achieve visually what the *Funeral Oration* aimed at orally: the depiction, explanation, and celebration of the Athenian imperial democracy" (Kagan, 1991, p. 161). The empire's steady stream of revenue became essential to individual well-being and inflamed the passion for continued imperial conquest. Pericles' policies were inducing a remarkable change in domestic ideology, one that was necessary to maintain Athens' empire.

PERICLES' TRANSFORMATION OF CITIZEN VIRTUE

Ancient Greek societies relied on civic-minded citizen virtue and piety. This virtue was essentially self-sacrifice and was lived out through a passionate attachment to the city. These small communities were constantly at war on account of existential uncertainty, jealousy, and the desire to affirm their supremacy. Thus, the core citizen virtue was martial courage in defense of the city. Courage was a necessary condition of being a true man, an *aner* or manly man; "a manly man is understood in contrast with a mere 'human being' (*anthropos*), the undistinguished mass of mankind, including women, children, slaves, and others who did not have the privilege of bearing arms" (Newell, 2003, p. 56).

Too much preoccupation with one's private life was enervating to a masculine spirit and was deemed base. Greek life, including war, had a competitive quality, and what was most admired was the heroic ethos of outstanding individuals. Greek men aspired to esteem and fame by showing their excellence through publicly recognized activities, like athletic contests. Furthermore, the battlefield provided the perfect arena for them to demonstrate their quality. Immortalized by Homer, Achilles is depicted as the peak of courage because he outshines all others and accepts death as a consequence in the pursuit of immortal fame. Virtue entails action, and the enterprising man is esteemed (Balot, 2001). Although courage was essential for the survival of the polis, it also tended to provoke an unrestrained love of glory. The irony is that excessive courage was also a danger to the political community. Spurred by men's desire for achievement and great honors, the polis was prone to excessive belligerence.

Pericles was born into a Greek culture that was deeply rooted in the agonistic view of nature and social relations. The desire for individual glory was ingrained in the habits and imagination of the Athenian citizen. The city's most ambitious leaders attested this desire's possibilities. Pericles, this model's paragon, actually sought to reduce the rarity of individual achievement and moderate its more zealous expressions. He understood that Athens' unique blend of democracy, empire, wealth, and extraordinary military, political, and cultural achievement stirred a passion for individual freedom among citizens, something unknown in the Greek world. He recognized both the virtue and danger in this particular kind of Athenian individualism. As a result, Pericles tried to direct the Athenians to attain a standard of virtue that did justice to their individualism but also fulfilled the expectation of public service. His shaping of the Athenian moral sense is given full expression in the most famous passage of Thucydides' (1996) *History*: *Pericles' Funeral Oration*.

Chronologically, the speech postdates the outbreak of the war, but I discuss it first because it is the clearest exposition of Pericles' transformative ambition. Pericles was chosen to give the *Funeral Oration* a year after the war's start to honor the first Athenian casualties. Although no great battle or momentous shift had occurred, it was a critical speech because it justified that the continued suffering was necessary, especially because Pericles had submitted the Athenians to a painful defensive strategy that allowed the Spartans to lay waste to Attica.

In his praise of Athenian courage, Pericles disavows Sparta's fabricated brand of this virtue. Spartan courage requires a systematic regimen of painful discipline at home and the exclusion of foreign influences (2.39.1). The Athenian version is something that Pericles thinks constitutes a broader characteristic, "the native spirit of [the] citizens" (2.39.1). The Athenians profit from freedom that flows from government to ordinary life, ease in private relations, the relaxation of the mind through games and festivals, and the enjoyment of pleasure (2.37–38). Although they live as they please, it is thanks to their spirit that the Athenians are still willing to encounter danger (2.39.4). What is important to note about Pericles' understanding of Athenian courage is that its basis is Athenian individualism, and he does not mention that it serves the common good, the reason why the Spartans subject themselves to such painful discipline.

Although courage is an impulse that the Athenians seem drawn to, Pericles devotes this speech toward encouraging bravery in war. Perhaps he deprecates Spartan self-sacrifice because traditional courage demands that one risk one's life for the interest of something other than oneself. The Spartans were ready to sacrifice for the city, while the Athenians were willing to encounter danger. But their zeal to do so is not as clear as the reason the Spartans face danger. Therefore the discussion of courage proves a tricky subject because Pericles has appealed to the Athenians' self-interest before notions of sacrifice and nobility.

Pericles abstracts further from traditional virtue by identifying the primary characteristics of the Athenian spirit: daring, and deliberation (2.40.3). The first defines the native ethos. While a singularly Athenian characteristic, it is also an expression of human nature that is unbridled by traditional restraints on behavior. Daring differs from courage because it has no extremes – courage is flanked by its vices, brashness and cowardice. Yet, Pericles does not say that the Athenians can have too much daring. There are no inhibitions placed on the Athenian spirit.

Pericles inspires the Athenians by praising the bold national character rather than the accomplishments of any single citizen. Moreover, he does not appeal to Homeric ideals, but, rather, invokes concrete proofs of Athenian power (2.41.4). The Athenians do not need to imitate Achilles as they force land and sea "to be the highway of their daring" (2.41.4). They have proven their versatility to others; they have smashed any conception of the limits of human power. Athens is the real teacher of human nature, which leads Pericles to say, "as a city we are the school of Hellas" (2.41). As a model city, Athens gets all the glory, and the eulogized Athenians fought nobly and died for the city's honor (2.41.5). On mentioning the dead soldiers' ambition for glory, Pericles first explicitly calls on surviving Athenians to be ready to suffer for the cause (2.41.5).

Thus, Pericles does not plead for the mere defense of the city; rather, he exhorts citizens to live up to their spirit for glory awaits them. Yet, his rhetorical move reveals a tension built into Athenian political culture. Athenian daring is a phenomenon that other Greeks can marvel at or fear. It created the empire and its subsequent greatness. Pericles thinks that Athens' excellence is noble and worth fighting for; he makes no mention of survival, as if such a pedestrian concern has no place in war. However, the neglect of survival points to Pericles' inability to ask the citizens to come to the city's common defense because the traditional bonds of Greek morality no longer hold it together.

Daring comes naturally to the Athenians, but the defense of the city does not. Why would Pericles go to such great lengths to promote the latter by emphasizing the former? The answer involves his transformative project both at the level of political psychology and in its practical dimension. Pericles has subjected the populace to an inglorious war strategy and must keep the people to it for as long as possible. I address this second issue later in the chapter.

Pericles' transformation ambition involves a moral balancing act that seeks to persuade the Athenians to evaluate their individual interests in light of that of the city. However, this evaluation does not "pivot on a norm of reciprocity between individuals and the city" (Monoson and Loriaux, 1998). A reciprocal relation depends on an individual's calculation about what he will receive for giving in turn. Athens provides citizens with a life where they can flourish as individuals. Indeed, it creates individuals. Yet, if one has to die for it, what good is Athens to the individual? Pericles must promise something that is not encapsulated by all the earthly goods Athens bestows. It must be greater than life itself and animate citizens' deepest passions. As Orwin argues, Pericles does not present the choice to risk one's life for Athens as rational (1994, p. 26).

Athenians can only reach their peak as individuals by exercising their daring, which effectively supports the city's imperial majesty. Pericles asks the citizens to bask in the greatness of this collective production. The exalted glory of the city is worth the risk of one's life because it is the only action that can confer immortality on the average citizen. The city's honor is superior to that of the individual because it alone endows ageless fame. The problem that Pericles faces, though, is that his appeal is to individuals who hunger for acclaim and are not necessarily interested in sharing it (Forde, 1986, p. 440).

Thus, his second and more unconventional appeal is to citizens' erotic attachments: "[y]ou must realize the power of Athens, and feed your eyes on her from day to day, till love of her fills your hearts; and then when all her greatness shall break upon you, you must reflect that it was by courage, sense of duty, and a keen feeling of honor in actions that men were enabled to win all this" (2.43.1). A love for one's country is a common sentiment, but Pericles makes a very unusual call to patriotism. Unlike the Spartan's self-abnegating, dutiful patriotism, an Athenian's passionate and selfish attachment to the city is the path toward patriotism. As Forde (1986) observes, "Erotic passion is individualistic, even egoistic, yet leads to the most intense devotion and willingness to sacrifice" (p. 439). This odd appeal shows just how distanced Athens' mores were from traditional Greek morality. One must imagine that Pericles either had a theoretical or intuitive sense of this new reality, and his rhetorical strategy hinges on interweaving Athenian self-interests and passions with a novel conception of the city.

In order to transform traditional self-sacrifice into the Periclean form, a fundamentally new way of thinking about the relationship between citizen and the polis had to emerge. The *Funeral Oration* does not imply a particular policy as much as a unique political understanding – what I have referred to throughout this chapter as Pericles' transformative ambition.

This speech reveals the consequential circumstances under which Pericles exercised leadership at the beginning of the war. Athens was at the peak of its political power, yet Pericles did not acknowledge that for Athens what still was at stake in the war is the perennial problem of power politics and basic survival. Instead, he sensed that domestic necessity was a greater issue, which is why he must urge his people to fight for Athens' exceptionality and the extraordinary character of its imperial rule.

Athens' unparalleled power helped Pericles gloss over its political abuses and heavy-handed approach toward its allies. For Pericles, Athens' singularity made it immune to the charges that it was acting unjustly toward its allies. Yet, Pericles reveals himself as a consummate imperialist: "we have forced every sea and land to be the highway of our daring, and everywhere whether for evil or good, have left imperishable monuments behind us" (2.41). I now examine Pericles' career at the international level through his contribution to the empire's growth, role in the run up to the war, and wartime strategy.

MANAGING THE EMPIRE: THE DELIAN LEAGUE AND IMPERIAL EXPANSION

The Delian League was formed in 478 BC, in the aftermath of the Persian wars. Headed by the Ionians, a voluntary coalition of Greek city-states requested that Athens become its leader after Pausanias' Spartan leadership became harsh and unpopular. Athens accepted this request, but self-interest figured into its calculations:

> These resorted to the Athenians and requested them as kinsmen to become their leaders, and to stop any attempt at violence on the part of Pausanias. The Athenians accepted their overtures, and determined to put down any attempt of the kind and to settle everything else as their interest might seem to demand. (1.95.2)

In 478 BC the allies met at Delos and agreed that the league would function to avenge Greek suffering by ravaging Persian territory, liberate

Greeks still under Persian rule, and swear to have the same friends and enemies. Three factors contributed to the league's founding: Greek cities in need of security against Persian ambitions, Sparta's conservative retrenchment, and Athens' greater political and commercial ambitions. Initially, the Athenians commanded autonomous allies, and the league's decisions were made in general congresses (1.96.2).

Between the conclusion of the Persian wars and the Peloponnesian War, Athens' power grew through successful military campaigns against Persia, against its allies in revolt, and against the Peloponnesians whom they encountered on many occasions (1.97). Athens' successes led to its problems with the allies. As the Persian threat receded, the allies were less compelled to support Athens' role as the policeman of the Aegean. As they became uneasy with Athenian leadership, Athens tightened its control over the league because the navy-intensive group was costly and demanded "a well-organized system for regular payments into the league treasury" (Kagan, 1969, p. 43). Only Chios and Lesbos contributed ships.

Pericles presided over the transition from league leader to imperial ruler, which conflicted with the identity of the free-ruling *polis*. By the Peloponnesian War, the Greek world saw Athens as an arrogant and aggressive city. The Peloponnesians' stated aim was to liberate Greece, restoring freedom to subjugated cities, and only a destruction of the Athenian Empire could accomplished this goal. Thucydides discusses how three critical foreign policies that were carried out during 476–467 BC show when Athens' imperial ambition took root.[2]

First, in 471 BC, Athens set a fundamental precedent when Naxos tried to leave the alliance: "it was the first instance of the confederation being forced to subjugate an allied city, a precedent which was followed by that of the rest in the order which circumstances prescribed" (1.98.4). Thereafter, Thasos' revolt in 465 BC was countered swiftly by Athens. Subdued rebellions also gave Athens the occasion to intervene in her allies' internal affairs. When a city's oligarchs had stoked an insurrection, Athens would supplant them and bring a democratic faction into power.

Second, under Cimon's command, the alliance won battles against Persia on land and at sea at Eurymedon in 469 BC. The Persian navy's defeat was so great that it no longer posed a threat in the Aegean. The league's focus then became the maintenance of the Athenian Empire, but more defection followed. The Thasians revolted, and Athens' besiegement of Thasos took over three years. In response to the uprising,

Athens sent 10 000 settlers from its own citizens and its allies to settle Ennea Hodoi (Amphipolis), which was opposite the coast of Thasos. The Thasians regarded the settlement as an act of hostility (1.100.3).

During the siege the Thasians turned to Sparta, which promised Thasos help. Unbeknownst to Athens, Sparta intended to invade Attica but was held back by a Helot revolt (101.1–2). The souring of relations between Athens and Sparta was occasioned by the Helot conflict when, in 462, the Athenians answered a Spartan call to aid them in a siege but were shockingly turned away soon after their arrival. This event had major political repercussions in Athens, which broke off its alliance with Sparta (the Hellenic alliance against Persia), laying the ground for Cimon's ostracism and the rise of the faction of Ephialtes and Pericles.

Soon after Pericles assumed power over the democratic faction, the Athenians committed to a major expedition in Egypt. Thucydides does not tell us who was responsible for the campaign. Although Pericles was not the author of the policy, it was in this critical moment for the empire that his real experience with foreign policy began. The conflict with the Peloponnesian cities was underway, and Athens was projecting its power in a high-risk expedition. After supporting an Egyptian rebellion against Persia for seven years, in 454 BC the Persian king sent a large army against Athens and the rebels. Athens lost at a terrible cost (40 ships and 8000 men), which also marked its first loss against the Persians.

Pericles embarked on a new imperial policy when in 454 BC he changed the Delian League's organization, moving the treasury from Delos to the Acropolis in Athens. The Conservative Party, now led by Thucydides, mounted a challenge. Pericles' new direction violated traditional religion and morality. The charge against Pericles took aim at his decision to transfer the treasury and the building campaign:

> Greece cannot but resent it as an insufferable affront, and consider herself to be tyrannized over openly, when she sees the treasure, which was contributed by her upon a necessity for war, wantonly lavished out by us upon our city, to gild her all over, and to adorn and set her forth, as it were some vain woman. (Plutarch, 2001, p. 211)

Pericles defended himself from the implied accusation that he was becoming a tyrant. He defended his policy by not apologizing at all. In Plutarch's explanation, as long as Athens successfully defended the Greeks against Persia, the citizens could decide their foreign policy in any way they pleased:

> They did not so much as supply one horse, man, or ship, but only found money for the service; which money, said [Pericles], is not theirs that give it, but theirs that receive it, if so be they perform the conditions upon which they receive it. And that it was good reason, that, now the city was sufficiently provided and stored with all things necessary for war, they should convert the overplus of its wealth to such undertaking as hereafter, when completed, give them eternal honour, and, for the present, while in process, freely supply all the inhabitants with plenty. (Plutarch, 2001, p. 211)

Pericles rebuffed the charges of moral impropriety and the abuse of imperial funds as he reminded people of the benefits they derived from the empire. His policies prevailed. In 443 BC, when he finally could secure adequate political backing, he called for Thucydides' ostracism. He succeeded, and secure in his policies without a considerable political figure to oppose him, he turned to consolidating the empire.

Athens had made sufficient progress against the Persian threat and sought peace with the enemy. Achieved in 449 BC, the Peace of Callias formally recognized the end of the war between Athens and Persia. It was in Pericles' interest to decrease the city's commitments against Persia, but the formal peace "eliminated the rationale for the Delian League and raised the question whether the alliance should be abandoned" (Fornara and Samons, 1991, p. 78).

The repercussions were immediate and dangerous for the empire as major allies began to revolt. Evidence of this can be found in the Athenians' tribute lists. In 447 BC, 171 cities are listed, and the following year shows only 156 (Kagan, 1969, p. 148). Pericles confronted the greatest foreign-policy test of his career to date as the sinews of Athens' power, the allied tribute, lay in the balance. He swiftly countered the major uprisings, personally directing the subjugation of Euboea and Megara in 446 BC. The problem was compounded when the Peloponnesian league took the rebellions as an opportunity to strike a blow against Athens. As Athenian forces were subduing multiple conflicts, the Peloponnesian army marched into Attica. This was an emergency of first order. Thucydides describes the events:

> Pericles had already crossed over with any army of Athenians to the island (Euboea), when news was brought to him that Megara had revolted, that the Peloponnesians were on the point of invading Attica, and that the Athenian garrison had been cut off by the Megarians … Meanwhile Pericles brought his army back in all haste from Euboea. After this the Peloponnesians, under the command of King Pleistonax son of Pausanias, marched into Attica as far as Eleusis and Thria, ravaging the country and without advancing further

returned home. The Athenians then crossed over again to Euboea under the command of Pericles, and subdued the whole of the island. While they settled all the rest of the island by means of agreed terms, they expelled the people of Histiaea and occupied the territories themselves. (1.114)

Pericles brought his army back from Euboea to meet the invading forces, but the Peloponnesians returned home without a fight, supposedly after Pericles bribed the Spartan King Pleistonax. No strong evidence supports this allegation, however. An important point about this episode is that Pericles was not willing to wage a war against Sparta in 446 BC. What changed to make him urge the Athenians to war in 431 BC?

In 446 BC, Pericles took his army to meet the invading Spartans. A conventional hoplite battle would have ensued, which the Peloponnesians were bound to win. Yet, by 431 BC the situation had changed. The threat of multiple allied revolts had faded, and Pericles was held in such esteem that he could direct policy unimpeded. He could fight the war against Sparta by using an unorthodox defensive strategy that principally relied on the strength of the navy and Athenian wealth.

PERICLES' SPARTA POLICY

In 445 BC, after Pericles successfully warded off a major military showdown with the Peloponnesians, Athens and Sparta agreed to a truce, which led to the negotiation of the Thirty Years' Peace. The treaty ended the first Peloponnesian War, and the peace lasted 14 years. The treaty stipulated that Athens give up any claims to territory in the Peloponnese while the Spartans tacitly recognized its rival's empire. To prevent future wars, they agreed to observe certain protocols: allies from one league could not defect to another side (the cause of the conflict in 445 BC), neutral cities were free to become allies of either side, and each side would submit any future disagreement to arbitration. The arbitration clause was unconventional in Greek relations; Pericles was likely behind this diplomatic innovation.

What did Pericles hope to gain through this peace? Kagan (1969) argues that Pericles sought a lasting peace, as opposed to biding his time for the inevitable war. He argues that, much like Otto von Bismarck and Augustus, Pericles became satisfied with what he had acquired and turned to a moderate diplomacy. Although these three statesmen might share some similarities, Kagan does not provide a sound basis for the analogy. Pericles faced a different strategic situation from the other leaders. Athens had not really concluded a major war with Sparta. While Athens still vied for Greek supremacy, Sparta was wary of losing its hold over the Peloponnese.

Kagan (1969) thinks that Pericles shifted his imperial policies after a long learning period that included past setbacks in Coronea, a disastrous Egyptian expedition, the Megarian defection, the revolt of Euboea, and the invasion of Attica. After these experiences, Pericles' imperial ambition waned; he shifted his goal to preserving the empire and did not want to endanger it with further growth (pp. 191–2). However, Kagan supports this claim by citing Pericles' advice to the Athenians to not expand the empire during the war against Sparta (1.144). Kagan concludes that Pericles' wartime policy of restraint was the same at the time of the Thirty Years' Peace.

There is reason to doubt Kagan's conclusion. Pericles cautioned the Athenians to suppress their expansionist aims during war; yet, there is no evidence of counseling them to not enlarge the empire indefinitely. His advice during the war was based on the strategic situation. Thus, it is a distinct possibility that if a clear opportunity for growth presented itself, Pericles would not warn against it. Such opportunities are imaginable if Athens proved victorious in the war. While Pericles' ambition fostered Athenian daring, imperialism, and power, Spartan hegemony, which symbolized how a great power could limit its international ambition, was an obstacle to the perpetuation and the expansion of the Periclean project.

Next, I discuss the series of events starting in 433 BC that precipitated the Peloponnesian War, in which I argue that Pericles played an independent role in fashioning events including the beginning of the conflict in 431 BC. At critical junctures he made decisive diplomatic moves that brought the Athenians closer to war. Thucydides describes his exacting policies toward Sparta: "for being the most powerful man of his time, and the leading Athenian statesman, he opposed the Spartans in everything, and would have no concessions, but ever urged the Athenians to war" (1.127).

The war originated in a dispute between two smaller powers, Corinth and Corcyra, over control of Epidamnus, which was a small city in a faraway corner of the Greek world. Prior to the disagreement, Corinth and Corcyra were on bad terms. Corcyra was originally a Corinthian colony, but as Corcyra's strength grew, so did its independence and pride. It failed to pay the customary reverence to its mother country, and

the two cities became bitter rivals. The conflict over Epidamnus escalated, and the two cities went to war.

In 433 BC, Corcyra appealed to Athens for help in what was becoming a dangerous conflict for it to undertake alone. Corinth was building
a large fleet to counter Corcyra's, and while Corinth was Sparta's ally,
Corcyra was neutral. Both cities sent ambassadors to Athens to plead
their cases. The majority of the assembly preferred to stay out of the
dispute because Corcyra was not an ally and remote Epidamnus lay
outside Athens' strategic interests.

Thucydides tells us that the debate lasted two days, and on the first
day, public opinion was disposed to reject Corcyra's plea. However, the
debate was not resolved, and the vote was postponed for the next day (a
delay on a vote was extremely rare). On the second day, public opinion
had shifted to intervention (1.44). Pericles and his associates had made
a case for the strategic worth in coming to Corcyra's aid in what they
were building up to be an inevitable war with Sparta.

Among the diplomatic hurdles to this measure, Corinth was in the
Peloponnesian League and Corcyra was a neutral state. The Corinthian
ambassadors had argued that Athenian intervention on Corcyra's behalf,
with the conflict underway, violated the Thirty Years' Peace. Although
Athens risked war with Sparta, it did not want to see Corcyra's fleet lost
to Corinth. A Corinthian victory at sea would embolden that city and
threaten Athens' command of the waters. Athens accepted the danger
since its attitude about the possibilities for a long peace with Sparta had
dimmed, while its expansionist ambitions had not:

> For it began to be felt that the coming of the Peloponnesian War was only a
> question of time, and no one was willing to see a naval power of such magni-
> tude as Corcyra sacrificed to Corinth; though if they could let them weaken
> each other by mutual conflict, it would be no bad preparation for the strug-
> gle which Athens might one day have to wage with Corinth and the other
> naval powers. At the same time the island seemed to lie conveniently on the
> coasting passage to Italy and Sicily. (1.44)

To avoid open war, however, Athens did not make a traditional alliance,
a fully offensive and defensive one, with Corcyra. Making such an
alliance would have been tantamount to declaring war on one of Sparta's
allies. Instead, the Athenians crafted an innovative defensive alliance
with Corcyra (one with no historical precedent). Pericles played a hand
in shifting public opinion to his view and designing the less provocative
alliance. It is very likely that without Pericles the Athenians would have

rejected the Corcyrean appeal for assistance, a fateful decision that put Athens and Sparta on the path to war.

The cautious Athenians only sent Corcyra ten ships (and three *strategoi*) to reinforce its fleet of 110. Yet, this small support still showed that Athens was serious about the alliance. Moreover, the mere sight of Athenian ships could act as a deterrent. Athens' generals were under strict instructions; "if they sailed to Corcyra and threatened a landing on her coast, or in any of her possessions, they were to do their utmost to prevent it" (1.45). The policy sought to hinder Corinth without fighting its military at sea because that would constitute the use of offensive force.

In the battle of Sybota in 433 BC, Corcyra and Corinth used primitive methods of trireme warfare and lacked discipline and tactical sense. As the battle wore on, the Athenians were drawn into the fight and began ramming Corinthian ships. However, they had waited too long and had to flee with the remaining Corcyrean vessels. Corinth then rowed out again, in attempt to strike a fatal blow to Corcyra's navy. Yet, in dramatic fashion Corinth retreated when a second fleet of Athenian ships approached over the horizon. It is likely that at the last minute, the assembly regretted its decision to send such few ships.

In the battle's aftermath, other cities were now embroiled with Athens. Megara had fought alongside Corinth, and Athens decided to punish it with a peacetime embargo against the city, which was another new policy. Again, this was most certainly one of Pericles' innovations since he fiercely defended it in the assembly. The Megarian Decree, as it is known, was also Pericles' most "striking, and in some ways most puzzling, measure" (Kagan, 2003, p. 207). Through the only peacetime embargo ever documented in the ancient world, Pericles showed Athenian resolve and the ability to punish cities in the Peloponnesian League.

Through the Megarian Decree, Pericles found another inventive way to skirt the application of offensive military force with another Spartan ally. Cut off from Athenian harbors, the embargo strangled the city's economy and offended the Megarians who now joined Corinth and a chorus of other aggrieved Greeks in an effort to make Sparta declare war against Athens.

What explains Pericles' alliance with Corcyra and his unpopular decision to bar Megara from Athenian harbors? A realist would argue that Pericles' decisions were imposed on him by the strategic reality of the inevitable war, which narrowed his choices. Thus, under situational pressures, Pericles would have perceived that he had limited options. I have argued, though, that the Athenians were not eager to ally with Corcyra until Pericles persuaded them otherwise. The Megarian Decree further stoked anti-Athenian sentiment. Pericles did not rescind the decree even as Spartan ambassadors promised that war would be avoided if Athens did so (1.139). In fact, he had a great deal of latitude and could determine Athens' strategic behavior. Unlike any other leader in Athens and Sparta – the Spartans had ignored King Archidamus' advice – Pericles shows that he could steer opinion to his position despite considerable opposition.

A realist could reply that Pericles' calculations were based on the balance of power. He was prescient about the reality of the looming war while lesser figures were merely fretful about the costs of war. Pericles, however, had a plan to fight Sparta, which was arguably designed free from situational pressures. Pericles took the long view. He scrupulously observed the Thirty Years' Peace but then decisively shifted to a hawkish posture toward the Spartans. This behavior points to his coolly rational, strategic understanding of international relations. He could prescribe restraint or aggression when necessary.

However, Pericles' transformative ambitions figured into his strategic decisions. The continued success of his domestic and imperial policies was undergirded by the requisite shift in the Greek balance of power to Athens. Pericles' realism was in service of his ambition. His transformative ambition, which is transmitted with rhetorical flourish in the *Funeral Oration*, fostered his city's daring character and brought it to its peak. However, for other states, the consequence of this national greatness is that they must contend with a restless, innovative, aggressive, and revolutionary regime. Next, I examine how the Athenians justified their behavior to other Greeks by appealing to contrary arguments: a rationalistic amoral foreign policy versus their rank superiority over others, which I compare with Pericles' position regarding the moral status of the empire.

ATHENIAN AND PERICLEAN REALISM: THE DEBATE AT SPARTA

Soon after the battle at Sybota, the Athenians and Corinthians fought again at Potidaea after the latter persuaded this city to rebel against Athens. The incident in distant Epidamnus had escalated, and conflict was reverberating throughout the Greek world, unsettling allies in both blocs. Whereas fear and anger against Athens was at a high, Sparta's credibility as the leader of the Peloponnesian League was being questioned. Although Sparta controlled the league's foreign policy, her poverty made her susceptible to Corinth's ascending ambitions. That city was wealthy and could equip a fleet of 100 triremes. In 432 BC the Spartans convened a congress in which her allies as well anyone who had a complaint against Athens gave voice to their grievances. Athenian envoys, who purportedly were in the city on some other business, attended and spoke at the debate. In contrast to Pericles' elevated defense of the Athenian way of life in the *Funeral Oration*, the Athenian speech frankly admits the city's pursuit of its self-interest in international relations, regardless of what justice demands (Pangle and Ahrensdorf, 1999).

The Athenians justified their dual pursuit of security and glory at the expense of justice in two opposing ways. The envoys did not bother to address grievances levied against Athens. Instead, they issued blunt amoral arguments such as that Athens, like all other states, was merely compelled to follow its interests. Acting in one's favor is a natural truth that is played out in practice. The creation and perpetuation of the empire are products of human impulses that are beyond the individual's control and lie outside the power of justice. States also feel these compelling pressures and act on them; they are "fear, honor, and interest" (Thucydides, 1.76). Athens may be a mighty empire, but its fear is identical to that of others. Self-interest is characterized by compulsion. The root of interest is psychological necessity that perceives that the world is circumscribed by necessity. The identification of the latter confirms that necessity and moral choice are irreconcilables in international relations.

However, the Athenians' amoral thesis about necessity was betrayed by their insistence that they, who were the more realistic of nations, do not fully succumb to such needs. The envoys' seeming candor that they were caught, like all others, in the necessities of the human condition was belied by their belief in Athenian exceptionality. The city carried itself in such a way that she was worthy of her position (1.76.2). The envoys argue that they did not transcend human nature but still showed a modicum of moderation: "praise is due to all who, if not so superior to human nature as to refuse dominion, yet respect justice more than their position compels them to do" (1.76). The envoys failed to communicate how they were capable of even a minimum of justice when they are convinced that a realistic order admits no moral choice.

Yet the Athenians' slippage from an amoral argument into one that demonstrates their superior values and willful exercise of them reveals that the logic of necessity is strained by another psychological compulsion that the envoys are unaware of, the belief that one's actions merit rewards or punishments. The Athenians want it both ways, impunity from moral wrongs committed on account of fear, honor, and interest, and praise for the restraint they show for reasons not linked to the former motives. However, as Ahrensdorf (1997) suggests, the Athenian position is unreasonable insofar as an appeal to amorality is inconsistent with one to nobility.

> A realist nation must never blame itself for acting unjustly, ignobly, or impiously in its pursuit of what it thinks is in its best interest, for it cannot reasonably expect itself to rise above or transcend its concern for its self-interest in any way (see 2.63.2–3; cf. 3.44–45 with 40.4). Therefore such a realist nation must never believe that it is morally superior in any way to any other nation. It must forswear the belief that it deserves rewards or benefits of any kind by virtue of its noble or just superiority to self-interest. It must deny itself the pleasure of believing that it is in any way a noble or just or holy nation. (p. 252)

The Athenians' disparagement of tradition and justice as well as the belief in their noble singularity concur with Pericles' thesis in the *Funeral Oration*. However, Pericles never admits that he believes in the envoys' amoralism; he was likely aware of such an idea though. As such, Pericles' thought tries to reconcile the inconsistent positions. He secularized nobility, and the Athenian project's worth was verified by the ground of its accomplishments. He does not admit to the amoral character of international relations but believes that Athens' noble purposes are shackled by conventional morality. Its moral superiority is witnessed through its ambition and the deeds of the daring Athenians. Pericles suggests that the Athenian citizen is part of an exceptional breed, an individual who has improved on mankind's pedestrian expressions of human nature (2.40). However, his inconsistency is revealed in his belief that Athens' moral greatness, which is proved by the power of the state, is so noble that it merits a transcendent gift, eternal fame for all individuals who die for the city (2.43.2). Even Pericles, who circumscribes the noble to earthly actions and power, succumbed to the moral hopes that he dismisses, a transcendent (divine) assurance that one's worth is justified.

After the contending parties spoke, the Spartan leadership deliberated on the issue. King Archidamus feared a protracted engagement with no clear outcome. Although he did not rule out war with Athens, he cautioned the Spartans not to declare war hastily. Archidamus proved prescient about the Athenians' resolve and the war's length. However, his advice was ignored. The aggrieved allies and the shocking candor of the Athenians inflamed the passions of Sparta's hawkish faction, which are summed up well by the Spartan ephor Sthenelaidas' rallying cry for war: "Vote therefore, Spartans, for war, as the honor of Sparta demands, and neither allow the further aggrandizement of Athens, nor betray our allies to ruin, but with the gods let us advance against the aggressors" (1.86). The majority voted that Athens had broken the treaty, and they declared war on Athens.

PERICLES' WAR STRATEGY

After the declaration of war, cooler tempers prevailed in Sparta. Over the course of a year, it seemed to try and avoid war by sending envoys to Athens with various requests. When the Athenians refused to entertain the Spartan demands, they made a final proposal that Athens give independence back to the subject cities, and "they proclaimed publicly and in the clearest language that there would be no war if the Athenians withdrew the Megarian Decree" (1.139).

The Athenians held a decisive assembly regarding Sparta's demands. They were divided into two camps, those who urged for war and others who believed that the Megarian decree was pure folly (1.139.4). Pericles came forward and gave the definitive speech.

He refused concessions to the Spartans on principle because Sparta had failed to abide by the legalistic clause of the Thirty Years' Peace, which stipulated that cities submit disputes to arbitration. Thus, any concession to Sparta amounted to direct interference in Athens' political affairs. Pericles warned that this was a slippery basis for negotiations because if they accommodated Sparta on the "trifle" that was the Megarian Decree, they "will instantly have to meet some greater demand, as having been frightened into obedience in the first instance; while a firm refusal will make them clearly understand that they must treat [the Athenians] as equals" (1.140.5).

Pericles was willing to incur the costs of war in 431 BC but not in 445 BC. Both times he knew that the Peloponnesians would likely prevail in a traditional land war. What changed in Athens' favor was that he could now persuade the citizens to fight an unconventional war and also hold them to it long term. He planned a long war at sea that relied on Athens' projection of power and wealth and exploited the enemies' weakness, which was a lack of naval experience and unfamiliarity with a protracted engagement.

Conventional Greek warfare was short and brutal and ended decisively. The Greeks understood war as a human activity that exercised a citizen's virtue and fulfilled his duty. War reflected the Greek moral code, which was inextricably tied to a conception that conflict was at work in nature. The city waging war did not intend to annihilate its adversary or even seek to destroy its army; rather, the object of challenging another city to fight was to "force it to acknowledge its superior strength as the outcome of a test as rule-bound as a tournament" (Vernant, 1995, p. 38).

As an invading army made its way into enemy territory, it began to lay waste to the countryside. Courage, honor, and sheer necessity demanded that the defending city's army go out to secure its territory. The decisive battle was fought on chosen ground that would make it easier for each hoplite army to form phalanxes. The soldier ranks held closely together and created a mass wall of shields that made frontal assaults difficult. Opposing phalanxes would collide against each other with the aim of maintaining the cohesion of one's front line while breaking the enemy's formation. The courage of the men in the front ranks made all the difference.

The hoplite soldier was a free adult male of the *polis* who had enough wealth to procure his own arms and armor. Citizens across classes were hoplites, yet they did not constitute the majority of the population. Still, hoplites held political power and moral authority above the common people. Marching in the phalanx epitomized the civic nature of the Greek military experience. The citizen-soldier army was a microcosm of the political community, and fighting forces represented the agonal clash of cities. In battle, each hoplite depended on the man next to him for his protection where he lay exposed. Hoplites were armed with a nine-foot pike and short sword, and they carried shields in their left hands that were three feet in diameter. The shield protected the soldier's left half, but not the right so he needed his neighbor's shield where he lay exposed. This is why hoplites fought in tight formations, as each man tried to keep behind his neighbor's shield (Lazenby, 2004, p. 9). To hold the line and control the field were enough to claim victory over one's adversary. The more disciplined and well-trained army usually succeeded, and the Spartan *polis* was fully dedicated to fielding the best army.

In order to win the war, the Athenians could not engage the Peloponnesian army on land. Pericles told the Athenians that they had no chance in a conventional battle: "in a single battle the Peloponnesians and their allies may be able to defy all Hellas" (1.141.6). However, there was no other proven way to win a war against a land force. Thus, Pericles sought to exploit the military and resource differences between Sparta and Athens:

> As to the war and the resources of either party, a detailed comparison will not show the inferiority of Athens. Personally engaged in the cultivation of their land, without funds either private or public, the Peloponnesians are also without experience in long wars across the sea, from the strict limit which poverty imposes on their attacks upon each other. Powers of this description are quite incapable of often manning a fleet or often sending out an army: they cannot afford the absence from their homes, the expenditure of their own funds; and, besides, they have not command of the sea. (1.141)

Pericles devised a fully defensive strategy against Sparta. The Athenians would never go out to meet the invading Peloponnesians. He would test the enemy's will, hoping to convince it that conventional tactics were futile. Sparta might march into Attica every summer and devastate Athens' countryside, but as long as Athens controlled the sea, it was invincible. In his speech Pericles advises the Athenians that if they "would remain quiet, take care of their fleet, refrain from trying to extend their empire in wartime and thus putting their city in danger, they would prevail" (2.65.7).

Pericles' defensive strategy would dampen Spartan morale by making them tire of invading Attica without inflicting any real harm. Athens' best shot at winning was through the empire. It could afford to import all the food it needed while maintaining the fleet for several years. Kagan has estimated how long Pericles planned to hold out. Considering the costs to the naval fleet, money in the treasury, and yearly revenue and tribute, he believes that Pericles planned the war to last no more than three years. Pericles was likely expecting that Sparta would recall the campaigns.

This strategy used Athens' fortifications, military capabilities, and vast resources. Its naval fleet was the largest and best trained in the Greek world. Long walls encircled the city and connected it to the port of Piraeus, which made it invulnerable to attack. Pericles had built a financial reserve that could sustain the fleet and the city's inhabitants.

Although these resources were unique to Athens, there is no reason that they naturally led to Pericles' war strategy. Consistent with his transformative ambition, Pericles abandoned traditional attachments. His leadership aimed at redefining the polity's conception of itself in such a way that citizens would value empire more than their territory and realize that the perpetuating the empire was above any private loss

> Consider for a moment. Suppose we were islanders: can you conceive a more impregnable position? Well, this in future should, as far as possible, be our conception of our position. Dismissing all thought of our land and houses, we must vigilantly guard the sea and city. No irritation that we may feel for the former must provoke us to a battle with the numerical superiority of the Peloponnesians. A victory would only be succeeded by another battle against the same superiority: a reverse involves the loss of our allies, the source of our strength, who will not remain quiet a day after we become unable to march against them. We must not cry over the loss of the houses and land but of men's lives; since houses and land do not gain men, but men them. And if I had thought I could persuade you, I would have bid you go out and lay them waste with your own hands, and show the Peloponnesians that this at any rate will not make you submit. (1.143.5)

Although Athens was a cosmopolitan city, most people lived in the countryside and were not happy to abandon their homes. The idea of laying waste to their private possessions was unthinkable. Thucydides says, "[D]eep was their trouble and discontent at abandoning their houses and the hereditary temples of the ancient state, and at having to change their habits of life and to bid farewell to what each regarded as his native city" (2.16). Pericles' speech demonstrates that he was not attached to any traditional mores, and the city-dwelling masses and naval rowers certainly must have favored his strategy. I think that we are left to infer that, owing to Pericles' reputation, persuasion, a bit of cajoling, and the preponderance of resources he poured into the walled city, his policy passed and citizens evacuated the countryside.

Kagan (1991) and Josiah Ober (1996) have argued that Pericles' strategy was not only original but also completely rational. Abandoning homes and a defensive strategy were unorthodox methods so contrary to the ordinary passions and attachments of Athens' citizens that, for Pericles to discharge them, Kagan has said, "his greatness lay not only in conceiving the plan and implementing it decisively by yielding all of Attica instead of taking half measures, but, most of all, in being able to put the plan through a democratic assembly by the force of his personality and to see that it was carried out" (1991, p. 230).

Pericles' plan not only changed the Hellenistic rules of war (Ober, 1996, pp. 51–71), it also was the beginning of a long-term strategic analysis of war planning and waging. He substituted tactics for grand strategy, brute force with financial resources, and the predominance of manly honor in agonal warfare with a psychological war of endurance. If it would not exact heavy losses on Sparta, Athens would project its power with the fleet around the Peloponnesus.

Kagan and Ober do not comment on how Pericles' radical policy did violence to the daring character that he had promoted throughout his leadership. If Pericles planned the war to last no more than three years, did he anticipate that glory-lusting individuals would accept being holed up within the city's walls for that long, especially if they began to suffer reverses? While Pericles had proven that he could articulate and mold the Athenian temper toward his imperial project in the *Funeral Oration*, he was now advocating a policy that cut against the grain of that temper and his own transformative project. Second, in the *Funeral Oration*, Pericles promotes the common defense via imperial aggrandizement. In reality, however, he asked the Athenians to defend the city for the sake of the empire but at substantial personal losses.

In addition, was this a sound strategy to win? Pericles used some of the Athenians' strategic advantages by sending expeditions and launching assaults from sea. Yet, he did not lay siege to other poleis, which is because his grand strategy rested on a psychological dimension that Spartan futility would wither away its commitment to the war.

Athens launched a series of hit-and-run operations against Peloponnesian coastal cities. With 100 ships, Pericles invaded Megara, which was in the Peloponnesian League. It was the largest Athenian force ever assembled, and it shows that in Pericles' mind it was a key component of his strategy (2.31.2). They ravaged the territory and then retired; subsequently, they invaded Megara annually, up until 424 BC (4.66). The goal of these invasions was to force the city to negotiate a separate peace or join the Athenian alliance: "their territory spanned the Isthmus, and even their neutrality would presumably have denied invading Peloponnesian armies passage to Attica" (Lazenby, 2004, p. 38).

However, without trying to seize and hold a ground, Pericles relied mostly on the expectations that Sparta's ineffectual invasions would require it to switch tactics or give up. As a result, Pericles put Sparta in the driver's seat. The defensive policy was rational, but he left victory to chance. Maybe Sparta would suffer reverses, its domestic system might strain, the Helots could revolt, and her allies might defect. Athens could have accelerated these problems by establishing a base in Spartan territory, which it finally did six years into the war and to much success.

Pericles did not match defense with a proper offensive strategy to make the war costly for Sparta. His rationalism took for granted that citizens would bear the costs of an empire at rest. The windfall of revenues, constant political activity, and daring that defined his and a younger generation of Athenians came to a complete halt.

However, the greatest reverse to his strategy was dealt by an event that Pericles could not have predicted. A plague decimated Athens' population and severely dampened morale. Allies defected from the league, and Pericles died from it two years into the war. The plague demolished Periclean ambition and cool rationalism. A third of the population also suffered excruciating deaths. People turned to selfishness and vice and disregarded each other, eroding the bonds of the community. It was so corrosive to Athens' social fabric that the people despaired; they turned on Pericles and sought peace with Sparta, which refused the ambassadors' entreaties.

Even Pericles adjusted his expectations after this incident. He abandoned his zealous goals for sober recommendations and substituted his praise for the Athenians character with harsh reprimands toward the unnerved citizens. He appealed to their egoistic interests, which reminded them that they could not meet these desires without the advantages of national greatness (2.60.2). Whereas the idea of survival is absent in the *Funeral Oration*, he now revisits the matter: "[s]ince then a state can support the misfortunes of private citizens, while they cannot support hers, it is surely the duty of everyone to be forward in her defense" (2.60.2).

Pericles plays on their concern for security but still argues that the nobility of the city's glory warrants their continued efforts (2.63). However, he admits the empire's superiority rests on ambiguous moral foundations. Despite a lot of anti-Athenian sentiment among allies and foes alike, he argues that the Athenians cannot just walk away, "for what [they] hold is, to speak somewhat plainly, a tyranny; to take it perhaps was wrong, but to let it go is unsafe" (2.64).

Pericles convinced the Athenians. Once they purged themselves of their need to punish someone for their ills, by fining their leader, they renewed their war efforts, and their confidence was restored in him.

CONCLUSION

Pericles was an imperialist, but a prudent one who calibrated imperial expansion and war strategy to Athens' resources, which he gauged accurately (2.65.5). He knew that his people were too enthusiastic, too whimsical, and obsessed with gain. However, he directed these impulses and engineered a moderate and conservative policy that brought the empire's greatness to its height (2.65.5).

Pericles' war strategy was not bold, but it did not hazard the city's security. After his death, his prudent course was lost amid the cacophony of policies that allowed "private ambitions and private interests, in matters apparently quite foreign to the war, to lead them into projects unjust both to themselves and to their allies" (2.65).

Lesser leaders such as Cleon, Nicias, and Alcibiades possessed strong attributes but lacked the Periclean blend that enabled him to exercise an independent control over the multitude, "to lead them instead of being led by them" (2.65.8). Cleon was patriotic but immoderate. Nicias was esteemed for his prudence. His conservative nature assuaged the public's uncertainty and fears, but his cautiousness was paralyzing. Alcibiades was bold and intelligent; his desire for personal glory knew no bounds. He embodied both the daring spirit and also the grander egoistic ambition of the Athenian; his statecraft stoked the imperial impulses that Pericles had so diligently tried to restrain during the war. Alcibiades' irrepressible ambitions and Nicias' trepidations led to the catastrophic Sicilian expedition.

This disaster exposed how the post-Periclean state failed to match resources and strategy to foreign-policy aims. Athens lost thousands of men, almost the entire fleet of ships, and the allies broke out in rebellion. This failure produced civil discord in the city, from which they finally fell victims too. Conversely, Sparta proved capable of waging a long-term war and adapted to naval warfare, scoring some surprising victories against Athens. In 404 BC, 27 years after the war started, Athens surrendered to Sparta: the fleet and alliance were dismantled, the city's wall turned down, and its foreign policy was commanded by Sparta, which then imposed the Thirty, the infamous oligarchic regime.

The missing element in Pericles' transformative ambition was that he relied so greatly on his statesmanship. He proved that he had a unique ability to guide Athens' imperial might and resolve tension between democracy and empire. But to whom could he pass the torch when he was gone?

The problem that leaders with transformative ambition, like Pericles, present to their polities and the world is that they can set forces in motion, which, if not entirely beyond the control of their less capable successors, can certainly overwhelm them. Transformative ambition and the reality of practical politics present a paradox. The former is willful; it seeks to bend the rules toward the demands of a single human being. The latter is indifferent to any particular desire or hope; it is the realm of impersonal and shifting circumstances. These two forces can align harmoniously or clash. Pericles of Athens experienced the duality of this phenomenon. He drew out the strengths and abated the weaknesses of democratic energy and freedom and in his lifetime achieved great things that brought the Athenian empire and democracy to their peaks. Yet, he learned how fragile the summits of human greatness are when an unpredictable calamity undermined his polity's character, nerve, and social bonds. While Pericles is proof that a statesman's intervening influence can fundamentally change the course of international and domestic politics, he also shows that in the long run transformative ambition may not produce its intended effects.

NOTES

1. An obol was a sixth of a drachma, and a drachma was the average daily wage in Athens.
2. These dates are provided by Robert Strassler (in Thucydides, 1996), but the chronology of the *Pentecontaetia* is debated. Strassler suggests that the dates should cover possibilities rather than record agreed facts (p. 53).

Conclusion

This book improves on the way current theories of international politics and leadership studies understand statesmanship by showing how leaders with transformative ambition confront the perennial issues that nations face in foreign affairs. Transformative ambition is a unique concept that helps us understand change in domestic and international politics. Leaders are the catalysts for change as they translate their ambition into policies that seek to shape the moral opinions and behaviors of their followers. In essence, these leaders override and transcend political structures and constraints, which results in new political practices. The changes they inaugurate do not translate into a wholesale transformation of the international system. In other words, they do not restructure the anarchic system into something altogether different. Leaders with transformative ambition aim for changes in their regime's domestic and foreign policy, and thereby alter the conventional rules of international politics of their day. As a result, these particular changes have system wide ramifications.

The fundamental problem with the way realists conceive of leaders is that they view them as inheriting an existing power position and relegate the range of leaders' possible actions to what they do or fail to do with that power. When the distribution of power is relatively stable, the test of leadership is how little action the statesman takes. Yet, when it is in flux, realist leaders must be perceptive and respond to shifts in the balance of power; they can anticipate and adapt to these changes, but the international world is not of their own making. The content and rules of international politics always stays the same.

While it is true that the world has not evolved into something other than an anarchic order, the realist bias for continuity over change makes it difficult to comprehend the ways in which political actors create new practices and rules. I have argued that realism's failure to account for such changes is partly caused by its inability to distinguish between structural constraints and the rules that statesmen consciously construct.

Bismarck, who is deemed the quintessential realist statesman, is in fact a clear example of a leader who fundamentally altered diplomacy and foreign affairs by challenging the rules of the day. Bismarck introduced realpolitik and by doing so he single-handedly overturned the rules of diplomacy. He introduced this change by straining and weakening the system he inherited rather than exhorting his contemporaries to live up to any particular principle, thus he displayed grand, although not trans-formative, ambition. Bismarck's contemporaries had long abided by the principles established by Metternich at the Congress of Vienna; once he had changed their world, they had to learn to live within a Bismarckian one. Bismarck did not meet realist expectations, he confounded them.

As I demonstrate in this book, international relations scholarship can benefit from paying attention to leaders whose ambitions exceed the necessities of realist politics, especially when their foreign policy is informed by domestic political projects. When transformative ambition meets the realities of politics, innovative methods to solve political problems emerge. Novel diplomatic tools are forged, grand domestic projects are envisioned, and the moral transformation of a polity takes place. Throughout this book, I have traced political change back to the intentions and influences of leaders. I believe there is ample opportunity and need for political scientists to pursue this exciting avenue of research.

The lesson of transformative ambition is that it manifests leaders who move fluidly between domestic and international politics. Pericles intro-duced various innovations into Athenian and Greek foreign affairs by seeking to harmonize Athens' domestic and foreign policy. In his edify-ing speeches to the Athenians he showed how both levels reinforced each other and amplified the effects of the Periclean project. The demo-cratic revolution that Pericles inaugurated primed the Athenians to extend the imperial project as more citizens realized the stakes they had in the empire.

Transformative ambition also illuminates leaders' circumspect under-standing of the citizenry's needs, hopes, and fears. Changes in the polity's perceptions and moral identity are anticipated by such leaders. Pericles not only managed the city's power but defined and directed the ethos of Athenian glory through his articulation of daring as the moral foundation of the regime. Pericles had an uncanny understanding of the pulse of the Athenians, and due to that understanding he pushed his regime's political and moral elements further, challenging and elevating them toward a good that had not yet been realized.

Studies of political leadership that rely solely on psychological and personality assessments prohibit scholars from distinguishing between transformative ambition and the personality traits of ordinary leaders. Certainly, every leader's personality matters. After all, the personality is composed of needs, motives, and unsatisfied desires that intrude on even the most sober and self-aware individuals. However, without a model that understands leaders with higher capacities of self-awareness, who can assess and direct their own ambition, scholars that use psychological models will continue to assume that all leaders are always a step behind their perceived ambitions. This project points to the necessity of recovering an Aristotelian psychology for the study of leadership. Leaders that fit Aristotle's model of magnanimity possess tact and acute self-awareness of themselves and others. Leaders of this ilk can articulate their ambition precisely and transcend egoistic passions.

Leaders with transformative ambition undergo a deeper and more fundamental psychological development as they migrate into politics. These leaders harness their ambitions and traits into a settled character and commit their genius to confronting the challenges of the politics of their day. Although Burns' transformational leadership theory offers an incisive view of such deeper development, it cannot grasp the complexity of ambition as a moral phenomenon. This is why revisiting Aristotle's idea of the magnanimous man is indispensable. It sheds light on the character of rare individuals who are molded by regime politics, yet whose virtue flourishes in such a way that they transcend the regime and influence its destiny. To understand leadership at its finest it is necessary to pay close attention to the interaction between high character and politics at both the domestic and international level.

My approach does not yield a parsimonious model. The transformative leaders examined here self-consciously reconciled their ambition with the good of their political communities. Although these leaders may seek the good of their communities, they try and achieve their goals by bending and overriding constraints of existing institutions, moral beliefs, and existing domestic and international practices.

In Pericles' case I made a sustained effort to show how leadership characteristics, and the policies that such qualities lend themselves to, are deeply intertwined with a host of political institutions and cultural practices. This is the example for future scholars to draw upon if they wish to systematically understand the interaction of political leadership and regime politics. Pericles' ambition and behavior that made him a successful leader cannot be circumscribed to Athens' formal political system.

My study of transformative ambition and leadership also raises a number of moral questions about the consequences of having these intermittent figures rise to power in political regimes. The first is the problem of unintended consequences. The problem that leaders with transformative ambition present to their polities and the world is that they can set forces in motion, which, if not entirely beyond the control of their less capable successors, can certainly overwhelm them. As established rules and old orders give way to new ones, lesser leaders may fail to hold together these new structures and captivate the moral imagination of their followers. Moreover, leaders with transformative ambition have a rare capaciousness of soul that includes their grand desire and the good of others. Pericles' immoderate successors could not handle the pressures of the protracted war, the unsettled demos, and the demand to stand above the morass of petty factionalized politics.

In addition, the projects that emerge from transformative ambition may be risky endeavors. Are such gambles good for particular nations and the international world? This is a question that must be addressed by moral philosophers and students of politics. Although I do not offer an ethics of transformative ambition here, this project points to a need to examine the ethics of transformation and its relationship to complex ambition.

Transformative ambition is not a relic of leaders in distant times and radically different political cultures. This phenomenon will continue to arise because of circumstances and the continuing belief across history and culture that human greatness and excellence are both necessary and beneficial to particular communities. Political circumstances are such that individual nations will always face internal and/or external peril that make the conditions ripe for extraordinary virtue and political genius, qualities that people naturally turn to in the imminence of danger. Not only will people continue to desire great leadership, human nature is such that a new crop of leaders with transformative ambition will always be waiting in the wings.

As Abraham Lincoln reminds us, despite the constraints imposed on leaders by political office, leaders with greater aspirations than to serve in an office will arise. Will they seek to fulfill their own ambition or will they put their energy and ardor toward noble purposes and in the service of the common good? The leaders discussed in this book took their bearings from what they believed were aims worthy of their ambition. For Pericles and de Gaulle, it was patriotic duty and self-denial of personal glory in the pursuit of higher principles. The American founders' lust for fame led them to design unprecedented political institutions. Bismarck's pursuit of Prussian power for the sake of having a stage for his ambition and genius produced a Bismarckian international order that changed history. Fidel Castro's hope to achieve mythical status and desire to bring about a Cuban revolution has led a small and enigmatic country in defiance of the largest superpower the world has ever known. Pericles' thirst to bring glory to Athens promoted the greatest cultural achievement of Western civilization and the first model for a society built upon the notion of individualism.

We must acknowledge that transformative ambition will continue to make its presence felt in political life and ever-changing circumstances will produce different expressions of it. As such, the phenomenon of transformative ambition and the change that it conduces to is worthy of further exploration and analysis.

References

Abente, D. (1987), 'The war of the triple alliance: three explanatory models', *Latin American Research Review*, **22** (2), 47–69.

Acemoglu D. and J. A. Robinson (2005), *Economic Origins of Dictatorship and Democracy*, New York: Cambridge University Press.

Adair, D. (1974), *Fame and the Founding Fathers*, T. Colbourn (ed.), New York: Norton.

Aho, J. A. (1975), *German Realpolitik and American Sociology: An Inquiry into the Sources and Political Significance of the Sociology of Conflict*, Lewisburg, PA: Bucknell University Press.

Ahrensdorf, P. J. (1997), 'Thucydides' realistic critique of realism', *Polity,* **30** (2), 231–65.

Alexander, R. J. (1977), 'The tyranny of General Stroessner', *Freedom at Issue,* **41**.

Ambrosius, L. E. (1987), *Woodrow Wilson and the American Diplomatic Tradition: The Treaty Fight in Perspective*, Cambridge: Cambridge University Press.

Aristotle (1935 [1992]), *The Athenian Constitution; The Eudemian Ethics; On Virtues and Vices*, translated by H. Rackham, Cambridge, MA: Harvard University Press.

Aristotle (1954 [1984]), *The Rhetoric and the Poetics of Aristotle,* translated by W. R. Roberts and I. Bywater, New York: Random House.

Aristotle (1997), *The Politics of Aristotle*, translated by P. Simpson, Chapel Hill, NC: University of North Carolina Press.

Aristotle (2002), *Nicomachean Ethics*, translated by J. Sachs, Newburyport, MA: Focus Publishing.

Bailey, T. A. (1945), *Woodrow Wilson and the Great Betrayal*, New York: The Macmillan Company.

Balot, R. (2001), 'Pericles' anatomy of democratic courage', *The American Journal of Philology*, **122** (4), 505–25.

Bass, B. M. (1985), *Leadership and Transformational Beyond Expectations*, New York: Free Press.

Bass, B. M. (1998), *Transformational Leadership: Industrial, Military, and Educational Impact*, Mahwah, NJ: Erlbaum.

Bass, B. M. and B. J. Avolio (1994), 'Transformational leadership and organizational culture', *The International Journal of Public Administration*, **17** (3–4), 541–554.

Bennis, W. and B. Nanus (1985), *The Strategies for Taking Charge: Leaders*, New York: Harper Row.

Berthon, S. (2001), *Allies at War: The Bitter Rivalry Among Churchill, Roosevelt, and de Gaulle*, New York: Carroll and Graf.

Boller, P. F. (1996), *Presidential Campaigns*, New York: Oxford University Press.

Burns, J. M. (1978), *Leadership*, New York: Harper and Row.

Castro, F. and I. Ramonet (2006), *Fidel Castro: My Life, A Spoken Autobiography*, New York: Scribner.

Centeno, M. A. (2002), *Blood and Debt: War and the Nation-state in Latin America*, University Park, PA: Pennsylvania State University Press.

Cerny, P. G. (1980), *The Politics of Grandeur: Ideological Aspects of de Gaulle's Foreign Policy*, Cambridge: Cambridge University Press.

Clements, K. A. (1987), *Woodrow Wilson: World Statesman*, Boston, MA: Twayne.

Cockcroft, J. D. (1922), 'Paraguay's Stroessner: the ultimate caudillo?', in H. M. Hammill (ed.), *Caudillos Dictators in Spanish America*, Norman, OK: University of Oklahoma Press, pp. 335–48.

Codevilla, A. (1981), 'De Gaulle: statesmanship in the modern state', in H. V. Jaffa (ed.), *Statesmanship: Essays in Honor of Sir Winston S. Churchill*, Durham, NC: Carolina Academic Press, pp. 213–34.

Conger, J. A. and R. N. Kanungo (1987), 'Toward a behavioral theory of charismatic leadership in organizational settings', *Academy of Management Review*, **12**, 637–47.

Conway, D. W. (1997), *Nietzsche and the Political*, New York: Routledge.

Cooper, J. M. (2009), *Woodrow Wilson: A Biography*, New York: Alfred A. Knopf.

Craig, G. A. and A. L. George (1995), *Force and Statecraft: Diplomatic Problems of our Time*, 3rd edn, New York: Oxford University Press.

Debs, A. and H. Goemans (2010), 'Regime type, the fate of leaders and war', *American Political Science Review*, **104** (4 Aug.), 430–45.

Dimock, M. E. (1957), 'Woodrow Wilson as legislative leader', *The Journal of Politics,* **19** (1), 3–19.

Doyle, M. W. (1997), *Ways of War and Peace: Realism, Liberalism, and Socialism*, New York: Norton.

Fagen, R. R. (1969), *The Transformation of Political Culture in Cuba*, Palo Alto, CA: Stanford University Press.

Faulkner, R. K. (2007), *The Case for Greatness: Honorable Ambition and its Critics*, New Haven, CT: Yale University Press.

Fearon, J. D. (1994), 'Domestic political audiences and the escalation of international disputes', *The American Political Science Review*, **88** (3), 577–92.

Forde, S. (1986), 'Thucydides on the causes of Athenian imperialism', *The American Political Science Review*, **80** (2), 433–48.

Forde, S. (1995), 'International realism and the science of politics: Thucydides, Machiavelli, and neorealism', *International Studies Quarterly*, **39** (2), 141–60.

Fornara, C. W. and L. J. Samons (1991), *Athens from Cleisthenes to Pericles*, Berkeley, CA: University of California Press.

Freud, S. and W. C. Bullitt (1967), *Thomas Woodrow Wilson, Twenty-eighth President of the United States: A Psychological Study*, London: Weidenfeld and Nicolson.

Gaulle, C. d. (1960), *The Edge of the Sword*, New York: Criterion Books.

George, A. L. and J. L. George (1964), *Woodrow Wilson and Colonel House: A Personality Study*, New York: Dover Publishing.

George, A. L. and J. L. George (1998), *Presidential Personality and Performance*, Boulder, CO: Westview Press.

George, J. L. and A. L. George (1981), 'Woodrow Wilson and Colonel House: a reply to Weinstein, Anderson, and Link', *Political Science Quarterly*, **96** (4), 641–65.

Gewirth, A. (2009), *Self-fulfillment*, Princeton, NJ: Princeton University Press.

Gilpin, R. G. (1988), 'The theory of hegemonic war', *Journal of Interdisciplinary History*, **18** (4), 591–613.

Glaser, C. L. and C. Kaufmann (1998), 'What is the offense–defense balance and can we measure it?', *International Security*, **22** (4), 44–82.

Gordon, P. H. (1993), *A Certain Idea of France: French Security Policy and the Gaullist Legacy*, Princeton, NJ: Princeton University Press.

Greenstein, F. (1969), *Personality and Politics*, Chicago, IL: Markham.

Guthrie, W. K. C. (1971), *The Sophists: The Fifth-century Enlightenment*, vol. 6, Cambridge: Cambridge University Press.

Hagedorn, A. (2007), *Savage Peace: Hope and Fear in America, 1919*, New York: Simon and Schuster.

Hale, J. R. (2009), *Lords of the Sea: The Epic Story of the Athenian Navy and the Birth of Democracy*, New York: Viking.

Halperin, M. (1972), *The Rise and Decline of Fidel Castro: An Essay in Contemporary History*, Los Angeles, CA: University of California Press.

Hamill, H. M. (1992), *Caudillos Dictators in Spanish America*, Norman, OK: University of Oklahoma Press.

Hater, J. and B. Bass (1988), 'Superiors' evaluation and subordinates' perceptions of transformational and transactional leadership', *Journal of Applied Psychology*, **73** (4), 695–702.

Hermann, M. G. (1980), 'Explaining foreign policy behavior using the personal characteristics of political leaders', *International Studies Quarterly*, **24** (1), 7–46.

Hermann, M. G. (2003), 'Saddam Hussein's leadership style', in J. M. Post (ed.), *The Psychological Assessment of Political Leaders*, Ann Arbor, MI: University of Michigan Press.

Hobbes, T. (1991), *Leviathan*, Richard Tuck (ed.), Cambridge: Cambridge University Press.

Holloway, C. (ed.), (2008), *Magnanimity and Statesmanship*, Lanham, MD: Lexington Books.

Hull, V. (2004), *The Battle of Puffendorf*, Missoula, MT: Pictorial Histories Pub. Co. Inc.

Hyman, J. E. (2006), *The Psychology of Nuclear Proliferation: Identity, Emotions, and Foreign Policy*, Cambridge: Cambridge University Press.

Jackson, J. (2003), *De Gaulle (Life and Times)*, London: Haus Publishing Ltd.

Jervis, R. (1976), *Perception and Misperception in International Politics*, Princeton, NJ: Princeton University Press.

Kagan, D. (1969), *The Outbreak of the Peloponnesian War*, Ithaca, NY: Cornell University Press.

Kagan, D. (1991), *Pericles of Athens and the Birth of Democracy*, New York: Free Press.

Kagan, D. (2003), *The Peloponnesian War: Athens and Sparta in Savage Conflict, 431–404 BC*, London: HarperCollins.

Kagan, D. (2009), *Thucydides: The Reinvention of History*, New York: Penguin Group.

Keohane, R. O. (1986), *Neorealism and its Critics*, New York: Columbia University Press.

Keynes, J. M. (1920), *Mr. Lloyd George's General Election*, London: Liberal Publication Department.

Kissinger, H. (1968), 'The white revolutionary: reflections on Bismarck', *Daedalus*, **97** (3), 888–924.

Kissinger, H. (1994), *Diplomacy*, New York: Simon and Schuster.

Kraig, R. A. (2004), *Woodrow Wilson and the Lost World of the Oratorical Statesman*, College Station, TX: Texas A&M University Press.

Lacouture, J. (1966), *De Gaulle*, New York: New American Library.

Lake, D. H. and R. Powell (eds) (1999), *Strategic Choice and International Relations*, Princeton, NJ: Princeton University Press.

Lambert, P. and A. Nickson (eds) (1997), *The Transition to Democracy in Paraguay*, Ipswich: The Ipswich Book Company Ltd.

Lang, D. (1995), 'Woodrow Wilson: diplomacy and the critique of equilibrium', paper presented at the International Studies Association 48th Annual Convention.

Lasswell, H. D. (1948), *Power and Personality*, New York: Norton.

Lazenby, J. F. (2004), *The Peloponnesian War: A Military Study*, New York: Routledge.

Lincoln, A. (1953 [1992]), *Selected Speeches and Writings of Abraham Lincoln I*, New York: Vintage Books/The Library of America.

Lloyd George, D. (1938), *The Truth about the Peace Treaties*, London: V. Gollancz.

Machiavelli, N. (1998), *The Prince*, 2nd edn, translated by H. C. Mansfield, Chicago, IL: University of Chicago Press.

Mahoney, D. J. (2000), *De Gaulle: Statesmanship, Grandeur, and Modern Democracy*, London: Transaction Publishers.

March, J. G. and J. P. Olsen (1984), 'The new institutionalism: organizational factors in political life', *The American Political Science Review*, **78** (3), 734–749.

Maslow, A. H. (1943), 'A theory of human motivation', *Psychological Review*, **50**, 370–396.

Maslow, A. H. (1950), 'Self-actualizing people: a study of psychological health', in *Personality Symposia: Symposium #1 on Values*, New York: Grune and Stratton.

Maslow, A.H. (1987), *Motivation and Personality*, 3rd edn, New York: Addison-Wesley.

McDonald, H. B. and R. Rosecrance (1985), 'Alliance and structural balance in the international system: a reinterpretation', *Journal of Conflict Resolution*, **29** (1), 57–82.

Mearsheimer, J. J. (2001), *The Tragedy of Great Power Politics,* New York: Norton.

Mesquita, B. B. d. and D. Lalman (1992), *War and Reason: Domestic and International Imperatives*, New Haven, CT: Yale University Press.

Mesquita, B. B. d., J. D. Morrow, R. M. Siverson, and A. Smith (2004), 'Testing novel implications from the selectorate theory of war', *World Politics*, **56** (3), 363–88.

Mesquita, B. B. d., A. Smith, R. M. Siverson, and J. D. Morrow (2003), *The Logic of Political Survival*, Cambridge, MA: MIT Press.

Monoson, S. S. and M. Loriaux (1998), 'The illusion of power and the disruption of moral norms: Thucydides' critique of Periclean policy', *The American Political Science Review*, **92** (2), 285–97.

Montesquieu, C. de (1989), *Montesquieu: The Spirit of the Laws*, A. M. Cohler, B. C. Miller and H. S. Stone (eds), Cambridge: Cambridge University Press.

Morgenthau, H. J. (1978), *Politics Among Nations: The Struggle for Power and Peace*, 5th edn, New York: Knopf.

Newell, W. R. (2000), *Ruling Passion: The Erotics of Statecraft in Platonic Political Philosophy*, Lanham, MD: Rowman and Littlefield.

Newell, W. R. (2009), *The Soul of a Leader: Character, Conviction, and Ten Lessons in Political Greatness*, New York: Harper.

Ober, J. (1993), 'Public speech and the power of the people in democratic Athens', *Political Science and Politics*, **26** (3), 481–86.

Ober, J. (1996), *The Athenian Revolution: Essays on Ancient Greek Democracy and Political Theory*, Princeton, NJ: Princeton University Press.

Orwin, C. (1994), *The Humanity of Thucydides*, Princeton, NJ: Princeton University Press.

Palmer, M. (1992), *Love of Glory and the Common Good: Aspects of the Political Thought of Thucydides*, Lanham, MD: Rowman and Littlefield Publishers.

Pangle, T. L. and P. J. Ahrensdorf (1999), *Justice Among Nations: On the Moral Basis of Power and Peace*, Lawrence, KS: University Press of Kansas.

Pelinka, Anton. (1999), *Politics of the Lesser Evil: Leadership, Democracy and Jaruzelski's Poland*, New Brunswick, NJ: Transaction Publishers.

Pflanze, O. (1958), 'Bismarck's "realpolitik"', *The Review of Politics*, **20** (4), 492–514.

Pflanze, O. (1972), 'Toward a psychoanalytic interpretation of Bismarck', *The American Historical Review*, **77** (2), 419–44.

Plato (1968 [1991]), *The Republic*, translated by Allan Bloom, New York: Basic Books.

Plato (1995), *Phaedrus*, translated by A. Nehamas and P. Woodruff, Indianapolis, IN: Hackett.

Plato (1998), *Gorgias*, translated by J. H. Nichols, Ithaca, NY: Cornell University Press.

Plutarch (2001), *Plutarch's Lives*, translated by J. Dryden, New York: Modern Library.

Popper, M. (2005), *Leaders who Transform Society: What Drives Them and Why We Are Attracted*, Westport, CT: Praeger Publishers.

Post, J. M. (2004), *Leaders and Their Followers in a Dangerous World: The Psychology of Political Behavior Psychoanalysis and Social Theory*, Ithaca, NY: Cornell University Press.

Putnam, R. D. (1988), 'Diplomacy and domestic politics: the logic of two-level games', *International Organization*, **42** (3), 427–60.

Rhodes, P. J. (1986), 'Political activity in classical Athens', *The Journal of Hellenic Studies*, **106**, 132–44.

Rieff, P. (2007), *Charisma: The Gift of Grace, and How It Has Been Taken Away From Us*, New York: Vintage Books.

Riker, W. H. (1986), *The Art of Political Manipulation*, New Haven, CT: Yale University Press.

Rose, G. (1998), 'Review: neoclassical realism and theories of foreign policy', *World Politics*, **51** (1), 144–72.

Saeger, J. S. (2007), *Francisco Solano López and the Ruination of Paraguay: Honor and Egocentrism*, Lanham, MD: Rowman and Littlefield.

Samuels, R. J. (2003), *Machiavelli's Children: Leaders and their Legacies in Italy and Japan*, Ithaca, NY: Cornell University Press.

Sartre, J.P. (1956), *Being and Nothingness: A Phenomenological Essay on Ontology*, New York: Washington Square Press.

Saunders, R. M. (1998), *In Search of Woodrow Wilson: Beliefs and Behavior*, Westport, CT: Greenwood Press.

Schweller, R. L. (1996), 'Neorealism's status-quo bias: what security dilemma?', *Security Studies*, **5** (3), 90–121.

Schweller, R. L. (2004), 'Unanswered threats: a neoclassical realist theory of underbalancing', *International Security*, **29** (2), 159–201.

Seymour, C. (1957), 'Woodrow Wilson: a political balance sheet', *Proceedings of the American Philosophical Society*, **101** (2), 135–141.

Sondrol, P. C. (1991), 'Totalitarian and authoritarian dictators: a comparison of Fidel Castro and Alfredo Stroessner', *Journal of Latin American Studies*, **23** (3), 599–620.

Steinberg, S. (2011), *Bismarck: A Life*, New York: Oxford University Press.

Stid, D. D. (1998), *The President as Statesman: Woodrow Wilson and the Constitution*, Lawrence, KS: University Press of Kansas.

Stromberg, R. N. (1963), *Collective Security and American Foreign Policy: From the League of Nations to NATO*, New York: Praeger.

Sweig, J. (2007), 'Fidel's final victory', *Foreign Affairs*, **86** (1), 39–56.

Szulc, T. (2000), 'Fidelismo: the unfulfilled ideology', in I. L. Horowitz and J. Suchlicki (eds), *Cuban Communism*, 10th edn, New Brunswick, NJ: Transaction Publishers, Rutgers, pp. 104–18.

Taliaferro, J. W. (2004), *Balancing Risk: Great Power Intervention in the Periphery*, Ithaca, NY: Cornell University Press.

Taylor, A. J. P. (1967), *Bismarck: The Man and the Statesman*, New York: Vintage Books.

Taylor, C. (1991), *The Ethics of Authenticity*, vol. 30, Cambridge, MA: Harvard University Press.

Thucydides (1996), *The Landmark Thucydides: A Comprehensive Guide to the Peloponnesian War*, R. B. Strassler (ed.), New York: Free Press.

Tulis, J. (1987), *The Rhetorical Presidency*, Princeton, NJ: Princeton University Press.

Walker, S. G. (1995), 'Psychodynamic processes and framing effects in foreign policy decision-making: Woodrow Wilson's operational code', *Political Psychology*, **16** (4), 697–717.

Waltz, K. (1979), *Theory of International Politics*, New York: McGraw-Hill.

Waltz, K. N. (1988), 'The origins of war in neorealist theory', *Journal of Interdisciplinary History*, **18** (4), 615–28.

Whigham, T. L. and B. Potthast (1999), 'The Paraguayan Rosetta Stone: new insights into the demographics of the Paraguayan War, 1864–1870', *Latin American Research Review*, **34** (1), 174–86.

Wight, M. (1978), *Power Politics*, New York: Holmes and Meier.

Wilson, W. (1897), 'Leaderless government', *The Virginia Law Register*, **3** (5), 337–354.

Wilson, W. (1914), 'Message to Congress', 63rd Cong., 2d Sess., Senate Doc. No. 566, Washington.

Winter, D. G. (2003), 'Assessing leaders' personalities: a historical survey of academic research studies', in J. M. Post (ed.), *The Psychological Assessment of Political Leaders with Profiles of Saddam Hussein and Bill Clinton*, Ann Arbor, MI: The University of Michigan Press, pp. 11–38.

Index

Achilles 149
Adair, Douglass 37
Ahrensdorf, Peter 133
Alcibiades 1–4, 60, 125, 170
Algeria
    Algiers 116, 122
    War of Independence (1954–62) 122–3
ambition 36–7, 96–8, 106, 109–10, 118, 124
    as potential cause of tyranny 40–41
    political 1–3, 7–9, 21–2, 26, 33, 35–7, 39, 45–6, 51, 54–9, 75–6, 79, 81–2, 94–5, 98, 100, 102–11, 118, 125, 127
    self-actualization as opposition to 95
    transformative 97–8, 101, 106
Ancient Greece 130
    Athens 2, 4, 10, 96–7, 125, 127–9, 131–2, 134–6, 138–9, 141–8, 151–60, 162–4, 166–8, 170, 173–4
    Attica 138, 150, 155, 158, 166–8
    Chios 154
    conventional warfare strategies of 165
    Corinth 158–9, 162
    Corcyra 158–9, 161
    Coronea 158
    culture of 149–51
    Delos 153
    Epidamnus 161–2
    Euboea 156–8
    Eurymedon 154
    Helots 130–31, 146, 155, 169
    Lesbos 154
    Megara 156
    Piraeus 166
    Sparta 10, 129, 131, 134–5, 137, 139, 142, 146, 150–52, 154–5, 157–9, 162–3, 165, 168–70
Archidamus 161, 163–4
Argentina 46, 50
Aristotle 82, 92–3, 103–4, 107, 111, 119, 129, 144, 146
    concept of magnanimity 2, 5–6, 9, 41, 79, 86, 100–104, 110–18, 124, 174
    concept of self-realization 93
    Ethics 100–102, 109, 111–12
    Eudemian Ethics 114–15
    Politics 116
    Rhetoric 109
    view of honor 58, 100
    view of magnificence 118
    view of political ambitions 106
    view of vanity 112
    virtue ethics of 86–8, 107, 116
Aron, Raymond 123
Augustus 157
Austria 11, 14, 26, 32
    Vienna 29
Austria–Hungary 14, 31
Austro-Prussian War (1866) 22
autocracies 57
    characteristics of 37, 45
    loss of power 45
    role of loyalty in 45
    strategic behaviour of 55

Bacon, Francis 42
Bass, Bernard M. 90–91

behaviour of leaders 54–5
  role of dominant motivation 56–7
  role of personality 55–6, 59–60
von Bismarck, Otto 7, 11–12, 22,
    24–7, 29–33, 121, 157, 176
  as example of offensive realism
    20
  foreign policies of 12–14, 27
  Kissigen Dictation (1877) 31
  May Laws (1873) 31
  speeches of 26
  transformative ambition of 13,
    25–6, 32
  use of *realpolitik* 22–5, 27–8,
    32–3, 173
Bolivia 48
Bonaparte, Napoleon (Napoleon I)
    3–4, 18, 31, 46, 120
  territory conquered by 65
Brazil 46, 50
Bueno de Mesquita, Bruce
  Logic of Political Survival, The
    35–6
Burns, James Macgregor 8–9, 88–9,
    92, 96
  concept of *engagé* 85, 94
  criticism of Aristotle's virtue
    ethics 87–8
  Leadership 82–3
  theory of transactional leadership
    95–6
  theory of transformational
    leadership 81–7, 93–5, 174
Bush, George W. 1, 108

Carter, Jimmy
  administration of 49
  foreign policy of 49
Castro, Fidel
  ambition of 46–7, 51, 176
  foreign policy of 48
  regime of 46–9
Chaco War (1932–5), belligerents of
    48
Chavez, Hugo 92–3
China Revolution (1946–50) 41
Churchill, Winston 1–2, 15, 91, 102,
    118, 120
  personality of 105

Cimon 138, 141–2
  banishment of 142, 147, 155
  family of 142
  military victories of 146, 154
classical realist leadership 14
  examples of 12
  view of role of statesman 16
Clemenceau, Georges, President of
    France 66
Clements, Kendrick 63
Cleomenes of Sparta 137
Cleon 170
Clinton, Hillary 108
Cold War 2, 49, 103, 119, 122–3
Collins, Susan, critique of Aristotlean
    magnanimity 116
Colorado Party (Paraguay) 48
competence
  definitions of 45–6
  role in strategic ambition 45
Congress of Vienna (1814–15) 11,
    173
  as example of balance-of-power
    diplomacy 65
Cuba 46, 51
  Revolution (1953–9) 47, 176

decline of regimes 41–2
  loss of power 45
defensive realism 21
  concept of 18
  leadership characteristics
    associated with 18,
    20–21
  view of international ambition
    36
Delian League 155–6
  formation of (478 BC) 153
  members of 153–4
Denmark 27
Diplomacy, balance-of-power 65
Dominican Republic, US occupation
    of (1965–6) 49
Doyle, Michael 131

Egypt 31, 40, 155
Eisenhower, Dwight D.,
    administration of 48

Ephialtes 142, 146, 155
Escalante, Anibal 46

Faulkner, Robert 105
    Case for Greatness: Honorable
        Ambition and Its Critics,
        The 103
Federation of North German States
    29–30
    Federal Government 29
First World War (1914–18) 63, 78,
    94
    belligerents of 14, 62, 66, 76
    Paris Peace Conference (1919)
        62, 73
    Treaty of Versailles (1919) 62,
        72–3, 77
Forde, Steven 133
France 6, 14–15, 20, 27, 30, 32, 65,
    116, 119, 121, 124
    Paris 62, 66–9
    Revolution (1789–99) 41
Franco–Prussian War (1870) 30
    Battle of Sedan 30
Franklin, Benjamin 43
Freud, Sigmund 24, 88, 105

Gandhi, Mahatma Mohandas 83,
    94
    background of 94
    shortcomings of 97
de Gaulle, Charles 4, 13, 23, 102–3,
    106, 116–20, 122–3, 175
    ambition of 124
    concept of French unity 6
    defence policies of 123
    Edge of the Sword, The 119
    Memoires de Guerre 121
    view of grandeur 119–20
George, Alexander
    Woodrow Wilson and Colonel
        House: A Personality Study
        61, 75–7
George, Juliet
    Woodrow Wilson and Colonel
        House: A Personality Study
        61, 75–7

von Gerlach, Leopold 27
German Progressive Party,
    representation of 25
Germany 7, 11, 13–14, 18, 32, 62,
    66, 69, 71
    borders of 12
    Diet of 22
    Landtag 26, 28
    territory of 30
    unification of 12–14
    Weltpolitik 20
Gilpin, Robert 130
Gladstone, William 64
Gorbachev, Mikhail 2
Gore, Al 1
Greco–Persian Wars (499–449 BC)
    130, 153–4
    Battle of Mycale (479 BC)
        136
    Peace of Callias (449 BC) 156

Hamilton, Alexander 43
Hermann, Margaret 57
    leadership personality type
        theories of 59–61
Herodotus
    Histories 137
Hitler, Adolf 1–2, 15, 18, 91
    as example of offensive realism
        20
    foreign policies of 15
    personality of 95
Hobbes, Thomas 95–6
Holloway, Carson 112
Homer 139, 149, 151
House, Colonel Edward 67
Hussein, Saddam 1

India 94
individualism 2, 22, 33, 82–3, 88,
    101, 116, 120, 128, 176
    Athenian 133, 150
    self-actualization 84–5
Israel 40
Italy 14, 31

Jefferson, Thomas 43

Kagan, Donald 128–9, 134–5
    observations of Pericles 144,
        157–8, 166–8
Kennedy, John F. 102
    administration of 48
Kissinger, Henry 12, 16, 63
    writings on Otto von Bismarck
        22–5, 27–8
    writings on Woodrow Wilson
        64–5

Lasswell, Harold, and theory of
        characteristics of political
        personalities 56, 61
leadership personalities 72–7, 174
    aggressive 59–61, 63
    conciliatory 59, 61
League of Nations 62–5, 67–71, 78
    Covenant of 52, 62, 68, 70–71
    failed US ratification of 8, 74,
        78
    members of 65, 70
Lee, Robert E. 106
Lenin, Vladimir 94
    political theories of 94–5
liberalism 84
    opposition to 28
Lincoln, Abraham 4, 102–3, 105–6,
        175
    Lyceum Address 3
    personality of 105
    political ambitions of 105
Lloyd George 66
Locke, John 85
Lodge, Cabot 67, 70, 72–3
Lopez, Francisco Solano 49–50
    background of 50
    family of 46
    foreign policy of 50–51
Louis XIV of France 18
loyalty 44, 48–9, 106
    concept of 37
    role in autocracies 45

Machiavelli, Niccòlo 2, 19, 36–7,
        39–40, 46, 86
    Prince, The 8, 39, 49, 86
Madison, James 43, 92

Mahoney, Daniel 121
Mandela, Nelson 103
Maslow, Abraham, and concept of
        self-actualization 88–90
McCain, John, presidential election
        campaign of (2008) 108–9
Mearshiemer, John 12, 33
    concept of offensive realism
        17–21
Melgarejo, Manuel Mariano 50
von Metternich, Klemens 11, 29,
        173
    principle of legitimacy 14
Mill, John Stuart 92
de Montesquieu, Charles 85
    Spirit of the Laws 96
Morgenthau, Hans 14, 16
Morrow, James D.
    Logic of Political Survival, The
        35–6
Moses 39–40

Napoleon III, capture of (1870)
        30
nationalism 13, 49
    ethnic 97
    French 123
    Prussian 28
Naxos 154
neorealist leadership 14, 21
    concept of 12
    view of role of statesman 15–17
Newell, Waller 106
    *Soul of a Leader: Character,
        Conviction, and Ten
        Lessons in Political
        Greatness, The* 104–5
Nicias 1, 170
Nietzsche, Friedrich 93
    concept of 'amoral will to power'
        89
    concept of 'self-creation' 90
concept of self-realization 93–4
    Genealogy of Morals 89
    Twilight of the Idols 89–90
North Atlantic Treaty Organization
        (NATO), French withdrawal
        from (1966) 123

Obama, Barack, presidential election
    campaign of (2008) 108–9
Ober, Josiah, observations of Pericles
    167–8
offensive realism
    leadership characteristics
        associated with 20–21
    view of international ambition 36
Orwin, Clifford 132

Pakistan 97
Pan-Hellenism 134–5
Pangle, Thomas 133
Paraguay 46, 49
    Ciudad del Este (Puerto
        Stroessner) 49
    Congress 51
    military of 50
Paraguayan War (1864–70)
    belligerents of 50
    casualties of 51
    Triple Alliance 50
Pausanias 153
Peloponnesian League, members of
    159–60, 168
Peloponnesian War (431–404 BC)
    138, 154, 158
    Battle of Potidaea (432 BC)
        161
    Battle of Sybota (433 BC)
        160–61
    belligerents of 129, 135, 154, 160
    Sicilian Expedition (415–413 BC)
        134
Pericles 2, 4, 6–7, 10, 13, 23, 102,
    125, 127–9, 133–5, 138–9,
    143–7, 149–52, 155, 157, 159,
    166, 170, 175
    death of 141
    domestic policies of 147
    family of 136–8, 140–41
    founding of Thurri 134
    Funeral Oration 128, 132–5, 139,
        149, 153, 161–3, 168–9
    imperial policies of 158, 164–5
    leadership qualities proposed by
        10
    Megarian Decree 160–61, 164

military strategies of 160–61, 164–5,
    167–70
    rationalism of 139–40, 144, 169
    transformative political ambitions
        of 59, 96–7, 131, 134–6,
        139, 145, 152, 158, 161,
        170–71, 173–4
Persian Empire 155
    navy of 154
Pflanze, Otto 24, 27
Plato 92, 129
    Gorgias 139, 144
Pleistonax 157
Plutarch 129, 137, 140–41, 155
Poland, Axis Invasion of (1939) 15
Prussia 11, 14, 31–2
    foreign policy of 28–9

realism and strategic perspective
    54–5
realist leaders 32–3, 38, 173
    defence concepts of 7
realpolitik 13, 32–3, 63
    application of 16, 22–5, 27–8, 32,
        173
    practitioners of 11, 27–8, 32
revolutionaries 38, 46, 49, 92, 94,
    101
    ideals of 47
    motivations of 42
Roosevelt, Franklin D. 120
Russian Empire 14, 20, 31–2
    February Revolution (1917) 41

Second World War (1939–45) 122
    Anschluss (1938) 15
    belligerents of 1, 15
    invasion of Poland (1939) 15
    Operation Barbarossa (1941)
        15
    Vichy France 117
self-actualization 8, 86, 88–9, 94
    altruistic 97
    collective 82, 90–91, 93–4
    opposition to ambition 95
    role in individualism 84–5
Sicial Expedition (AD 415–413) 1
Sicily, polis of Melos 134, 136

Siverson, Randolph
  Logic of Political Survival, The
    35–6
Smith, Alastair
  Logic of Political Survival, The
    35–6
Socrates 139–40, 144
South Africa 94
Soviet Union 48, 119, 123–4
  Axis invasion of (1941) 15
  Red Army 15
  territorial influence of 2, 48
Spain 31
statesmanship 64, 79, 118, 170,
    172
  magnanimous 115
  relationship with leaders'
    behaviour 54–5
  relationship with magnanimity
    103
Steidlmeier, Paul 90–91
Steinberg, Jonathan 27
Sthenelaidas 164
strategic ambition 41
  examples of 43–4
  role of competence in 45
  role of incentive in 43–6
Stroessner, Alfredo 46, 51
  ambition of 49–50
  background of 48
  regime of 48–9

Talleyrand (Charles Maurice de
    Talleyrand-Périgord) 65
Thasian Rebellion (465 BC) 154
  belligerents of 155
Third Reich (1933–45) military 15
Thirty Years' Peace 157, 161
  clauses of 164
Three Emperors League, members of
    31
Thucydides 125, 129, 131–2, 134–5,
    139, 143, 159
  History 128, 130, 150
  theory of hegemonic warfare
    130
de Tocqueville, Alexis 92
transformational leadership 81, 83–6,
    91, 174

aristocratic 93
authentic 90–91
critiques of 82, 92
relationship with self-actualization
    86–8
transformative political ambition 8,
    13, 23–4, 38, 51, 81, 125, 172,
    175
  driving forces of 4–5, 107
  examples of 6, 13, 25–6, 32, 40,
    46–7, 59, 96–7, 131, 134,
    136, 139–40, 145, 152,
    161, 170–71, 173–4
  potential danger of 171
  relationship with study of regimes
    9
Triple Entente, formation of 32
Tulis, Jeffrey 78

United Kingdom 14, 31–2
  Glorious Revolution (1688) 41–2
United States of America 48, 76, 119,
    123–4
  Civil War (1861–5) 105–6
Congress 62, 65, 67–70, 72–3, 75,
    77, 108
  Democratic Party 69, 72, 77
  military of 49
  Monroe Doctrine 68
  Republican Party 67–9, 71, 73
  Revolutionary War (1775–83)
    41–3
  Washington DC 67, 72
Uruguay 46

Venezuela 92–3
Vietnam War (1955–75)
  belligerents of 49

Waltz, Kenneth 12, 33
  concept of neorealism 16
  concept of structural realism
    17–18
Washington, George 43, 102–3
  political ambitions of 103–4
Wilhelm II, Kaiser 15, 18
  as example of offensive realism
    20

William I, King 28, 30
Wilson, Joseph Ruggles, family of
    75
Wilson, Woodrow 2, 13, 52, 61–4,
    71–6, 79
    Article X 70–71, 78
    Congressional Government 78

family of 75
foreign policy of 8, 62–4, 69
Fourteen Points 66–9
personality of 61–2, 73–8
Winter, David 58

Xanthippus, family of 136–8